Learning Spring Boot 2.0

Second Edition

Simplify the development of lightning fast applications based on microservices and reactive programming

Greg L. Turnquist

BIRMINGHAM - MUMBAI

Learning Spring Boot 2.0

Second Edition

First published: November 2014

Second edition: November 2017

Production reference: 1311017

Published by Packt Publishing Ltd.
Livery Place
35 Livery Street
Birmingham
B3 2PB, UK.

ISBN 978-1-78646-378-4

www.packtpub.com

Credits

Author
Greg L. Turnquist

Reviewer
Zoltan Altfatter

Commissioning Editor
Aaron Lazar

Acquisition Editor
Chaitanya Nair

Content Development Editor
Siddhi Chavan

Technical Editor
Abhishek Sharma

Copy Editor
Sonia Mathur

Project Coordinator
Prajakta Naik

Proofreader
Safis Editing

Indexer
Francy Puthiry

Graphics
Abhinash Sahu

Production Coordinator
Nilesh Mohite

About the Author

Greg L. Turnquist has been a software professional since 1997. In 2002, he joined the senior software team that worked on Harris' $3.5 billion FAA telco program, architecting mission-critical enterprise apps while managing a software team. He provided after-hours support to a nation-wide system and is no stranger to midnight failures and software triages. In 2010, he joined the SpringSource division of VMware, which was spun off into Pivotal in 2013.

As a test-bitten script junky, Java geek, and JavaScript Padawan, he is a member of the Spring Data team and the lead for Spring Session MongoDB. He has made key contributions to Spring Boot, Spring HATEOAS, and Spring Data REST while also serving as editor-at-large for Spring's *Getting Started Guides*.

Greg wrote technical best sellers *Python Testing Cookbook* and *Learning Spring Boot, First Edition*, for Packt. When he isn't slinging code, Greg enters the world of magic and cross swords, having written the speculative fiction action and adventure novel, *Darklight*.

He completed his master's degree in computer engineering at Auburn University and lives in the United States with his family.

About the Reviewer

Zoltan Altfatter (@altfatterz) is a software engineer, passionate about the JVM and Spring ecosystem. He has several years of industry experience working at small startups and big consultancy firms.

You can find more about him on his blog: http://zoltanaltfatter.com.

www.PacktPub.com

For support files and downloads related to your book, please visit www.PacktPub.com.

Did you know that Packt offers eBook versions of every book published, with PDF and ePub files available? You can upgrade to the eBook version at www.PacktPub.com and as a print book customer, you are entitled to a discount on the eBook copy. Get in touch with us at service@packtpub.com for more details.

At www.PacktPub.com, you can also read a collection of free technical articles, sign up for a range of free newsletters and receive exclusive discounts and offers on Packt books and eBooks.

www.packtpub.com/mapt

Get the most in-demand software skills with Mapt. Mapt gives you full access to all Packt books and video courses, as well as industry-leading tools to help you plan your personal development and advance your career.

Why subscribe?

- Fully searchable across every book published by Packt
- Copy and paste, print, and bookmark content
- On demand and accessible via a web browser

Customer Feedback

Thanks for purchasing this Packt book. At Packt, quality is at the heart of our editorial process. To help us improve, please leave us an honest review on this book's Amazon page at https://www.amazon.com/dp/1786463784.

If you'd like to join our team of regular reviewers, you can e-mail us at customerreviews@packtpub.com. We award our regular reviewers with free eBooks and videos in exchange for their valuable feedback. Help us be relentless in improving our products!

Table of Contents

Preface

When *Learning Spring Boot, First Edition*, by Packt, made its debut, it was the first Spring Boot book to hit the international market. The user community ate it up, which is evidence of the popularity of Spring Boot. And today, Spring Boot is driven by the same, core principal stated in that book's preface, "How can we make Spring more accessible to new developers?"

By focusing on developers, community, and customers, Spring Boot has alleviated untold hours of time normally spent plumbing infrastructure. Andrew Clay Shafer, Pivotal's Senior Directory of Technology, has presented a most famous conference slide, "'Great job configuring servers this year'—No CEO Ever." We don't get bonus points for wasting time configuring web containers, database connectors, template view resolvers, and other mind-numbing infrastructure. However, we've done it for so long, we all assume it's a part and parcel of our trade.

Spring Boot has upset that apple cart and shown that we can, in fact, focus on building features our customers want on day one. As James Watters, Senior Vice President at Pivotal, has stated in countless presentations, when you focus on things above the value line, you build real confidence with your customers. This is demonstrated by the latest Zero Turnaround whitepaper showing that 46%, or almost one of every two Java developers, is using some part of the Spring portfolio. Spring Boot is solving problems for legions of customers, and this book can help you close the gap in your understanding.

What this book covers

Chapter 1, *Quick Start with Java*, explains how to rapidly craft a web application running on an embedded web container, access some data, and then deploy it into the cloud using minimal amounts of code and build settings.

Chapter 2, *Reactive Web with Spring Boot*, shows how to start building a social media service to upload pictures using Spring WebFlux, Project Reactor, and the Thymeleaf template engine.

Chapter 3, *Reactive Data Access with Spring Boot*, explains how we can pick up Spring Data MongoDB as a reactive-power data store and hook it to our social media platform. You'll find out how Spring Boot autoconfigures our app to persist data.

Chapter 4, *Testing with Spring Boot*, explains how we can write unit tests with JUnit, slice tests where small parts of our app uses real components, and full-blown embedded container testing. Also, you will see how to write an autoconfiguration policy for a browser-driving test toolkit and test that as well.

Chapter 5, *Developer Tools for Spring Boot Apps*, puts several tools in our hands to enhance developer experience, such as DevTools, LiveReload, and connecting our IDE to the cloud.

Chapter 6, *AMQP Messaging with Spring Boot*, explains how to use RabbitMQ as our message broker and reactively build up a reliable, streaming message service between components.

Chapter 7, *Microservices with Spring Boot*, introduces Spring Cloud and the ability to break up our social media platform into smaller, more manageable apps, dynamically talking to each other.

Chapter 8, *WebSockets with Spring Boot*, shows how to enhance the user experience by sending updates to all interested parties from various microservices. You will also see how to route all WebSocket messages through a RabbitMQ broker.

Chapter 9, *Securing Your App with Spring Boot*, lets us secure the social media platform for production with both URL-based and method-based tactics, so only registered users can get online, and only authorized admins and owners can actually delete uploaded pictures.

Chapter 10, *Taking Your App to Production with Spring Boot*, shows us how to bundle up our application and deploy to production without breaking the bank by using profile-based configurations to distinguish between local and cloud-based situations and creating custom properties to tailor application settings without rewriting code for every environment.

What you need for this book

- Spring Boot 2.0 requires Java Developer Kit (JDK) 8 or higher
- A modern IDE (IntelliJ IDEA or Spring Tool Suite) is recommended

- RabbitMQ 3.6 or higher must be installed (check out `https://www.rabbitmq.com/download.html`, or, when using Mac Homebrew, brew install RabbitMQ)
- MongoDB 3.0 or higher must be installed (check out `https://www.mongodb.com/download-center`, or, when using Mac Homebrew, brew install MongoDB)

Who this book is for

This book is designed for both novices and experienced Spring developers. It will teach you how to override Spring Boot's opinions and frees you from the need to define complicated configurations.

Conventions

In this book, you will find a number of text styles that distinguish between different kinds of information. Here are some examples of these styles and an explanation of their meaning.

Code words in text, database table names, folder names, filenames, file extensions, pathnames, dummy URLs, user input, and Twitter handles are shown as follows:

"The `@Data` annotation from Lombok generates getters, setters, a `toString()` method, an `equals()` method, a `hashCode()` method, and a constructor for all required (that is, `final`) fields."

A block of code is set as follows:

```
public interface MyRepository {
    List<Image> findAll();
}
```

Any command-line input or output is written as follows:

```
$ java -jar build/libs/learning-spring-boot-0.0.1-SNAPSHOT.jar
```

New terms and **important words** are shown in bold. Words that you see on the screen, for example, in menus or dialog boxes, appear in the text like this: "When the first user clicks on **Submit**, the message automatically appears on the second user's window."

 Warnings or important notes appear like this.

Tips and tricks appear like this.

Reader feedback

Feedback from our readers is always welcome. Let us know what you think about this book--what you liked or disliked. Reader feedback is important for us as it helps us develop titles that you will really get the most out of.

To send us general feedback, simply email feedback@packtpub.com, and mention the book's title in the subject of your message.

If there is a topic that you have expertise in and you are interested in either writing or contributing to a book, see our author guide at www.packtpub.com/authors.

Customer support

Now that you are the proud owner of a Packt book, we have a number of things to help you to get the most from your purchase.

Downloading the example code

You can download the example code files for this book from your account at http://www.packtpub.com. If you purchased this book elsewhere, you can visit http://www.packtpub.com/support and register to have the files emailed directly to you.

You can download the code files by following these steps:

1. Log in or register to our website using your email address and password.
2. Hover the mouse pointer on the **SUPPORT** tab at the top.
3. Click on **Code Downloads & Errata**.
4. Enter the name of the book in the **Search** box.
5. Select the book for which you're looking to download the code files.
6. Choose from the drop-down menu where you purchased this book from.
7. Click on **Code Download**.

Once the file is downloaded, please make sure that you unzip or extract the folder using the latest version of:

- WinRAR / 7-Zip for Windows
- Zipeg / iZip / UnRarX for macOS
- 7-Zip / PeaZip for Linux

The code bundle for the book is also hosted on GitHub at `https://github.com/PacktPublishing/Learning-Spring-Boot-2.0-Second-Edition`. We also have other code bundles from our rich catalog of books and videos available at `https://github.com/PacktPublishing/`. Check them out!

Downloading the color images of this book

We also provide you with a PDF file that has color images of the screenshots/diagrams used in this book. The color images will help you better understand the changes in the output. You can download this file from `https://www.packtpub.com/sites/default/files/downloads/LearningSpringBoot2.0_ColorImages.pdf`.

Errata

Although we have taken every care to ensure the accuracy of our content, mistakes do happen. If you find a mistake in one of our books--maybe a mistake in the text or the code-- we would be grateful if you could report this to us. By doing so, you can save other readers from frustration and help us improve subsequent versions of this book. If you find any errata, please report them by visiting `http://www.packtpub.com/submit-errata`, selecting your book, clicking on the **Errata Submission Form** link, and entering the details of your errata. Once your errata are verified, your submission will be accepted and the errata will be uploaded to our website or added to any list of existing errata under the Errata section of that title.

To view the previously submitted errata, go to `https://www.packtpub.com/books/content/support` and enter the name of the book in the search field. The required information will appear under the **Errata** section.

Piracy

Piracy of copyrighted material on the internet is an ongoing problem across all media. At Packt, we take the protection of our copyright and licenses very seriously. If you come across any illegal copies of our works in any form on the internet, please provide us with the location address or website name immediately so that we can pursue a remedy.

Please contact us at copyright@packtpub.com with a link to the suspected pirated material.

We appreciate your help in protecting our authors and our ability to bring you valuable content.

Questions

If you have a problem with any aspect of this book, you can contact us at questions@packtpub.com, and we will do our best to address the problem.

1

Quick Start with Java

Working with Spring Boot is like pair-programming with the Spring developers.

— *Josh Long @starbuxman*

Perhaps you've heard about Spring Boot? It's cultivated the most popular explosion in software development in years. Clocking millions of downloads *per month*, the community has exploded since its debut in 2013.

I hope you're ready for some fun, because we are going to take things to the next level as we use Spring Boot to build a social media platform. We'll explore its many valuable features, all the way from the tools designed to speed up development efforts to production-ready support as well as cloud-native features.

Despite some rapid fire demos you might have caught on YouTube, Spring Boot isn't just for quick demos. Built atop the de facto standard toolkit for Java, the Spring Framework, Spring Boot will help us build this social media platform with lightning speed and stability.

Also, this book will explore a new paradigm introduced in Spring Framework 5, **reactive programming**. In this day and age, as we build bigger systems, iterate faster, and host fleets of distributed microservices, it has become critical that we switch from a classic blocking programming style. As Josh Long would point out, this is nothing new. The network stacks of today's OSs are inherently asynchronous, but the JVM is *not*. Only in recent years have people realized the need to chop up tasks in a asynchronous, non-blocking fashion. However, the programming paradigm to handle potentially unlimited streams of data coming at fluctuating times requires a new programming model, which we will explore carefully alongside the power of Spring Boot itself.

In this chapter, we'll get a quick kick off with Spring Boot using the Java programming language. Maybe that makes you chuckle? People have been dissing Java for years as being slow, bulky, and not a good language for agile shops. In this chapter, we'll see how that is *not* the case.

In this chapter, we will cover the following topics:

- Creating a bare project using the Spring Initializr found at `http://start.spring.io`
- Exploring Spring Boot's management of third-party libraries
- Seeing how to run our app straight inside our **Integrated Development Environment (IDE)** with no standalone containers
- Using Spring Boot's property support to make external adjustments
- Packaging our app into a self-contained, runnable JAR file
- Deploying our app into the cloud
- Adding out-of-the-box production-grade support tools

 At any time, if you're interested in a more visual medium, feel free to check out my *Learning Spring Boot [Video]* at `https://www.packtpub.com/application-development/learning-spring -boot-video`.

Getting started

What is step one when we get underway with a project? We visit Stack Overflow and look for an example project to help us build our project!

Seriously, the amount of time spent adapting another project's build file, picking dependencies, and filling in other details adds up to a lot of wasted time.

No more.

At the **Spring Initializr** (https://start.spring.io), we can enter minimal details about our app, pick our favorite build system and the version of Spring Boot we wish to use, and then choose our dependencies off a menu. Click the **Generate Project** button, and we have a free-standing, ready-to-run application.

In this chapter, we'll take a quick test drive, and build a small web app. We can start by picking **Gradle** from the drop-down menu. Then select **2.0.0.M5** as the version of Spring Boot we wish to use.

Next, we need to pick our application's coordinates, as follows:

- Group - com.greglturnquist.learningspringboot
- Artifact - learning-spring-boot

Now comes the fun part. We pick the ingredients for our application, like picking off a delicious menu. If we start typing, say, Web, into the **Dependencies** box, we'll see several options appear. To see all the available options, click on the **Switch to the full version** link toward the bottom.

There are lots of overrides, such as switching from JAR to WAR, or using an older version of Java. You can also pick Kotlin or Groovy as the primary language for your application. For starters, in this day and age, there is no reason to use anything older than Java 8. JAR files are the way to go. WAR files are only needed when applying Spring Boot to an old container.

To build our social media platform, we need these few ingredients:

- Reactive Web (embedded Netty + Spring WebFlux)
- Reactive MongoDB (Spring Data MongoDB)
- Thymeleaf template engine
- Lombok (to simplify writing POJOs)

The following screenshot shows us picking these options:

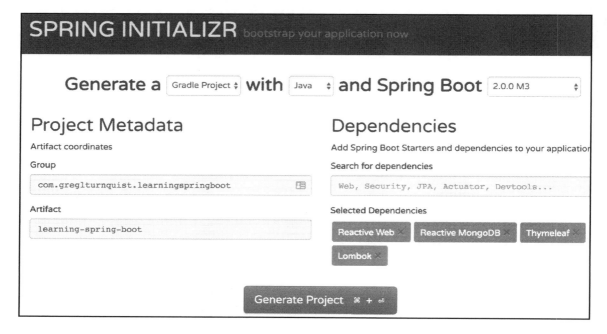

With these items selected, click on **Generate Project**.

 There are *lots* of other tools that leverage this site. For example, IntelliJ IDEA lets you create a new project inside the IDE, giving you the same options shown here. It invokes the website's REST API, and imports your new project. You can also interact with the site via curl or any other REST-based tool.

Now, let's unpack that ZIP file, and see what we've got. You will find the following:

- A `build.gradle` build file
- A Gradle wrapper, so there's no need to install Gradle
- A `LearningSpringBootApplication.java` application class
- An `application.properties` file
- A `LearningSpringBootApplicationTests.java` test class

We built an empty Spring Boot project. Now what? Before we sink our teeth into writing code, let's take a peek at the build file. It's quite terse, but carries some key bits.

Let's take a look, starting from the top:

```
buildscript {
  ext {
    springBootVersion = '2.0.0.M5'
  }
  repositories {
    mavenCentral()
    maven { url "https://repo.spring.io/snapshot" }
    maven { url "https://repo.spring.io/milestone" }
  }
  dependencies {
    classpath(
        "org.springframework.boot:spring-boot-gradle-
        plugin:${springBootVersion}")
  }
}
```

This preceding build file contains the basis for our project:

- `springBootVersion` shows us we are using Spring Boot **2.0.0.M5**
- The Maven repositories it will pull from are listed next (Maven central plus Spring's snapshot and milestone repositories)
- Finally, we see the `spring-boot-gradle-plugin`, a critical tool for any Spring Boot project

The first piece, the version of Spring Boot, is important. That's because Spring Boot comes with a curated list of 140 third-party library versions, extending well beyond the Spring portfolio and into some of the most commonly used libraries in the Java ecosystem. By simply changing the version of Spring Boot, we can upgrade all these libraries to newer versions known to work together. (See `https://github.com/spring-projects/spring-boot/blob/master/spring-boot-project/spring-boot-dependencies/pom.xml` for a complete list.)

There is an extra project, the Spring IO Platform (`http://platform.spring.io/platform/`), which includes an additional 134 curated versions, bringing the total to 274.

The repositories aren't as critical, but it's important to add milestones and snapshots if fetching a library that hasn't been released to Maven central, or is hosted on some vendor's local repository. Thankfully, Spring Initializr does this for us based on the version of Spring Boot selected on the site.

Finally, we have `spring-boot-gradle-plugin` (and there is a corresponding `spring-boot-maven-plugin` for Maven users). This plugin is responsible for linking Spring Boot's curated list of versions with the libraries we select in the build file. That way, we don't have to specify the version number.

Additionally, this plugin hooks into the build phase and bundles our application into a runnable über JAR, also known as a shaded or fat JAR.

Java doesn't provide a standardized way of loading nested JAR files into the classpath. Spring Boot provides the means to bundle up third-party JARs inside an enclosing JAR file, and properly load them at runtime. Read more at `http://docs.spring.io/spring-boot/docs/2.0.0.M5/reference/htmlsingle/#executable-jar`.

With an über JAR in hand, we only need put it on a thumb drive. We can carry it to another machine, to a hundred virtual machines in the cloud, our data center, or anywhere else. It runs anywhere we can find a JVM.

Peeking a little further down in `build.gradle`, we can see the plugins that are enabled by default:

```
apply plugin: 'java'
apply plugin: 'eclipse'
apply plugin: 'org.springframework.boot'
apply plugin: 'io.spring.dependency-management'
```

- The `java` plugin indicates the various tasks expected for a Java project
- The `eclipse` plugin helps generate project metadata for Eclipse users
- The `org.springframework.boot` plugin is where the actual `spring-boot-gradle-plugin` is activated
- The `io.spring.dependency-management` plugin supports Maven **Bill of Materials (BOM)** manifests, allowing usage of libraries that manage the sets of library versions in our Gradle build. (Because Maven supports this natively, there is no Maven equivalent plugin.)

An up-to-date copy of IntelliJ IDEA can read a plain old Gradle-build file just fine without extra plugins.

This brings us to the final ingredient used to build our application--**Dependencies**.

Spring Boot starters

No application is complete without specifying dependencies. A valuable feature of Spring Boot is its virtual packages. These are published packages that don't contain any code, but simply list other dependencies instead.

The following code shows all the dependencies we selected on the Spring Initializr site:

```
dependencies {
    compile('org.springframework.boot:spring-boot-starter-data-
    mongodb-reactive')
    compile('org.springframework.boot:spring-boot-starter-thymeleaf')
    compile('org.springframework.boot:spring-boot-starter-webflux')

    compile('org.projectlombok:lombok')
    compile('de.flapdoodle.embed:de.flapdoodle.embed.mongo')
    testCompile('org.springframework.boot:spring-boot-starter-test')
}
```

You might have noticed that most of these packages are Spring Boot starters:

- `spring-boot-starter-data-mongodb-reactive` pulls in Spring Data MongoDB with the reactive bits enabled
- `spring-boot-starter-thymeleaf` pulls in the Thymeleaf template engine
- `spring-boot-starter-webflux` pulls in Spring WebFlux, Jackson JSON support, and embedded Netty

These starter packages allow us to quickly grab the bits we need to get up and running. Spring Boot starters have become so popular that many other third-party library developers are crafting their own.

In addition to starters, we have the following three extra libraries:

- Project Lombok (`https://projectlombok.org`) makes it dead simple to define POJOs without getting bogged down in getters, setters, and other details.
- Flapdoodle is an embedded MongoDB database that allows us to write tests, tinker with a solution, and get things moving before getting involved with an external database.

 At the time of writing, Flapdoodle isn't listed on the website. We must add it manually, as shown previously.

- `spring-boot-starter-test` pulls in Spring Boot Test, JSONPath, JUnit, AssertJ, Mockito, Hamcrest, JSONassert, and Spring Test, all within test scope.

The value of this last starter, `spring-boot-starter-test`, cannot be overstated. With a single line, the most powerful test utilities are at our fingertips, allowing us to write unit tests, slice tests, and full-blown our-app-inside-embedded-Netty tests. It's why this starter is included in all projects without checking a box on the Spring Initializr site.

Now, to get things off the ground, we need to shift focus to the tiny bit of code written for us by the Spring Initializr.

Running a Spring Boot application

The fabulous `https://start.spring.io` website created a tiny class, `LearningSpringBootApplication`, as shown here:

```
package com.greglturnquist.learningspringboot;

import org.springframework.boot.SpringApplication;
import
 org.springframework.boot.autoconfigure.SpringBootApplication;

@SpringBootApplication
public class LearningSpringBootApplication {

  public static void main(String[] args) {
    SpringApplication.run(
      LearningSpringBootApplication.class, args);
  }
}
```

This preceding tiny class is actually a fully operational web application!

- The `@SpringBootApplication` annotation tells Spring Boot, when launched, to scan recursively for Spring components inside this package and register them. It also tells Spring Boot to enable **autoconfiguration**, a process where beans are automatically created based on classpath settings, property settings, and other factors. We'll see more of this throughout the book. Finally, it indicates that this class itself can be a source for Spring bean definitions.
- It holds `public static void main()`, a simple method to run the application. There is no need to drop this code into an application server or servlet container. We can just run it straight up, inside our IDE. The amount of time saved by this feature, over the long haul, adds up fast.

- `SpringApplication.run()` points Spring Boot at the leap-off point--in this case, this very class. But it's possible to run other classes.

This little class is runnable. Right now! In fact, let's give it a shot:

```
  .   ____          _            __ _ _
 /\\ / ___'_ __ _ _(_)_ __  __ _ \ \ \ \
( ( )\___ | '_ | '_| | '_ \/ _` | \ \ \ \
 \\/  ___)| |_)| | | | | || (_| |  ) ) ) )
  '  |____| .__|_| |_|_| |_\__, | / / / /
 =========|_|==============|___/=/_/_/_/
 :: Spring Boot ::    (v2.0.0.M5)
2017-08-02 15:34:22.374: Starting LearningSpringBootApplication
on ret...
2017-08-02 15:34:22.377: Running with Spring Boot
v2.0.0.BUILD-SNAPSHO...
2017-08-02 15:34:22.378: No active profile set, falling back
to defaul...
2017-08-02 15:34:22.433: Refreshing
org.springframework.boot.web.react...
2017-08-02 15:34:23.717: HV000184: ParameterMessageInterpolator
has be...
2017-08-02 15:34:23.815: HV000184: ParameterMessageInterpolator
has be...
2017-08-02 15:34:23.953: Cannot find template location:
classpath:/tem...
2017-08-02 15:34:24.094: Mapped URL path [/webjars/**] onto
handler of...
2017-08-02 15:34:24.094: Mapped URL path [/**] onto handler of
type [c...
2017-08-02 15:34:24.125: Looking for @ControllerAdvice:
org.springfram...
2017-08-02 15:34:24.501: note: noprealloc may hurt performance
in many...
2017-08-02 15:34:24.858: 2017-08-02T15:34:24.858-0500 I
NETWORK  [init...
2017-08-02 15:34:24.858: start
de.flapdoodle.embed.mongo.config.Mongod...
2017-08-02 15:34:24.908: Cluster created with settings
{hosts=[localho...
2017-08-02 15:34:24.908: Adding discovered server
localhost:65485 to c...
2017-08-02 15:34:25.007: 2017-08-02T15:34:25.006-0500 I
NETWORK  [init...
2017-08-02 15:34:25.038: Opened connection
[connectionId{localValue:1,...
2017-08-02 15:34:25.040: Monitor thread successfully
connected to serv...
```

```
2017-08-02 15:34:25.041: Discovered cluster type of STANDALONE
2017-08-02 15:34:25.145: Cluster created with settings
 {hosts=[localho...
2017-08-02 15:34:25.145: Adding discovered server
 localhost:65485 to c...
2017-08-02 15:34:25.153: Opened connection
 [connectionId{localValue:2,...
2017-08-02 15:34:25.153: Monitor thread successfully connected
 to serv...
2017-08-02 15:34:25.153: Discovered cluster type of STANDALONE
2017-08-02 15:34:25.486: Registering beans for JMX exposure
 on startup
2017-08-02 15:34:25.556: Started HttpServer on
 /0:0:0:0:0:0:0:0:8080
2017-08-02 15:34:25.558: Netty started on port(s): 8080
2017-08-02 15:34:25.607: Started in 3.617 seconds (JVM
 running for 4.0...
```

Scrolling through the preceding output, we can see these several things:

- The banner at the top gives us a read-out of the version of Spring Boot. (By the way, you can create your own ASCII art banner by creating either `banner.txt` or `banner.png` and putting it in the `src/main/resources/` folder.)
- Embedded Netty is initialized on port `8080`, indicating that it's ready for web requests.
- It's slightly cut off, but there are signs that Flapdoodle, our embedded MongoDB data store, has come up.
- And the wonderful **Started LearningSpringBootApplication in 3.617 seconds** message can be seen too.

Spring Boot uses embedded Netty, so there's no need to install a container on our target machine. Non-web apps don't even require that. The JAR itself is the new container that allows us to stop thinking in terms of old-fashioned servlet containers. Instead, we think in terms of apps. All these factors add up to maximum flexibility in application deployment.

How does Spring Boot use embedded Netty among other things? As mentioned earlier, it has autoconfiguration, which means that it defines Spring beans based on different conditions. When Spring Boot sees Netty on the classpath, it creates an embedded Netty instance along with several beans to support it.

When it spots Spring WebFlux on the classpath, it creates view resolution engines, handler mappers, and a whole host of other beans needed to help us write a web application. This lets us focus writing routes, not doddling around configuring infrastructure.

With Flapdoodle on the classpath as well as the Reactive MongoDB drivers, it spins up an in-memory, embedded MongoDB data store and connects to it with its state-of-the-art drivers.

Spring Data MongoDB will cause Spring Boot to craft a `MongoOperations` bean along with everything else needed to start speaking Mongo Query Language and make it available if we ask for it, letting us focus on defining repositories.

At this stage, we have a running web application, albeit an empty one. There are no custom routes, and no means to handle data. But we can add some real fast.

Let's start by drafting a simple REST controller as follows:

```
package com.greglturnquist.learningspringboot;

import org.springframework.web.bind.annotation.GetMapping;
import org.springframework.web.bind.annotation.RequestParam;
import org.springframework.web.bind.annotation.RestController;

@RestController
public class HomeController {

  @GetMapping
  public String greeting(@RequestParam(required = false,
  defaultValue = "") String name) {
    return name.equals("") ? "Hey!" : "Hey, " + name + "!";
  }

}
```

Let's examine this tiny REST controller in detail:

- The `@RestController` annotation indicates that we don't want to render views, but write the results straight into the response body instead.
- `@GetMapping` is Spring's shorthand annotation for `@RequestMapping(method = RequestMethod.GET)`. In this case, it defaults the route to `/`.
- Our `greeting()` method has one argument-- `@RequestParam(required=false, defaultValue="") String name`. It indicates that this value can be requested via an HTTP query (`?name=Greg`)--the query isn't required, and in case it's missing, it will supply an empty string.
- Finally, we return one of two messages depending on whether or not the `name` is an empty string, using Java's ternary operator.

If we relaunch `LearningSpringBootApplication` in our IDE, we'll see this new entry in the console:

```
2017-08-02 15:40:00.741: Mapped "{[],methods=[GET]}" onto
public java....
```

We can then ping our new route in the browser at `http://localhost:8080` and `http://localhost:8080?name=Greg`. Try it out!

(By the way, it sure would be handy if the system could detect this change and relaunch automatically, right? Check out Chapter 5, *Developer Tools for Spring Boot Apps* to find out how.)

That's nice, but since we picked Spring Data MongoDB, how hard would it be to load some sample data and retrieve it from another route? (Spoiler alert--Not hard at all.)

We can start out by defining a simple `Chapter` entity to capture book details, as follows:

```java
package com.greglturnquist.learningspringboot;

import lombok.Data;

import org.springframework.data.annotation.Id;
import org.springframework.data.mongodb.core.mapping.Document;

@Data
@Document
public class Chapter {

  @Id
  private String id;
  private String name;

  public Chapter(String name) {
    this.name = name;
  }

}
```

This preceding little POJO lets us look at the details about the chapter of a book as follows:

- The `@Data` annotation from Lombok generates getters, setters, a `toString()` method, an `equals()` method, a `hashCode()` method, and a constructor for all required (that is, `final`) fields
- The `@Document` annotation flags this class as suitable for storing in a MongoDB data store

- The `id` field is marked with Spring Data's `@Id` annotation, indicating this is the primary key of our Mongo document
- Spring Data MongoDB will, by default, create a collection named `chapters` with two fields, `id` and `name`
- Our field of interest is `name`, so let's create a constructor call to help insert some test data

To interact with this entity and its corresponding collection in MongoDB, we could dig in and start using the autoconfigured `MongoOperations` supplied by Spring Boot. But why do that when we can declare a repository-based solution?

To do this, we'll create an interface defining the operations we need. Check out this simple interface:

```
package com.greglturnquist.learningspringboot;

import org.springframework.data.repository
  .reactive.ReactiveCrudRepository;

public interface ChapterRepository
  extends ReactiveCrudRepository<Chapter, String> {

}
```

This last declarative interface creates a Spring Data repository as follows:

- `ReactiveCrudRepository` extends `Repository`, a Spring Data Commons marker interface that signals Spring Data to create a concrete implementation based on the reactive paradigm while also capturing domain information. It also comes with some predefined CRUD operations (`save`, `delete`, `deleteById`, `deleteAll`, `findById`, `findAll`, and more).
- It specifies the entity type (`Chapter`) and the type of the primary key (`String`).
- We could also add custom finders, but we'll save that for `Chapter 3`, *Reactive Data Access with Spring Boot*.

Spring Data MongoDB will automatically wire up a concrete implementation of this interface.

 Spring Data doesn't engage in code generation. Code generation has a sordid history of being out of date at some of the worst times. Instead, Spring Data uses proxies and other mechanisms to support these operations. Never forget--the code you don't write has no bugs.

With `Chapter` and `ChapterRepository` defined, we can now preload the database, as shown in the following code:

```java
package com.greglturnquist.learningspringboot;

import reactor.core.publisher.Flux;

import org.springframework.boot.CommandLineRunner;
import org.springframework.context.annotation.Bean;
import org.springframework.context.annotation.Configuration;

@Configuration
public class LoadDatabase {

  @Bean
  CommandLineRunner init(ChapterRepository repository) {
    return args -> {
      Flux.just(
        new Chapter("Quick Start with Java"),
        new Chapter("Reactive Web with Spring Boot"),
        new Chapter("...and more!"))
        .flatMap(repository::save)
        .subscribe(System.out::println);
    };
  }

}
```

This preceding class will be automatically scanned by Spring Boot and run in the following way:

- `@Configuration` marks this class as a source of beans.
- `@Bean` indicates that the return value of `init()` is a Spring Bean--in this case, a `CommandLineRunner` (utility class from Spring Boot).
- Spring Boot runs all `CommandLineRunner` beans after the entire application is up and running. This bean definition requests a copy of `ChapterRepository`.
- Using Java 8's ability to coerce the `args → {}` lambda function into `CommandLineRunner`, we are able to gather a set of `Chapter` data, save all of them and then print them out, preloading our data.

We aren't going to delve into the intricacies of `Flux`, `flatMap`, and `subscribe` yet. We'll save that for Chapter 2, *Reactive Web with Spring Boot* and Chapter 3, *Reactive Data Access with Spring Boot*.

With all this in place, the only thing left is to write a REST controller to serve up the data!

```java
package com.greglturnquist.learningspringboot;

import reactor.core.publisher.Flux;

import org.springframework.web.bind.annotation.GetMapping;
import org.springframework.web.bind.annotation.RestController;

@RestController
public class ChapterController {

  private final ChapterRepository repository;

  public ChapterController(ChapterRepository repository) {
    this.repository = repository;
  }

  @GetMapping("/chapters")
  public Flux<Chapter> listing() {
    return repository.findAll();
  }
}
```

This preceding controller is able to serve up our data as follows:

- `@RestController` indicates that this is another REST controller.
- Constructor injection is used to automatically load it with a copy of `ChapterRepository`. With Spring, if there is only one constructor call, there is no need to include an `@Autowired` annotation.
- `@GetMapping` tells Spring that this is the place to route `/chapters` calls. In this case, it returns the results of the `findAll()` call found in `ReactiveCrudRepository`. Again, if you're curious what `Flux<Chapter>` is, we'll tackle that at the top of the next chapter. For now, think of it being like a `Stream<Chapter>`.

If we relaunch our application and visit `http://localhost:8080/chapters`, we can see our preloaded data served up as a nicely formatted JSON document, as seen in this screenshot:

```
[
    - {
          id: 1,
          name: "Quick start with Java"
      },
    - {
          id: 2,
          name: "Reactive Web with Spring Boot"
      },
    - {
          id: 3,
          name: "...and more!"
      }
]
```

This may not be very elaborate, but this small collection of classes has helped us quickly define a slice of functionality. And, if you'll notice, we spent zero effort configuring JSON converters, route handlers, embedded settings, or any other infrastructure.

Spring Boot is designed to let us focus on functional needs, not low-level plumbing.

Delving into Spring Boot's property support

We just got things off the ground with an operational application, but that isn't the only killer feature of Spring Boot.

Spring Boot comes with a fistful of prebuilt properties. In fact, just about every autoconfigured component has some property setting (`http://docs.spring.io/spring-boot/docs/2.0.0.M5/reference/htmlsingle/#common-application-properties`) allowing you to override just the parts you like.

Many of these autoconfigured beans will back off if Boot spots us creating our own. For example, when Spring Boot spots reactive MongoDB drivers on the classpath, it automatically creates a reactive `MongoClient`. However, if we define our own `MongoClient` bean, then Spring Boot will back off and accept ours.

This can lead to other components switching off. But sometimes, we don't need to swap out an entire bean. Instead, we may wish to merely tweak a single property of one of these autoconfigured beans.

Let's try to make some adjustments to `src/main/resources/application.properties` as follows:

```
# Override the port Tomcat listens on
server.port=9000

# Customize log levels
logging.level.com.greglturnquist=DEBUG
```

This preceding changes will cause Spring Boot to launch Netty on port `9000`, as shown here:

```
2017-08-02 15:40:02.489: Netty started on port(s): 9000
```

It will also bump up the log level for package `com.greglturnquist` to `DEBUG`.

 Many modern IDEs include **code completion** to find various properties.

While it's handy to externalize configuration settings into property files, it wouldn't be a big advantage if they were only embeddable inside our app's JAR file.

That's why, Spring Boot comes with property override support. The following list shows all the locations from which we can override properties, the first being the highest priority:

- The `@TestPropertySource` annotation on test classes
- Command-line arguments
- The properties found inside `SPRING_APPLICATION_JSON` (inline JSON embedded in an `env` variable or system property)
- The `ServletConfig` init parameters
- The `ServletContext` init parameters
- The JNDI attributes from `java:comp/env`
- The Java System properties (`System.getProperties()`)
- The OS environment variables
- A `RandomValuePropertySource` that only has properties in `random.*`

- Profile-specific properties outside the packaged JAR file (`application-{profile}.properties` and YAML variants)
- Profile-specific properties inside the packaged JAR file (`application-{profile}.properties` and YAML variants)
- Application properties outside the package JAR file (`application.properties` and YAML variants)
- Application properties inside the packaged JAR file (`application.properties` and YAML variants)
- The `@PropertySource` annotation on any `@Configuration` classes
- Default properties (specified using `SpringApplication.setDefaultProperties`)

For an example of the same overrides in YAML format as our `application.properties` file, we could put the following in `application.yml` in `src/main/resources`:

```
server:
  port: 9000
logging:
  level:
    com:
      greglturnquist: DEBUG
```

This would do the exact same thing that we already saw with `application.properties`. The only difference is the formatting.

What are the benefits of YAML over properties? If we need to override lots of settings, it avoids duplication of various keys.

Spring properties can also reference other properties, as shown in this fragment:

```
app.name=MyApp
app.description=${app.name} is a Spring Boot application
```

In this preceding example, the second property, `app.description`, references the first property, `app.name`.

This isn't the end of options with property overrides. It's just the beginning. Throughout this book, we'll expand on the options provided by Spring Boot's property support.

For now, let's focus on getting our app to production!

Bundling up the application as a runnable JAR file

We've hacked out a suitable application. Now it's time to take it to production. As Spring Developer Advocate Josh Long likes to say, production is the happiest place on earth.

The good ol' `spring-boot-gradle-plugin` has built-in hooks to handle that for us. By invoking Gradle's `build` task, it will insert itself into the build process, and create a JAR file.

```
$ ./gradlew clean build
:clean
:compileJava
:processResources
:classes
:findMainClass
:jar
:bootRepackage
:assemble
:compileTestJava
:processTestResources UP-TO-DATE
:testClasses
:test
... test output ...
:check
:build
BUILD SUCCESSFUL
Total time: 10.946 secs
```

If we peek at the output, we'll find the original JAR file (non-FAT) along with the rebundled one containing our application code as well as the third-party dependencies, as shown here:

```
$ ls build/libs
learning-spring-boot-0.0.1-SNAPSHOT.jar
learning-spring-boot-0.0.1-SNAPSHOT.jar.original
```

If you wish to check out the newly minted JAR's contents, type `jar tvf build/libs/learning-spring-boot-0.0.1-SNAPSHOT.jar`. We won't show it here because of space constraints.

The über JAR is nicely loaded up with our custom code, all of our third-party dependencies, and a little Spring Boot code to allow us to run it. Why not try that out right here?

Let's type the following command:

```
$ java -jar build/libs/learning-spring-boot-0.0.1-SNAPSHOT.jar
```

We can expect the same output as before, which is as seen in this image:

```
  .   ____          _            __ _ _
 /\\ / ___'_ __ _ _(_)_ __  __ _ \ \ \ \
( ( )\___ | '_ | '_| | '_ \/ _` | \ \ \ \
 \\/  ___)| |_)| | | | | || (_| |  ) ) ) )
  '  |____| .__|_| |_|_| |_\__, | / / / /
 =========|_|==============|___/=/_/_/_/
 :: Spring Boot ::    (v2.0.0.M5)
2017-09-19 20:41:20.036: Starting LearningSpringBootApplication
 on ret...
...
... the rest has been cut for space ...
```

By invoking the JAR using Java's -jar option, we can launch the application with nothing more than the JVM on our machine.

With our JAR file in hand, we can take our application anywhere. If we need to override any settings, we can do it without cracking it open and making alterations.

Suppose we alter our command slightly, like this:

```
$ SERVER_PORT=8000 java
  -jar build/libs/learning-spring-boot-0.0.1-SNAPSHOT.jar
```

We can now expect the results to be a little different, as seen in this image:

```
  .   ____          _            __ _ _
 /\\ / ___'_ __ _ _(_)_ __  __ _ \ \ \ \
( ( )\___ | '_ | '_| | '_ \/ _` | \ \ \ \
 \\/  ___)| |_)| | | | | || (_| |  ) ) ) )
  '  |____| .__|_| |_|_| |_\__, | / / / /
 =========|_|==============|___/=/_/_/_/
 :: Spring Boot ::    (v2.0.0.M5)
...
2017-08-03 15:40:02.489: Netty started on port(s): 8000
...
```

From the command line, we override server.port using an alternative notation (SERVER_PORT) and run it on port 8000.

This lends us the ability to deploy it into the cloud.

Deploying to Cloud Foundry

Cloud-native applications are becoming the norm, as companies accelerate their rate of releasing to production (`https://pivotal.io/cloud-native`).

> *Cloud Native describes the patterns of high performing organizations delivering software faster, consistently and reliably at scale. Continuous delivery, DevOps, and microservices label the why, how and what of the cloud natives. In the the most advanced expression of these concepts they are intertwined to the point of being inseparable. Leveraging automation to improve human performance in a high trust culture, moving faster and safer with confidence and operational excellence.*

Many cloud platforms thrive under releasing self-contained applications. The open source Cloud Foundry platform, with its support for many technologies and runnable JAR files, is one of the most popular ones.

To get started, we need either a copy of Cloud Foundry installed in our data center, or an account at **Pivotal Web Services (PWS)**, a Cloud Foundry hosting provider (`https://run.pivotal.io/`). Assuming we have a PWS account (pronounced *p-dubs*), let's install the tools and deploy our app.

On macOS X, we can type this:

```
$ brew tap cloudfoundry/tap
$ brew install cf-cli
=> Installing cf-cli from cloudfoundry/tap
==> Downloading
    https://cli.run.pivotal.io/stable?release=macosx64-bin...
==> Downloading from
    https://s3-us-west-1.amazonaws.com/cf-cli-release...
    ####################################################
    ####################...
==> Caveats
    Bash completion has been installed to:
    /usr/local/etc/bash_completion.d
==> Summary
    /usr/local/Cellar/cf-cli/6.32.0: 6 files, 16.7MB,
    built in 10 seco...
```

For Linux, we can fetch a tarball like this:

```
$ wget -O cf-linux.tgz "https://cli.run.pivotal.io/stable?
  release=linux64-binary&source=github"
$ tar xvfz cf-linux.tgz
$ chmod 755 ./cf
```

This preceding code will download and enable a Linux-based `cf` tool.

 Before using the `cf` tool, you must register for an account at PWS.

For more installation details, visit
`https://docs.run.pivotal.io/cf-cli/install-go-cli.html`.

Using the `cf` tool, let's deploy our application. To kick things off, we need to log into PWS, as follows:

```
$ cf login
API endpoint: https://api.run.pivotal.io
Email> gturnquist@pivotal.io
Password>
Authenticating...
OK
Select an org (or press enter to skip):
... your organizations will be listed here ...
Org> 2
Targeted org FrameworksAndRuntimes
Select a space (or press enter to skip):
... your spaces will be listed here ...
Space> 1
Targeted space development
API endpoint:    https://api.run.pivotal.io (API version: 2.62.0)
User:            gturnquist@pivotal.io
Org:             FrameworksAndRuntimes
Space:           development
```

We are logged in and targeting a logical space inside an organization.

 Your `Org` and `Space` will certainly be different.

Time to deploy! We can do so with the `cf push` command. At a minimum, we specify the name of our application and the artifact with the `-p` option (and use a different name than `learning-spring-boot`, since it's been taken by this book!):

```
$ cf push learning-spring-boot -p build/libs/learning-spring-boot-
  0.0.1-SNAPSHOT.jar
Creating app learning-spring-boot in org FrameworksAndRuntimes
```

```
/ space development as gturnquist@pivotal.io...
OK
Creating route learning-spring-boot.cfapps.io...
OK
Binding learning-spring-boot.cfapps.io to learning-spring-boot...
OK
Uploading learning-spring-boot...
...
...
Staging complete
Uploading droplet, build artifacts cache...
Uploading build artifacts cache...
Uploading droplet...
Uploaded build artifacts cache (108B)
Uploaded droplet (76.7M)
Uploading complete
Destroying container
Successfully destroyed container
0 of 1 instances running, 1 starting
0 of 1 instances running, 1 starting
0 of 1 instances running, 1 starting
1 of 1 instances running
App started
OK
...
...
requested state: started
instances: 1/1
usage: 1G x 1 instances
urls: learning-spring-boot.cfapps.io
last uploaded: Tue Sep 20 02:01:13 UTC 2017
stack: cflinuxfs2
buildpack: java-buildpack=v3.9-offline-
https://github.com/cloudfoundry/java-buildpack.git#b050954 java-main
open-jdk-like-jre=1.8.0_101 open-jdk-like-memory-
calculator=2.0.2_RELEASE spring-auto-reconfiguration=1.10.0_RELEASE
     state    since                    cpu      memory       disk
#0   running  2017-09-19 09:01:59 PM   243.7%   503.5M of 1G  158.1M of 1G

     details
```

We have pushed our JAR file to PWS, let the Java buildpack (automatically selected) register it with a URL, and start it up. Now, we can visit its registered URL at `http://learning-spring-boot.cfapps.io`:

```
$ curl http://learning-spring-boot.cfapps.io?name=Greg
  Hey, Greg!
```

We've taken our application to production.

The next step is to handle what are sometimes referred to as *Day 2 situations*. This is where we must now monitor and maintain our application, and Spring Boot is ready to provide us just what we need.

Adding production-ready support

We've created a Spring web app with minimal code and released it to production. This is the perfect time to introduce production-grade support features.

There are some questions that often arise in production, and these are as follows:

- What do we do when the system administrator wants to configure his or her monitoring software to ping our app to see if it's up?
- What happens when our manager wants to know the metrics of people hitting our app?
- What are we going to do when the ops center supervisor calls us at 2:00 a.m. and we have to figure out what went wrong?

The last feature we are going to introduce in this chapter is Spring Boot's **Actuator** module. This module provides some super slick Ops-oriented features that are incredibly valuable in a production environment.

We start by adding this dependency to our `build.gradle` as follows:

```
compile('org.springframework.boot:spring-boot-starter-actuator')
```

When you run this version of our app, the same business functionality is available that we saw earlier, but there are additional HTTP endpoints; these are listed in the following table:

Actuator Endpoint	Description
`/application/autoconfig`	This reports what Spring Boot did and didn't autoconfigure, and why
`/appplication/beans`	This reports all the beans configured in the application context (including ours as well as the ones autoconfigured by Boot)
`/application/configprops`	This exposes all configuration properties
`/application/dump`	This creates thread dump report

`/application/env`	This reports on the current system environment
`/application/health`	This is a simple endpoint to check the life of the app
`/application/info`	This serves up custom content from the app
`/application/metrics`	This shows counters and gauges on web usage
`/application/mappings`	This gives us details about all Spring WebFlux routes
`/application/trace`	This shows the details about past requests

Endpoints, by default, are disabled. We have to *opt in*. This is accomplished by setting `endpoints.{endpoint}.enabled=true` inside `src/main/resources/application.properties`, like this:

```
endpoints.health.enabled=true
```

This line added to `application.properties` mentions the endpoint, health, and enables it. If we restart the application, we can ping for its health, as shown in the next section.

Pinging our app for general health

Each of these endpoints can be visited using our browser or using other tools like `curl`:

```
$ curl localhost:9000/application/health
{
  "status": "UP",
  "details": {
    "mongo": {
      "status": "UP",
      "details": {
        "version": "3.2.2"
      }
    },
    "diskSpace": {
      "status": "UP",
      "details": {
        "total": 498937626624,
        "free": 66036432896,
        "threshold": 10485760
      }
    }
  }
}
```

This preceding health status gives us the following:

- An overall UP status
- The status of MongoDB
- The status of the diskspace

When other components are added, they may, optionally, add their own health checks.

This immediately solves our first need listed previously. We can inform the system administrator that he or she can write a management script to interrogate our app's health.

Be warned that each of these endpoints serve up a compact JSON document. Generally speaking, command-line curl probably isn't the best option. While it's convenient on *nix and Mac systems, the content is dense and hard to read. It's more practical to have the following:

- a JSON plugin installed in our browser (such as JSON Viewer at https://github.com/tulios/json-viewer)
- a script that uses a JSON parsing library if we're writing a management script (such as Groovy's JsonSlurper at http://docs.groovy-lang.org/latest/html/gapi/groovy/json/JsonSlurper.html or JsonPath at https://code.google.com/p/json-path)

Metrics

To really get operational, we need metrics. Most production systems have metrics in one form or another. Thankfully, we don't have to start from scratch. There is a metric endpoint in Spring Boot Actuator. If we add this following setting to application.properties:

```
endpoints.metrics.enabled=true
```

With this property setting, if we restart the application, we can get a quick read out on thing.

Assuming we have JSON Viewer installed, it's easy to surf to http://localhost:9000/application/metrics and get a listing on all sorts of metrics. We even have counters for every good/bad web hit, broken down on a per-page basis, as shown here:

```
{
  "names": [
    "jvm.buffer.memory.used",
```

```
        "jvm.memory.used",
        "jvm.buffer.count",
        "logback.events",
        "process.uptime",
        "jvm.memory.committed",
        "jvm.buffer.total.capacity",
        "jvm.memory.max",
        "process.starttime",
        "http.server.requests"
    ]
}
```

We can visit any one of these metrics by appending it's name to the metrics URL. For example, to view the `http.server.requests`, visit `http://localhost:9000/application/metrics/http.server.requests`:

```
{
    "name": "http.server.requests",
    "measurements": [
        {
            "statistic": "TotalTime",
            "value": 3.53531643E8
        },
        {
            "statistic": "Count",
            "value": 57.0
        }
    ],
    "availableTags": [
        {
            "tag": "exception",
            "values": [
                "none",
                "none",
                "none",
                "none"
            ]
        },
        {
            "tag": "method",
            "values": [
                "GET",
                "GET",
                "GET",
                "GET"
            ]
        },
        {
```

```
      "tag": "uri",
      "values": [
        "/application/metrics/{requiredMetricName}",
        "/application/metrics/{requiredMetricName}",
        "/application/metrics",
        "/favicon.ico"
      ]
    },
    {
      "tag": "status",
      "values": [
        "200",
        "404",
        "200",
        "200"
      ]
    }
  ]
}
```

This provides a basic framework of metrics to satisfy our manager's needs. It's important to understand that metrics gathered by Spring Boot Actuator aren't persistent across application restarts. To gather long-term data, we have to write them elsewhere (http://docs.spring.io/spring-boot/docs/2.0.0.M5/reference/htmlsingle/#producti on-ready-metrics).

If you have used Spring Boot 1.x, then this may look very different. That's because a newer, more sophisticated version of metrics has arrived-- **Micrometer**. It's currently in development, and may change quite a bit, so stay tuned at http://micrometer.io/, and be sure to follow @micrometerio on Twitter, as the ability to craft highly detailed and advanced metrics comes to Spring Boot.

Summary

In this chapter, we rapidly crafted a Spring Web application using the Spring stack on top of Netty with little configuration from our end. We plugged in Spring Boot's Actuator module, configuring it with metrics, health, and management features so that we can monitor it in production by merely adding two lines of extra code.

In the next chapter, we'll get underway building our social media platform using these scalable APIs built on top of Reactive Streams.

Reactive Web with Spring Boot

2

The more and more I use #SpringBoot the more I like it.

– Derek Stainer @dstainer

In the previous chapter, we saw how quickly an application can be created with just a few lines of code. In this chapter, we are going to embark upon a journey. We will build a social media application where users can upload pictures and write comments.

In this chapter, we will build the web layer for our social media application doing the following:

- Creating a reactive web application with Spring Initializr
- Learning the tenets of reactive programming
- Introducing Reactor types
- Switching from Apache Tomcat to Embedded Netty
- Comparing reactive **Spring WebFlux** against classic Spring MVC
- Showing some Mono/Flux-based endpoints
- Creating a reactive ImageService
- Creating a reactive file controller
- Showing how to interact with a Thymeleaf template
- Illustrating how going from async to sync can be easy, but the opposite is not

Creating a reactive web application with Spring Initializr

In the last chapter, we took a quick tour through the Spring Initializr site at `http://start.spring.io`. Let's go back there and pick some basic ingredients to start building our social media site by picking the options needed as shown in the following screenshot:

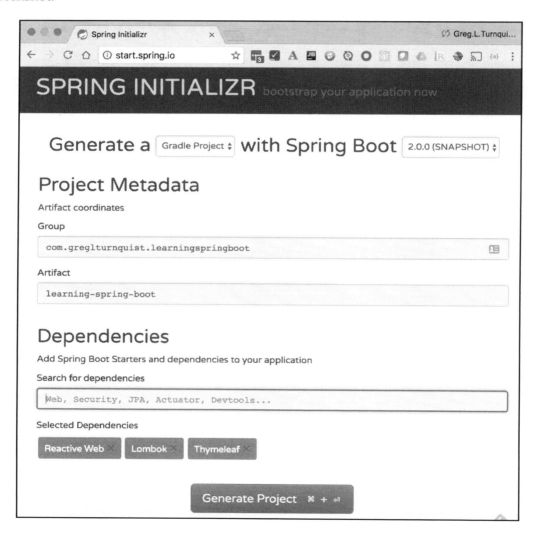

As shown in the preceding screenshot, we've picked the following options:

- **Build system**: Gradle
- **Spring Boot Version**: 2.0
- **Group**: com.greglturnquist.learningspringboot
- **Artifact**: learning-spring-boot

For dependencies, we are going to use these:

- **Reactive Web**: This pulls in Reactive Spring, something we'll explore here and through the rest of this book
- **Lombok**: This is a tiny library that keeps Java interesting by handling getters, setters, toString, equals, hashCode, and more
- **Thymeleaf**: This is not Boot's only supported template library, but a powerful one that includes reactive support as well as strict HTML compliance.

From here, we merely need to click on the **Generate Project** button and a zipped up project will be downloaded. Import it into our IDE, and we're ready to get rolling.

(We will add more dependencies to our project in later chapters.)

We won't list the entire Gradle build file generated by the site, but the dependencies are listed as follows:

```
dependencies {
    compile('org.springframework.boot:spring-boot-starter-webflux')
    compile("org.springframework.boot:spring-boot-starter-thymeleaf")
    compile('org.synchronoss.cloud:nio-multipart-parser:1.1.0')
    compile('org.projectlombok:lombok')
    testCompile('org.springframework.boot:spring-boot-starter-test')
}
```

The following dependencies are included in the build file:

- spring-boot-starter-webflux: This is the foundation for a Reactive Spring web applications
- spring-boot-starter-thymeleaf: This brings in Thymeleaf's template engine
- nio-multipart-parser: This is a third-party library from Synchronoss, which supports reactive multipart file uploads

- `lombok`: This is a convenient library to create mutable and immutable value objects among other things
- `spring-boot-starter-test`: This is a collection of test libraries including JUnit, Spring Boot Test, Mockito, AssertJ, JSONassert, and Hamcrest

What version of Spring Boot are we using? That can be spotted toward the top of `build.gradle` inside the `buildscript` fragment, as seen here:

```
ext {
    springBootVersion = '2.0.0.M5'
}
```

The version is specified at the top to feed both `spring-boot-gradle-plugin` as well as in the dependencies.

The Gradle build additionally uses the Spring team's Dependency Management Gradle plugin (available here: `https://github.com/spring-gradle-plugins/dependency-management-plugin`), which includes several Maven-like dependency management features. It includes the ability to consume any Maven **Bills of Materials (BOMs)** while also handling direct and transitive dependencies.

With our build file in place, we can now dive into *reactive programming*.

Learning the tenets of reactive programming

To launch things, we are going to take advantage of one of Spring Boot's hottest new features--Spring Framework 5's reactive support. The entire Spring portfolio is embracing the paradigm of reactive applications, and we'll focus on what this means and how we can cash in without breaking the bank.

Before we can do that, the question arises--what *is* a reactive application?

In simplest terms, reactive applications engage in the concept of non-blocking, asynchronous operations. Asynchronous means that the answer comes later, whether by polling or by an event pushed backed to us. Non-blocking means not waiting for a response, implying we may have to poll for the results. Either way, while the result is being formed, we don't hold up the thread, allowing it to service other calls.

The side effect of these two characteristics is that applications are able to accomplish more with existing resources.

There are several flavors of reactive applications going back to the 1970s, but the current one gaining resonance is **Reactive Streams** due its introduction of **backpressure**.

Backpressure is another way of saying volume control. The consumer controls how much data is sent by using a pull-based mechanism instead of a traditional push-based solution. For example, imagine requesting a collection of images from the system. You could receive one or a hundred thousand. To prevent the risk of running out of memory in the latter case, people often code page-based solutions. This ripples across the code base, causing a change in the API. And it introduces another layer of handling.

To expand on this example, the following solution would depict that risky collection:

```
public interface MyRepository {
  List<Image> findAll();
}
```

This preceding repository could indeed return one `Image` or a hundred thousand. There's no way to tell. The most common solution, as mentioned, would be to switch to something like this instead:

```
public interface MyRepository {
  Page<Image> findAll(Pageable p);
}
```

The first solution is simple. We know how to iterate over it. The second solution is also iterable (Spring Data Commons's `Page` type implements Java's `Iterable` interface), but requires passing in a parameter to our API, specifying how big a page is and which page we want. While not hard, it introduces a fundamental change in our API.

Reactive Streams is much simpler--return a container that lets the client choose how many items to take. Whether there is one or thousands, the client can use the exact same mechanism and take however many it's ready for. To do this, we would use the following method signature:

```
public interface MyRepository {
  Flux<Image> findAll();
}
```

A `Flux`, which we'll explore in greater detail in the next section, is very similar to a Java 8 `Stream`. We can take as many as we want and it lazily waits until we subscribe to it to yield anything. There is no need to put together a `PageRequest`, making it seamless to chain together controllers, services, and even remote calls.

Introducing Reactor types

We've mentioned Reactive Streams with little detail. There is a spec for Reactive Streams (`http://www.reactive-streams.org/`), but it's important to understand that it is quite primitive. In fact, it's so primitive that it's not very effective for building applications. That may sound counterintuitive, but it wasn't written so much for end users as it was for framework developers. To build reactive applications, we'll use Project Reactor (`http://projectreactor.io/`), the core library that Spring Framework 5 uses for its reactive programming model.

To introduce Reactor's core types, we'll begin with the one we just saw in the previous section, `Flux`, and some code like this:

```
Flux.just("alpha", "bravo", "charlie");
```

This simple creation of a Reactor `Flux` can be detailed as follows:

- `Flux` is Reactor's base type, a container holding *0..N* items, none of which will be reached until the client calls the reactive stream's `subscribe()` method. In this case, the container holds a set of strings.
- `just()` is a static helper method to construct a fixed collection. Other static helpers are also available, like `fromArray()`, `fromIterable()`, and `fromStream()`. This makes it easy to bridge existing Java collections.

 There are additional methods to convert a `Flux` to a Java `Stream` and an `Iterable`. But since these types are generally blocking, it's best to avoid them if possible.

Exactly what does a `Flux` embody? How is it different from a Java `List` or `Stream`? A `Flux` keenly represents multiple values coming, in the future, asynchronously. When those values are coming is not specified nor can it be assumed they are all arriving on the same thread.

In the past, Java has made it possible to represent either a single value or a collection of values that are coming right now in synchronous, blocking APIs. We've also had single value types for asynchronous values (`Future` and `CompletableFuture`). But Java has yet to create a value type for multiple, asynchronous values. That is what Project Reactor and Reactive Streams is all about--processing multiple, asynchronous, non-blocking values in a cohesive fashion.

To consume a `Flux`, we have to either `subscribe` or let the framework do it for us. Here's an example of subscribing for the results:

```
Flux.just("alpha", "bravo", "charlie")
  .subscribe(System.out::println);
```

This last code creates a `Flux` with three items, subscribes for the results, and prints each value out to the screen as follows:

```
alpha
bravo
charlie
```

This may not appear impressive, especially when compared to the existing Java collection builders like `Arrays.asList("alpha", "bravo", "charlie")`. Looks the same, right?

A difference can be seen when we start leveraging Java 8 lambdas and function types. That's when we can chain together a series of function calls, all of which are delayed until that exact element is extracted. Look at the following fragment:

```
Flux.just(
    (Supplier<String>) () -> "alpha",
    (Supplier<String>) () -> "bravo",
    (Supplier<String>) () -> "charlie")
      .subscribe(supplier -> System.out.println(supplier.get()));
```

This `Flux` contains the equivalent in values of our earlier `Flux.just()` except that each one is wrapped inside a Java 8 `Supplier`. This means that, actually, **retrieving** each value is delayed until subscription and only when each individual value is fetched through Reactor's `onNext()` method. This is also known as **lazy**.

Sure this example is contrived, but we'll see more of this paradigm as we explore reactive programming throughout this book.

Another facet of Project Reactor is over 160 operations rooted in functional programming including some of the most well known ones such as `map`, `flatMap`, `filter`, and `then`.

To wrap up this section, let's pick an example a little more complex in nature. What if we took the sample data that we have been poking at and count up how many of each letter we have. Check it out:

```
Flux.just("alpha", "bravo", "charlie")
  .map(String::toUpperCase)
  .flatMap(s -> Flux.fromArray(s.split("")))
  .groupBy(String::toString)
  .sort((o1, o2) -> o1.key().compareTo(o2.key()))
```

```
.flatMap(group -> Mono.just(group.key()).and(group.count()))
.map(keyAndCount ->
  keyAndCount.getT1() + " => " + keyAndCount.getT2())
  .subscribe(System.out::println);
```

We can take apart this preceding flow as follows:

- This **flow** starts with the same values as shown earlier in this chapter, `alpha`, `bravo`, and `charlie` bundled into a Reactor `Flux`.
- Each entry is converted to uppercase using `String::toUpperCase` ensuring we'll count lowers and uppers together.
- The entries are then flatMapped into individual letters. To visualize flatMapping, look at this example--`["alpha", "bravo"]` is mapped by `s.split("")` into a collection of collections, `[["a", "l", "p", "h", "a"], ["b", "r", "a", "v", "o"]]`, and then flattened into a single collection, `["a", "l", "p", "h", "a", "b", "r", "a", "v", "o"]`.
- Then we group by the string value, which will combine all the `"a"` entries into one subgroup, and so on and so forth.
- Next, we sort by the key value, because the group type doesn't implement `Comparable`.

 The underlying type of `groupBy()` is a `GroupedFlux`, a `Flux` with a key value that doesn't implement `Comparable`.

- We flatMap the group's key and count value into a pair of `Mono` objects. (More on `Mono` further in this chapter.)
- We unpack the tuple, and convert it into a string showing key and count.
- We subscribe to the entire flow, printing out the results.

The output can be seen as follows:

```
A => 4
B => 1
C => 1
E => 1
H => 2
I => 1
L => 2
O => 1
```

```
P => 1
R => 2
V => 1
```

Now that's a lot to take in all at once. Reactor flows, much like Java 8 streams, can pack a lot of functionality. But that is their key benefit. By spending little time on language ceremony, we, instead, focus on strong functional definitions. If needed, it can be handy to read each step in that flow again, using the bullet points to help decode it.

After chatting about `Flux` and all of its operations, something else has leaked into our code--Mono. What is that? It's a Reactor container for *0..1* items, a subset of `Flux`. It implements the same Reactive Streams interface, `Publisher`, which means that we only get its results when we invoke `subscribe()`. It has a few API differences from `Flux` like `flatMap()` versus `flatMapMany()`, but apart from that, it is not hard to grok.

It turns out, a lot of use cases involve handling single values, making it worthwhile capturing this type. In the flow we just walked through, it turns out that the `count()` of a group is stored in a `Mono<Long>`, indicating that we can't know the value until the subscribe is applied at the end. So we have to bundle it up along with the key and map over it to effectively unpack it.

Given that we just walked through a chain of Reactor operations, it's handy to review some of the most commonly used ones. Look at this quick guide:

Operation	Description
map()	Converts one `Flux` into another `Flux` of identical size using a function applied to each element
flatMap()	Converts one `Flux` into another `Flux` of a different size by first mapping, and then removing any nesting
filter()	Converts one `Flux` into a smaller `Flux` with elements removed based on a filtering function
groupBy()	Converts the `Flux` into a bundled set of subgroups based on the grouping function
sort()	Converts one `Flux` into a sorted `Flux` based on the sorting function

Several of these operations listed in the previous table also exist for `Mono`. There are others, but these are the big ones.

What's the big picture in all this? Essentially, every step of this flow *could* be an asynchronous, non-blocking, remote call to another service. With Reactor, we don't have to worry about thread management unless we really want to get into it. It's handled for us. And soon, we'll start doing just that.

 There's a myth that is possibly as old as Java itself: **To make things run faster, we must use threads**. And the corollary would be: **The more threads, the faster**. But this is not born out of empirical research. In fact, using threads can lead to concurrent faults and using too many threads can introduce context switching overhead. JavaScript developers, in an environment where there is but one thread, have developed many reactive solutions that are very efficient at handling things. That is because using queues and event loops combined with asynchronous, non-blocking APIs that don't hold up the thread, actually results in accomplishing a lot with few resources.

If this introductory taste of Project Reactor, `Flux`, and `Mono` is still confusing, please read the following blog articles for more detailed information on reactive programming:

- `http://bit.ly/reactive-part-1`
- `http://bit.ly/reactive-part-2`
- `http://bit.ly/reactive-part-3`
- `http://bit.ly/reactive-types`

Switching from Embedded Netty to Apache Tomcat

By default, Spring Boot is geared up to use embedded Netty (`http://netty.io`). Why? Because it's one of the most popular solutions for reactive applications. And when it comes to reactive applications, it's critical that the entire stack be reactive.

However, it's possible to switch to another embedded container. We can experiment with using Apache Tomcat and its asynchronous Servlet 3.1 API. All we have to do is to make some tweaks to the dependency settings in `build.gradle`, as follows:

```
compile('org.springframework.boot:spring-boot-starter-webflux') {
    exclude group: 'org.springframework.boot',
    module: 'spring-boot-starter-reactor-netty'
}
compile('org.springframework.boot:spring-boot-starter-tomcat')
```

What's happening in the preceding code? This can be explained as follows:

- `spring-boot-starter-webflux` excludes `spring-boot-starter-reactor-netty`, taking it off the classpath
- `spring-boot-starter-tomcat` is added to the classpath
- Spring Boot's `TomcatAutoConfiguration` kicks in, and configures the container to work using `TomcatReactiveWebServerFactory`

It's important to point out that there are these other containers available:

- Jetty
- Undertow

For the rest of this title, we'll stick with Spring Boot's default, Netty.

 It's interesting to refer to these as containers given that they are *contained* inside our application. It used to be standard practice to install Apache Tomcat (or whatever container we picked) and install the application into it. But Spring Boot has made embedded containers a core feature, inverting this concept of apps inside containers and putting the container inside the app instead. For an entertaining presentation on how this change has swept the Java community, check out Eberhard Wolff's Java Application Servers Are Dead (`http://www.slideshare.net/ewolff/java-application-servers-are-dead`) presentation.

Comparing reactive Spring WebFlux against classic Spring MVC

Ever heard of Spring MVC? It's one of the most popular web frameworks used by the Java community. Since Spring Framework 3, it has utilized an annotation-driven programming style, sometimes known as `@MVC`.

But we aren't going to use that in this book. Instead, we are going to use something new, Spring WebFlux. WebFlux is an alternative module in the Spring Framework focused on reactive handling of web requests. A huge benefit is that it uses the same annotations as `@MVC`, along with many of the same paradigms while also supporting Reactor types (`Mono` and `Flux`) on the inputs and outputs. This is NOT available in Spring MVC. The big thing to understand is that it's just a module name--`spring-webflux` versus `spring-webmvc`.

Why is Spring doing this?

Spring MVC is built on top of Java EE's Servlet spec. This specification is inherently blocking and synchronous. Asynchronous support has been added in later versions, but servlets can still hold up threads in the pool while waiting for responses, defying our need for non-blocking. To build a reactive stack, things need to be reactive from top to bottom, and this requires new contracts and expectations.

Certain things, like HTTP status codes, a `ResponseBody`, and the `@GetMapping`/`@PostMapping`/`@DeleteMapping`/`@PutMapping` annotations are used by both modules. But other things under the hood must be rewritten from scratch. The important point is that this doesn't impact the end developer.

By switching to Reactive Spring, we can immediately start coding with `Flux` and `Mono`, and don't have to stop and learn a totally new web stack. Instead, we can use the popular annotation-based programming model while we invest our effort in learning how to make things reactive. It's also important to know that Spring MVC isn't going away or slated for end of life. Both Spring WebFlux *and* Spring MVC will stay as actively supported options inside the Spring portfolio.

Showing some Mono/Flux-based endpoints

Let's start with a simple HTTP GET. Similar to Spring MVC endpoints, Spring WebFlux supports Flux operations as shown here:

```
@GetMapping(API_BASE_PATH + "/images")
Flux<Image> images() {
  return Flux.just(
    new Image("1", "learning-spring-boot-cover.jpg"),
    new Image("2", "learning-spring-boot-2nd-edition-cover.jpg"),
    new Image("3", "bazinga.png")
  );
}
```

This preceding controller can be described as follows:

- Using the same `Flux.just()` helper, we return a rather contrived list
- The Spring controller returns a `Flux<Image>` Reactor type, leaving Spring in charge of properly subscribing to this flow when the time is right

Before we can move forward, we need to define this `Image` data type like this:

```
@Data
@NoArgsConstructor
public class Image {

  private String id;
  private String name;

  public Image(String id, String name) {
    this.id = id;
    this.name = name;
  }
}
```

The preceding POJO class can be described as follows:

- `@Data` is a Lombok annotation that generates getters, `toString`, `hashCode`, `equals` as well as setters for all non-final fields
- `@NoArgsConstructor` is a Lombok annotation to generate a no-argument constructor
- It has `id` and `name` fields for storing data
- We have crafted a custom constructor to load up fields of data

With this simple data type, we can now focus on reactively interacting with them.

Nothing is simple without creating new data. To do that, we can write an HTTP POST operation as follows:

```
@PostMapping(API_BASE_PATH + "/images")
Mono<Void> create(@RequestBody Flux<Image> images) {
  return images
    .map(image -> {
      log.info("We will save " + image +
      " to a Reactive database soon!");
      return image;
    })
    .then();
}
```

The last code can be described as follows:

- `@PostMapping` indicates this method will respond to HTTP `POST` calls. The route is listed in the annotation.
- `@RequestBody` instructs Spring to fetch data from the HTTP request body.
- The container for our incoming data is another `Flux` of `Image` objects.
- To consume the data, we map over it. In this case, we simply log it and pass the original `Image` onto the next step of our flow.
- To wrap this logging operation with a promise, we invoke `Flux.then()`, which gives us `Mono<Void>`. Spring WebFlux will make good on this promise, subscribing to the results when the client makes a request.

If we run this code and submit some JSON, we can check out the results.

First, let's use HTTPie (`https://httpie.org`):

```
http --json -v POST localhost:8080/api/images id=10 name=foo
```

The verbose results are easy to read and are as follows:

```
POST /api/images HTTP/1.1
Accept: application/json, */*
Accept-Encoding: gzip, deflate
Connection: keep-alive
Content-Length: 27
Content-Type: application/json
Host: localhost:8080
User-Agent: HTTPie/0.9.8
{
    "id": "10",
    "name": "foo"
}
HTTP/1.1 200
Content-Length: 0
Date: Sat, 28 Jan 2017 20:14:35 GMT
```

In this case, HTTPie nicely sent a single item and our Spring WebFlux controller parsed it perfectly, like this:

```
... c.g.learningspringboot.ApiController ... We will save
  Image(id=10, name=foo) to a Reactive database soon!
```

Single entry `Flux` has been nicely handled.

If we want to send a JSON array, we can either embed the JSON array in a file or just send it directly with `curl`, as follows:

```
curl -v -H 'Content-Type:application/json' -X POST -d '[{"id":10,
"name": "foo"}, {"id":11, "name":"bar"}]' localhost:8080/api/images
```

Ta-dah!

```
c.g.learningspringboot.ApiController ... We will save Image(id=10,
name=foo) to a Reactive database soon!
c.g.learningspringboot.ApiController ... We will save Image(id=11,
name=bar) to a Reactive database soon!
```

 Whether we send a single JSON item or an array of JSON items, Spring WebFlux maps both onto Reactor's `Flux` with no issue. In classic Spring MVC, we'd have to choose either `Image` or `List<Image>` and encode things properly or write two handlers.

Want to dial up the log levels? With Spring Boot, adjusting logging levels is a snap. Rename the `application.properties` file supplied by `start.spring.io` as `application.yml`, and edit it to look like this:

```
logging:
  level:
    io:
      netty: DEBUG
    reactor: DEBUG
```

The preceding code will punch up Netty and Project Reactor to spit out DEBUG level messages.

If we fetch the list of images again (`http localhost:8080/api/images`), we can see stuff like this in the server logs:

```
    2017-01-28 15:46:23.470 DEBUG 28432 --- [ctor-http-nio-4]
r.i.n.http.server.HttpServerOperations   : New http connection, requesting
read
    2017-01-28 15:46:23.471 DEBUG 28432 --- [ctor-http-nio-4]
r.ipc.netty.http.server.HttpServer       : [id: 0x9ddcd1ba,
L:/0:0:0:0:0:0:0:1:8080 - R:/0:0:0:0:0:0:0:1:65529] RECEIVED: 145B
          +-------------------------------------------------+
          | 0  1  2  3  4  5  6  7  8  9  a  b  c  d  e  f |
          +-------------------------------------------------+----------
-----+
  |00000000| 47 45 54 20 2f 61 70 69 2f 69 6d 61 67 65 73 20 |GET
/api/images |
  |00000010| 48 54 54 50 2f 31 2e 31 0d 0a 48 6f 73 74 3a 20
```

```
|HTTP/1.1..Host: |
    |00000020| 6c 6f 63 61 6c 68 6f 73 74 3a 38 30 38 30 0d 0a
|localhost:8080..|
    |00000030| 55 73 65 72 2d 41 67 65 6e 74 3a 20 48 54 54 50  |User-Agent:
HTTP|
    |00000040| 69 65 2f 30 2e 39 2e 38 0d 0a 41 63 63 65 70 74
|ie/0.9.8..Accept|
    |00000050| 2d 45 6e 63 6f 64 69 6e 67 3a 20 67 7a 69 70 2c  |-Encoding:
gzip,|
    |00000060| 20 64 65 66 6c 61 74 65 0d 0a 41 63 63 65 70 74 4  |
deflate..Accept|
    |00000070| 3a 20 2a 2f 2a 0d 0a 43 6f 6e 6e 65 63 74 69 6f  |:
*/*..Connectio|
    |00000080| 6e 3a 20 6b 65 65 70 2d 61 6c 69 76 65 0d 0a 0d  |n: keep-
alive...|
    |00000090| 0a                                               |.
|
    +--------+------------------------------------------------+----------
-----+
    2017-01-28 15:46:23.471 DEBUG 28432 --- [ctor-http-nio-4]
r.ipc.netty.channel.ChannelOperations    : [HttpServer] handler is being
applied:
org.springframework.http.server.reactive.ReactorHttpHandlerAdapter@3a950f21
```

This shows the incoming web request to GET /api/images, headers and all. The output can also be read, but given the volume of data from Netty, its verbose output is not shown. Nevertheless, these log levels provide a handy means to debug traffic on the wire.

 DON'T DO THIS if the request or the results are HUGE! I once switched this on when I was uploading a 300 MB JAR file. The logging broke the application.

Creating a reactive ImageService

The first rule of thumb when building web apps is to keep Spring controllers as light as possible. We can think of them as converters between HTTP traffic and our system.

To do that, we need to create a separate `ImageService`, as shown here, and let it do all the work:

```
@Service
public class ImageService {

    private static String UPLOAD_ROOT = "upload-dir";

    private final ResourceLoader resourceLoader;

    public ImageService(ResourceLoader resourceLoader) {
        this.resourceLoader = resourceLoader;
    }
    ...
}
```

This last Spring service can be described as follows:

- `@Service`: This indicates this is a Spring bean used as a service. Spring Boot will automatically scan this class and create an instance.
- `UPLOAD_ROOT`: This is the base folder where images will be stored.
- `ResourceLoader`: This is a Spring utility class used to manage files. It is created automatically by Spring Boot and injected to our service via **constructor injection**. This ensures our service starts off with a consistent state.

Now we can start creating various utility methods needed to service our application.

Let's kick things off by loading up some mock image files loaded with test data. To do that, we can add the following method to the bottom of our newly minted `ImageService` class:

```
/**
 * Pre-load some test images
 *
 * @return Spring Boot {@link CommandLineRunner} automatically
 *         run after app context is loaded.
 */
@Bean
CommandLineRunner setUp() throws IOException {
    return (args) -> {
        FileSystemUtils.deleteRecursively(new File(UPLOAD_ROOT));

        Files.createDirectory(Paths.get(UPLOAD_ROOT));

        FileCopyUtils.copy("Test file",
          new FileWriter(UPLOAD_ROOT +
            "/learning-spring-boot-cover.jpg"));
```

```
      FileCopyUtils.copy("Test file2",
        new FileWriter(UPLOAD_ROOT +
          "/learning-spring-boot-2nd-edition-cover.jpg"));

      FileCopyUtils.copy("Test file3",
        new FileWriter(UPLOAD_ROOT + "/bazinga.png"));
    };
  }
```

The preceding little nugget of initializing code is described as follows:

- @Bean indicates that this method will return back an object to be registered as a Spring bean at the time that ImageService is created.
- The bean returned is a CommandLineRunner. Spring Boot runs ALL CommandLineRunners after the application context is fully realized (but not in any particular order).
- This method uses a Java 8 lambda, which gets automatically converted into a CommandLineRunner via Java 8 **SAM (Single Abstract Method)** rules.
- The method deletes the UPLOAD_ROOT directory, creates a new one, then creates three new files with a little bit of text.

With test data in place, we can start interacting with it by fetching all the existing files in UPLOAD_ROOT *reactively* by adding the following method to our ImageService:

```
public Flux<Image> findAllImages() {
  try {
    return Flux.fromIterable(
      Files.newDirectoryStream(Paths.get(UPLOAD_ROOT)))
      .map(path ->
        new Image(path.hashCode(),
                  path.getFileName().toString()));
  } catch (IOException e) {
    return Flux.empty();
  }
}
```

Let's explore the preceding code:

- This method returns Flux<Image>, a container of images that only gets created when the consumer subscribes.

- The Java NIO APIs are used to create a `Path` from `UPLOAD_ROOT`, which is used to open a lazy `DirectoryStream` courtesy of `Files.newDirectoryStream()`. `DirectoryStream` is a lazy iterable, which means that nothing is fetched until `next()` is called, making it a perfect fit for our Reactor `Flux`.
- `Flux.fromIterable` is used to wrap this lazy iterable, allowing us to only pull each item as demanded by a reactive streams client.
- The `Flux` maps over the paths, converting each one to an `Image`.
- In the event of an exception, an empty `Flux` is returned.

It's important to repeat that the stream of directory paths is lazy as well as the `Flux` itself. This means that nothing happens until the client subscribes, that is, starts pulling for images. At that point, the flow we just wrote will *react*, and start performing our data transformation. And it will only process each entry as each entry is pulled.

The next piece we need in our `ImageService` is the ability to fetch a single image so it can be displayed, and we can use this to do so:

```
public Mono<Resource> findOneImage(String filename) {
  return Mono.fromSupplier(() ->
    resourceLoader.getResource(
      "file:" + UPLOAD_ROOT + "/" + filename));
}
```

This last code can easily be described as follows:

- Since this method only handles one image, it returns a `Mono<Resource>`. Remember, `Mono` is a container of one. `Resource` is Spring's abstract type for files.
- `resourceLoader.getResource()` fetches the file based on `filename` and `UPLOAD_ROOT`.
- To delay fetching the file until the client subscribes, we wrap it with `Mono.fromSupplier()`, and put `getResource()` inside a lambda.

Until now, we've seen `Mono.just()` used to illustrate Reactor's way of initializing single items. However, if we wrote `Mono.just(resourceLoader.getResource(...))`, the resource fetching would happen immediately when the method is called. By putting it inside a Java 8 `Supplier`, that won't happen until the lambda is invoked. And because it's wrapped by a `Mono`, invocation won't happen until the client subscribes.

There is another `Mono` operation that is very similar to `fromSupplier()`--`defer()`. The difference is that `Mono.defer()` is invoked individually by every downstream subscriber. It's best used not for fetching resources like our situation but for something like polling status instead.

Having written code to fetch all images and a single image, it's time we introduce the ability to create new ones. The following code shows a reactive way to handle this:

```
public Mono<Void> createImage(Flux<FilePart> files) {
    return files.flatMap(file -> file.transferTo(
        Paths.get(UPLOAD_ROOT, file.filename()).toFile())).then();
}
```

The last code can be described as follows:

- This method returns a `Mono<Void>` indicating that it has no resulting value, but we still need a handle in order to subscribe for this operation to take place
- The incoming `Flux` of `FilePart` objects are flatMapped over, so we can process each one
- Each file is tested to ensure it's not empty
- At the heart of our chunk of code, Spring Framework 5's `FilePart` transfers the content into a new file stored in `UPLOAD_ROOT`
- `then()` lets us wait for the entire `Flux` to finish, yielding a `Mono<Void>`

Our last image-based operation to add to `ImageService` is to implement the means to delete images, as shown here:

```
public Mono<Void> deleteImage(String filename) {
    return Mono.fromRunnable(() -> {
        try {
            Files.deleteIfExists(Paths.get(UPLOAD_ROOT, filename));
        } catch (IOException e) {
            throw new RuntimeException(e);
        }
    });
}
```

The preceding code can be described as follows:

- Because this method doesn't care about return values, its return type is `Mono<Void>`.

- To hold off until subscribe, we need to wrap our code with
  `Mono.fromRunnable()`, and use a lambda expression to coerce a `Runnable`.
  This lets us put our code off to the side until we're ready to run it.
- Inside all of that, we can use Java NIO's handy `Files.deleteIfExists()`.

If wrapping every return type in either a `Flux` or a `Mono` is starting to
bend your brain, you are not alone. This style of programming may take a
little getting used to but it's not that big of a leap. Once you get
comfortable with it, I guarantee you'll spot blocking code all over the
place. Then you can set out to make it reactive without descending into
callback hell.

Creating a reactive file controller

With our reactive image service in place, we can start to work on the reactive file controller.

For starters, let's create a `HomeController` as shown here:

```
@Controller
public class HomeController {

  private static final String BASE_PATH = "/images";
  private static final String FILENAME = "{filename:.+}";

  private final ImageService imageService;

  public HomeController(ImageService imageService) {
    this.imageService = imageService;
  }
```

The preceding code can be described as follows:

- `@Controller`: This indicates that it is a web controller, and will be registered by
  Spring Boot to handle web requests.
- `BASE_PATH`: This is a static string used to define the base of many routes.
- `FILENAME`: This is a pattern for filenames where the `"."` is included. Otherwise,
  Spring WebFlux will use the suffix as part of content negotiation (for example,
  `.json` would try to fetch a JSON response, while `.xml` would try to fetch an
  XML response).
- `ImageService`: This is injected via constructor injection so that we can tap our
  reactive image handling code we just wrote.

With this in place, we can code the handler for displaying a single image on the web page like this:

```
@GetMapping(value = BASE_PATH + "/" + FILENAME + "/raw",
 produces = MediaType.IMAGE_JPEG_VALUE)
@ResponseBody
public Mono<ResponseEntity<?>> oneRawImage(
  @PathVariable String filename) {
    return imageService.findOneImage(filename)
      .map(resource -> {
        try {
          return ResponseEntity.ok()
            .contentLength(resource.contentLength())
            .body(new InputStreamResource(
              resource.getInputStream()));
        } catch (IOException e) {
          return ResponseEntity.badRequest()
            .body("Couldn't find " + filename +
            " => " + e.getMessage());
        }
    });
}
```

The last code can be explained as follows:

- `@GetMapping` defines a route mapping for `GET BASE_PATH + "/" + FILENAME + "/raw"`. It also sets the `Content-Type` header to properly render it as an image.
- `@ResponseBody` indicates that this method's response will be written directly into the HTTP response body.
- `@PathVariable` flags that the input `filename` will be extracted from the route's `{filename}` attribute.
- `Mono<ResponseEntity<?>>` shows that we are returning a single response, reactively. `ResponseEntity<?>` describes a generic HTTP response.
- The code taps our image service's `findOneImage()` using `filename`.

 It's possible to have incoming arguments wrapped in Reactor types such as `Mono<String>`. Since this argument comes from the route and not the request body, there is nothing gained in this situation.

- Since `findOneImage` returns a `Mono<Resource>`, we map over it, transforming this Spring `Resource` into a `ResponseEntity` including a `Content-Length` response header as well as the data embedded in the body.
- In the event of an exception, it will return an *HTTP Bad Response*.

This one controller handler method demonstrates many features provided by Reactive Spring. We see route handling, delegating to a separate service, converting the response into a suitable format for clients, and error handling.

This code also shows it being done reactively. Generating the *HTTP OK / HTTP BAD REQUEST* response doesn't happen until `map()` is executed. This is chained to the image service fetching the file from disk. And none of that happens until the client subscribes. In this case, subscribing is handled by the framework when a request comes in.

 I thought you said to keep controllers light! That is true. Maybe this looks not so light? To take the `ResponseEntity` wrapping and move it into the `ImageService` would be wrong, because that service doesn't know anything about the web layer. This controller's focus is to make the data presentable to web clients, which is exactly what we've coded.

The next controller method we can add to `HomeController` is the handler for uploading new files, as shown here:

```
@PostMapping(value = BASE_PATH)
public Mono<String> createFile(@RequestPart(name = "file")
 Flux<FilePart> files) {
    return imageService.createImage(files)
     .then(Mono.just("redirect:/"));
}
```

The preceding method is described as follows:

- A collection of incoming `FilePart` objects is represented as a `Flux`
- The flux of files is handed directly to the image service to be processed
- `.then()` indicates that once the method is complete, it will then return a `redirect:/` directive (wrapped in a `Mono`), issuing an HTML redirect to `/`

It's important to remember that we aren't issuing `.then()` against the flux of files. Instead, the image service hands us back a `Mono<Void>` that signals when it has completed processing all the files. It is that `Mono` which we are chaining an additional call to return back the redirect.

The next thing we need to add to our `HomeController` is the ability to handle requests for deleting images. This is done as follows:

```
@DeleteMapping(BASE_PATH + "/" + FILENAME)
public Mono<String> deleteFile(@PathVariable String filename) {
  return imageService.deleteImage(filename)
    .then(Mono.just("redirect:/"));
}
```

The previous code can be described like this:

- Using Spring's `@DeleteMapping` annotation, this method is ready for HTTP DELETE operations
- It's keyed to the same `BASE_PATH + "/" + FILENAME` pattern
- It taps the image service's `deleteImage()` method
- It uses `then()` to wait until the delete is done before returning back a mono-wrapped `redirect:/` directive

The last bit to add to our `HomeController` is the call to serve up a list of images in a template. For that, we need this general GET handler for the root:

```
@GetMapping("/")
public Mono<String> index(Model model) {
  model.addAttribute("images", imageService.findAllImages());
  return Mono.just("index");
}
```

The preceding handler can be described as follows:

- `@GetMapping` is used to explicitly map the `"/"` route.
- It accepts a `Model` object, giving us a place to load data *reactively*.
- `addAttribute()` lets us assign the image service's `findAllImages() Flux` to the template model's `images` attribute.
- The method returns `"index"` wrapped in a `Mono`, ensuring the whole thing is chained together, top to bottom, to kick off when Spring WebFlux subscribes to render the template.

It's important to understand that we don't assign a list of images to the template model's `images` attribute. We assign a lazy `Flux` of images, which means that the model won't be populated with real data until Reactive Spring subscribes for the data. Only then will the code actually start fetching image data.

Perhaps, at this stage, you're wondering amidst all the lambdas, Fluxes, Monos, and subscriptions, exactly what is happening from a threading perspective. Project Reactor is **concurrency agnostic**. It doesn't enforce a certain concurrency model, but leaves you in command instead. Reactor has several schedulers that support a multitude of options. This includes running in the current thread, running in a single worker thread, running on a per-call dedicated thread, an elastic pool of threads, a fixed pool of worker threads tuned for parallel work, and a time-aware scheduler capable of scheduling tasks in the future. Additionally, Reactor allows creating a scheduler out of any ExecutorService. We aren't going to delve into that in this work, but it's definitely something to investigate when you build a real application and want to govern how things scale.

Why use reactive programming?

At this stage, you've gotten a good taste of how to whip up a file-handling controller, and hitch it to a service that reads and writes files to disk. But the question that often arises is *why do I need to do this reactively?*

With imperative programming, the process of taking inputs, building intermediate collections and other steps often leaves us with lots of intermediate states--some of it potentially blocking in bad places.

Using the functional style as we've explored so far moves away from the risk of inefficiently building up this state, and switches to building a stream of data instead. And Reactor's operations let us have one stream feed another in lots of different ways. We can merge streams, filter streams, and transform streams.

When we engage in reactive programming, the level of abstraction moves up a level. We find ourselves focusing on creating tiny functions to perform various operations, and chaining them together. We think more along integration of the items in our streams rather than the lower-level implementation details.

By building up these flows of chained operations, tying inputs to outputs, Reactor is able to do the heavy lifting of invoking code when needed, and requesting/releasing resources as effectively as possible.

Additionally, by having an inherently asynchronous, non-blocking nature, our framework of choice (Reactor) is able to manage talking to the scheduler for us. We can focus on *what* happens during the flow while the framework handles *when* it happens.

For yet another metaphor to describe reactive operations chained together, imagine a train with lots of cars. Each car is a different operation to be applied to our data, and we can easily see the order in which things must happen. We can carefully lay out each car with its defined purpose, but nothing moves until the locomotive moves. And then, the whole chain of cars moves as expected. Adding/removing/inserting cars is the nature of building a reactive data flow.

To summarize, reactive programming helps us in the following:

- Avoid inefficient, intermediate state
- Focus on building streams of data
- Gives us ability to merge, filter, and transform streams of data
- Focus on *what* happens at each step while Reactor decides *when*

Interacting with a Thymeleaf template

Having put Thymeleaf on the classpath, an entire reactive view resolver has already been configured for us. The last step in putting together the web layer for our social media platform is to create the Thymeleaf template itself. We can do that by putting the following content into `index.html` underneath `/src/main/resources/templates`:

```html
<!DOCTYPE html>
<html xmlns:th="http://www.thymeleaf.org">
<head>
  <meta charset="UTF-8" />
  <title>Learning Spring Boot: Spring-a-Gram</title>
  <link rel="stylesheet" href="/main.css" />
</head>
<body>

<h1>Learning Spring Boot - 2nd Edition</h1>

<div>
  <table>
    <thead>
    <tr>
        <th>Id</th><th>Name</th><th>Image</th><th></th>
    </tr>
    </thead>
    <tbody>
    <tr th:each="image : ${images}">
        <td th:text="${image.id}" />
        <td th:text="${image.name}" />
```

```
                <td>
                    <a th:href="@{'/images/' + ${image.name} + '/raw'}">
                        <img th:src="@{'/images/'+${image.name}+'/raw'}"
                            class="thumbnail" />
                    </a>
                </td>
                <td>
                    <form th:method="delete"
                            th:action="@{'/images/' + ${image.name}}">
                        <input type="submit" value="Delete" />
                    </form>
                </td>
        </tr>
        </tbody>
    </table>

    <form method="post" enctype="multipart/form-data"
                                    action="/images">
        <p><input type="file" name="file" /></p>
        <p><input type="submit" value="Upload" /></p>
    </form>
</div>

</body>
</html>
```

Key parts of the preceding template are described here:

- All of the Thymeleaf directives are tagged with a th prefix, making the entire template HTML compliant
- `<tr th:each="image : ${images}" />` is Thymeleaf's for-each directive, where we read images from the template model and iterate over it, forming one table row element per image
- `<a th:href="@{'/images/' + ${image.name} + '/raw'}">` shows how to create a link by splicing together strings with the image.name attribute
- The whole thing builds a table with a row for each image, showing ID, name, image, and a delete button
- At the bottom is a single upload form for creating new images

A critical thing to remember is that the name of the template must be index.html, matching our controller's return of Mono.just("index") combined with the default configuration settings of Spring Boot for Thymeleaf.

Spring Boot autoconfigures view resolvers based on the templating solution we pick. Spring Boot supports many including Thymeleaf, Mustache, Groovy Templates, and even Apache FreeMarker. By default, they all come with a conventional location to put templates, in this case, `src/main/resources/templates/<template name>.html`.

Since we want a bare amount of CSS, we can drop the following into `src/main/resources/static/main.css`:

```
table {
  border-collapse: collapse;
}

td, th {
  border: 1px solid #999;
  padding: 0.5rem;
  text-align: left;
}

.thumbnail {
  max-width: 75px;
  max-height: 75px;
}
```

Let's tear the preceding small bit of CSS apart:

- The borders of the table are collapsed
- A little spacing is defined for the table entries
- A special class is created to render images with a small thumbnail size

Of course, this is primitive CSS, but our focus is to learn about Spring Boot not CSS3. The important thing to observe here is that Spring Boot will automatically serve up all content underneath `src/main/resources/static` as web resources. We can put CSS, JavaScript, favicons, and images for our site. Anything that needs to be statically served can be put here, and will be available from the root of the web application's context path.

Throughout this book, we'll add to this web page, enhancing the user experience. But for now, we should have enough to get off the ground.

The only thing remaining is to code a `public static void main()`; however, we don't have to! The Spring Initializr site has already created one for us, which is as follows:

```
@SpringBootApplication
public class LearningSpringBootApplication {
```

```
public static void main(String[] args) {
  SpringApplication.run(
    LearningSpringBootApplication.class, args);
}

@Bean
HiddenHttpMethodFilter hiddenHttpMethodFilter() {
  return new HiddenHttpMethodFilter();
}

}
```

This last code is almost identical to the application class we created in Chapter 1, *Quick Start with Java*. But there is one difference--we must add a HiddenHttpMethodFilter Spring bean to make the HTTP DELETE methods work properly.

 DELETE is not a valid action for an HTML5 FORM, so Thymeleaf creates a hidden input field containing our desired verb while the enclosing form uses an HTML5 POST. This gets transformed by Spring during the web call, resulting in the @DeleteMapping method being properly invoked with no effort on our end.

Illustrating how going from async to sync can be easy, but the opposite is not

Invariably, the question comes along--*Do I need a synchronous or asynchronous API?*

It's important to understand that reactive programming is not very effective unless the *entire* stack is reactive. Otherwise, we're simply blocking at some point, which causes the backpressure to not achieve much. That's a long-winded way of saying there is little value in making the web layer reactive if the underlying services are not.

However, it is *very* likely that we may produce a chunk of code that must be tapped by a non-reactive layer, hence, we have to wrap our asynchronous, non-blocking code with the means to block.

Let's explore async-to-sync by creating a BlockingImageService. This service will, basically, leverage the already written ImageService, but *not* include any of Reactor's Flux or Mono types in its method signatures.

We can start with a class definition as follows:

```
public class BlockingImageService {

  private final ImageService imageService;

  public BlockingImageService(ImageService imageService) {
    this.imageService = imageService;
  }
```

This preceding class definition can be described as follows:

- The class has no annotation, hence, it won't be automatically scanned and activated by Spring Boot. However, it can appear in a configuration class somewhere via a @Bean-annotated method.
- It will contain a constructor injected ImageService.

With this in place, we can look at wrapping the findAllImages() method with blocking semantics, like this:

```
public List<Image> findAllImages() {
  return imageService.findAllImages()
    .collectList()
    .block(Duration.ofSeconds(10));
}
```

Let's dig into the details of the last code:

- ImageService.findAllImages() has no arguments, and returns a Flux<Image>. The simplest mechanism is collectList(), which transforms it into a Mono<List<Image>>. This means that instead of signaling the arrival of each image, there is one single (Mono) for a list of ALL images.
- To ask for the result, we use block(). Reactor's block() can either wait forever for the next signal, or we can supply it with a timeout limit. In this case, we have selected ten seconds as the longest that we'll wait.

Reactor's block() API is what we do when we want to transform a Mono<T> into just T. It's a simple one-to-one concept. Inside the method, it invokes the reactive streams' subscribe() API, meaning it will cause any chain of operations to take effect.

Flux has no block() because it represents multiple values. Flux *does* come with blockFirst() and blockLast() if we wanted the first or the last item. But to get the whole collection entails a bigger semantic scope. Hence, the need to collectList() into a Mono followed by blocking for it.

It's usually a good idea to set a timeout limit for *any* async call to avoid deadlock situations or waiting for a response that may never come.

Fetching a single image is a bit simpler and can be done using the following code:

```
public Resource findOneImage(String filename) {
    return imageService.findOneImage(filename)
        .block(Duration.ofSeconds(30));
}
```

`ImageService.findOneImage()` has one argument, the filename, but it isn't wrapped with any Reactor types. The return type is `Mono<Resource>`, so a simple `block()` is all we need to transform it into a `Resource`. In this case, we've picked thirty seconds as the maximum time to wait for an answer.

When it comes to uploading new images, that is a little more complicated.

```
public void createImage(List<FilePart> files) {
    imageService.createImage(Flux.fromIterable(files))
        .block(Duration.ofMinutes(1));
}
```

The last code can be described as follows:

- The image service's input is `Flux<FilePart>` and the return type is `Mono<Void>`. This makes things doubly interesting, having to massage both the input *and* the output.
- The preceding code assumes we are uploading multiple files. To transform it into a `Flux`, we use `Flux.fromIterable(files)`. If the input had been a single `FilePart`, we could have used `Flux.just(file)`.
- The return type is `void`, meaning we don't have to return anything. Simply invoking image service's `create()` method may seem hunky dory. But remember--*nothing* happens with Reactor types until we subscribe, so it's critical that we invoke `block()` even if we aren't going to return it.

We'll leave it as an exercise for the reader to implement a blocking version of `deleteImage()`.

Summary

We're off to a good start by building the web layer of our social media platform. We used the Spring Initializr to create a bare bones Reactive Spring application with Gradle support. Then we explored the basics of reactive programming by creating a reactive image handling service and wrapping it with a reactive web layer. And we drafted a Thymeleaf template to show thumbnails, allow deleting of images and uploading of new images.

In the next chapter, we will see how to build a data layer and make it reactive as well.

3

Reactive Data Access with Spring Boot

Very impressed with @springboot so far, 10 mins to get a REST service up and running, now to add MongoDB. No black magic under the covers!

– Graham Rivers-Brown @grahamrb

In the previous chapter, we started putting together the frontend bits of our social media platform using Spring WebFlux. The missing critical ingredient was a data store. Few applications exist that don't touch a database. In fact, data storage is arguably one of the most critical components we encounter with app development. In this chapter, we'll learn how to persist information in a reactive data store (MongoDB), and learn how to interact with it.

In this chapter, we will be doing the following:

- Getting underway with a reactive data store
- Wiring up Spring Data repositories with Spring Boot
- Creating a reactive repository
- Pulling data through a Mono/Flux and chain of operations
- Creating custom finders
- Querying by example
- Querying with MongoOperations
- Logging reactive operations

Getting underway with a reactive data store

Since this book is aimed at the cutting edge of Spring Boot 2.0 and its Reactive Streams support, we have to pick something a little more up to date than JPA. The JPA spec doesn't cover reactive programming. Hence, its APIs are not reactive. However, MongoDB has reactive drivers, and will be perfect.

To get going, we need to install the latest version of MongoDB 3.4 (for reactive support).

If you're using macOS X, installing MongoDB is as simple as this:

```
$ brew install mongodb
==> Installing mongodb
==> Downloading https://homebrew.bintray.com/bottles/mongodb-
3.4.6.el_capitan.bottle.tar.gz
######################################################### 100.0%
==> Pouring mongodb-3.4.6.el_capitan.bottle.tar.gz
==> Summary
/usr/local/Cellar/mongodb/3.4.6: 18 files, 267.5MB
```

With MongoDB installed, we can launch it as a service, like this:

```
$ brew services start mongodb
==> Successfully started `mongodb` (label: homebrew.mxcl.mongodb)
```

 For other operating systems, check out the download links at https://www.mongodb.com/download-center. For more details about installing MongoDB, visit https://docs.mongodb.com/manual/installation/.

Assuming that we have MongoDB installed and running, we can now delve into writing a little code.

To write any MongoDB code, we need to add Spring Data MongoDB to our classpath. We can do so by updating our build file with the following:

```
compile('org.springframework.boot:spring-boot-starter-
    data-mongodb-reactive')
```

The preceding, new compile-time dependency pulls in the following:

- Spring Data MongoDB
- MongoDB's core components + Reactive Stream drivers

It's important to point out that both `spring-boot-starter-webflux` *and* `spring-boot-starter-data-mongodb-reactive` transitively bring in Project Reactor. Spring Boot's `dependency-management` plugin is responsible for ensuring they both pull in the same version.

With all these things on the classpath, Spring Boot will get busy configuring things for us. But first, what *is* the problem we are trying to solve?

Solving a problem

In this day and age, why are we still writing queries like this:

```
SELECT *
FROM PERSON
WHERE FIRST_NAME = %1
```

That type of query must be thirty years old! The ANSI spec for SQL was released in 1986, and its effects can be seen in countless languages.

So, is it any better to write something more like this:

```
SELECT e
FROM Employee e
WHERE e.firstName = :name
```

The last bit of code is **JPA (Java Persistence API)**, based upon the open source Hibernate project (which has become JPA's reference implementation). Is this Java's improvement over writing pure SQL?

Maybe this fragment below is an enhancement?

```
create
  .select()
  .from(EMPLOYEE)
  .where(EMPLOYEE.FIRST_NAME.equal(name))
  .fetch()
```

That last code snippet is **jOOQ**, and can help with code completion, but it seems that we are, basically, doing the same thing we've been doing for decades.

Especially, considering that we could do the same thing by merely creating this:

```
interface EmployeeRepository
  extends ReactiveCrudRepository<Employee, Long> {

    Flux<Employee> findByFirstName(Mono<String> name);
}
```

This preceding declarative interface does the exact same thing, but without writing a single query in any language.

By extending Spring Data's `ReactiveCrudRepository`, we are granted an out-of-the-box set of CRUD operations (`save`, `findById`, `findAll`, `delete`, `deleteById`, `count`, `exists`, and more). We also have the ability to add custom finders purely by method signature (`findByFirstName` in this example).

When Spring Data sees an interface extending its `Repository` marker interface (which `ReactiveCrudRepository` does), it creates a concrete implementation. It scans every method, and parses their method signatures. Seeing `findBy`, it knows to look at the rest of the method name, and start extracting property names based on the domain type (`Employee`). Because it can see that `Employee` has `firstName`, it has enough information to fashion a query. This also tips it off about expected criteria in the arguments (`name`). Finally, Spring Data looks at the return type to decide what result set to assemble--in this case, a Reactor `Flux` that we started to explore in the previous chapter. The entire query (*not* the query *results*), once assembled, is cached, so, there is no overhead in using the query multiple times.

In a nutshell, by following a very simple convention, there is no need to handwrite a query at all. And while this book is focused on MongoDB and its corresponding Mongo Query Language, this concept applies to SQL, JPA, Cassandra Query Language, or any other supported data store.

 Spring Data does not engage in **code generation** of any code. Code generation has had a flaky history. Instead, it uses various tactics to pick a base class that handles the minimum set of operations while wrapping it with a proxy that implements the declared interface, bringing onboard the dynamic query handler.

This mechanism of managing data is revolutionary, making Spring Data one of the most popular Spring portfolio projects, second only to the Spring Framework itself and Spring Security (and of course Spring Boot).

Wait a second, didn't we just mention using MongoDB earlier?

Yup. That's why Spring Data's query-neutral approach is even better. Changing data stores doesn't require throwing away absolutely everything and starting over. The interface declared previously extends Spring Data Commons, not Spring Data MongoDB. The only data store details are in the domain object itself.

Instead of `Employee` being some JPA-based entity definition, we can work on a MongoDB document-based one instead, like this:

```
@Data
@Document(collection="employees")
public class Employee {
  @Id String id;
  String firstName;
  String lastName;
}
```

This preceding MongoDB POJO can be described as follows:

- The `@Data` Lombok annotation takes care of getters, setters, `toString`, `equals`, and `hashCode` functions.
- `@Document` is an optional annotation that lets us spell out the MongoDB collection that this domain object will be stored under (`"employees"`).
- `@Id` is a Spring Data Commons annotation that flags which field is the key. (NOTE: When using Spring Data JPA, the required annotation is `javax.persistence.Id`, whereas, all other Spring-Data-supported stores utilize `org.springframework.data.annotation.Id`).

What is Spring Data Commons? It's the parent project for all Spring Data implementations. It defines several concepts implemented by every solution. For example, the concept of parsing finder signatures to put together a query request is defined here. But the bits where this is transformed into a native query is supplied by the data store solution itself. Spring Data Commons also provides various interfaces, allowing us to reduce coupling in our code to the data store, such as `ReactiveCrudRepository`, and others that we'll soon see.

Nothing else is needed to start writing `Employee` objects into the `employees` collection of our MongoDB database.

Wiring up Spring Data repositories with Spring Boot

Normally, wiring up a repository requires not only defining a domain object and a repository, but also activating Spring Data. Each data store comes with an annotation to activate it for repository support. In our case, that would be `@EnableReactiveMongoRepositories`, since we are using MongoDB's reactive drivers.

However, with Spring Boot, we don't have to lift a finger!

Why?

Because the following code, lifted from Spring Boot itself, shows how MongoDB reactive repository support is enabled:

```
@Configuration
@ConditionalOnClass({ MongoClient.class,
 ReactiveMongoRepository.class })
@ConditionalOnMissingBean({
   ReactiveMongoRepositoryFactoryBean.class,
    ReactiveMongoRepositoryConfigurationExtension.class })
@ConditionalOnProperty(prefix = "spring.data.mongodb.reactive-
   repositories", name = "enabled",
   havingValue = "true", matchIfMissing = true)
@Import(MongoReactiveRepositoriesAutoConfigureRegistrar.class)
@AutoConfigureAfter(MongoReactiveDataAutoConfiguration.class)
public class MongoReactiveRepositoriesAutoConfiguration {

}
```

The preceding autoconfiguration policy can be described as follows:

- `@Configuration`: This indicates that this class is a source of bean definitions.
- `@ConditionalOnClass`: This lists ALL the classes that must be on the classpath for this to kick in--in this case, MongoDB's reactive `MongoClient` (Reactive Streams version) and `ReactiveMongoRepository`, which means that it only applies if Reactive MongoDB and Spring Data MongoDB 2.0 are on the classpath.

- `@ConditionalOnMissingBean`: This indicates that it only applies if there isn't already a `ReactiveMongoRepositoryFactoryBean` and a `ReactiveMongoRepositoryConfigurationExtension` bean.
- `@ConditionalOnProperty`: This means that it requires that the `spring.data.mongodb.reactive-repositories` property must be set to `true` for this to apply (which is the default setting if no such property is provided).
- `@Import`: This delegates all bean creation for reactive repositories to `MongoReactiveRepositoriesAutoConfigureRegistrar`.
- `@AutoConfigureAfter`: This ensures that this autoconfiguration policy is only applied after `MongoReactiveDataAutoConfiguration` has been applied. That way, we can count on certain infrastructure being configured.

When we added `spring-boot-starter-data-mongodb-reactive` to the classpath, this policy kicked in, and created critical beans for interacting reactively with a MongoDB database.

It's left as an exercise for the reader to pull up `MongoReactiveRepositoriesAutoConfigureRegistrar`, and see how it works. What's important to note is that nestled at the bottom of that class is the following:

```
@EnableReactiveMongoRepositories
private static class EnableReactiveMongoRepositoriesConfiguration {
}
```

This aforementioned little class means that we don't have to enable reactive MongoDB repositories. Spring Boot will do it for us automatically when Reactive MongoDB and Spring Data MongoDB 2.0+ are on the classpath.

Creating a reactive repository

So far, we have been dabbling with Spring Data using our sample domain of employees. We need to shift our focus back to the social media platform that we started building in the previous chapter.

Before we can work on a reactive repository, we need to revisit the `Image` domain object we defined in the last chapter. Let's adjust it so that it works nicely with MongoDB:

```
@Data
@Document
public class Image {

  @Id final private String id;
  final private String name;
}
```

This preceding definition is almost identical to what we saw in the previous chapter, with the following differences:

- We use `@Document` to identify this is a MongoDB domain object, but we accept Spring Data MongoDB's decision about what to name the collection (it's the short name of the class, lowercase, that is, `image`)
- `@Data` creates a constructor for all final fields by default, hence, we've marked both `id` and `name` as `final`
- We have also marked both fields `private` for proper encapsulation

With that in place, we are ready to declare our social media platform's reactive repository as follows:

```
public interface ImageRepository
  extends ReactiveCrudRepository<Image, String> {

  Mono<Image> findByName(String name);
}
```

This code for the reactive repository can be described as follows:

- Our interface extends `ReactiveCrudRepository`, which, as stated before, comes with a prepackaged set of reactive operations including `save`, `findById`, `exists`, `findAll`, `count`, `delete`, and `deleteAll`, all supporting Reactor types
- It includes a custom **finder** named `findByName` that matches on `Image.name` based on parsing the name of the method (not the input argument)

Each of the operations inherited from `ReactiveCrudRepository` accepts direct arguments or a Reactor-friendly variant. This means, we can invoke either `save(Image)` or `saveAll(Publisher<Image>)`. Since `Mono` and `Flux` both implement `Publisher`, `saveAll()` can be used to store either.

ReactiveCrudRepository has ALL of its methods returning either a Mono or a Flux based on the situation. Some, like delete, simply return Mono<Void>, meaning, there is no data to return, but we need the operation's handle in order to issue the Reactive Streams' subscribe call. findById returns a Mono<Image>, because there can be only one. And findAll returns a Flux<Image>.

Before we can get our feet wet in using this reactive repository, we need to preload our MongoDB data store. For such operations, it's recommended to actually use the *blocking* API. That's because when launching an application, there is a certain risk of a thread lock issue when both the web container as well as our hand-written loader are starting up. Since Spring Boot also creates a MongoOperations object, we can simply grab hold of that, as follows:

```
@Component
public class InitDatabase {
  @Bean
  CommandLineRunner init(MongoOperations operations) {
    return args -> {
      operations.dropCollection(Image.class);

      operations.insert(new Image("1",
        "learning-spring-boot-cover.jpg"));
      operations.insert(new Image("2",
        "learning-spring-boot-2nd-edition-cover.jpg"));
      operations.insert(new Image("3",
        "bazinga.png"));

      operations.findAll(Image.class).forEach(image -> {
        System.out.println(image.toString());
      });
    };
  }
}
```

The preceding code is detailed as follows:

- @Component ensures that this class will be picked up automatically by Spring Boot, and scanned for bean definitions.
- @Bean marks the init method as a bean definition requiring a MongoOperations. In turn, it returns a Spring Boot CommandLineRunner, of which all are run after the application context is fully formed (though in no particular order).

- When invoked, the command-line runner will use `MongoOperations`, and request that all entries be deleted (`dropCollection`). Then it will insert three new `Image` records. Finally, it will fetch with (`findAll`) and iterate over them, printing each out.

With sample data loaded, let's hook things into our reactive `ImageService` in the next section.

Pulling data through a Mono/Flux and chain of operations

We have wired up a repository to interface with MongoDB through Spring Data. Now we can start hooking it into our `ImageService`.

The first thing we need to do is inject our repository into the service, like this:

```
@Service
public class ImageService {

  ...

  private final ResourceLoader resourceLoader;

  private final ImageRepository imageRepository;

  public ImageService(ResourceLoader resourceLoader,
    ImageRepository imageRepository) {
    this.resourceLoader = resourceLoader;
    this.imageRepository = imageRepository;
  }
  ...
}
```

In the previous chapter, we loaded Spring's `ResourceLoader`. In this chapter, we are adding `ImageRepository` to our constructor.

Previously, we looked up the names of the existing uploaded files, and constructed a `Flux` of `Image` objects. That required coming up with a contrived `id` value.

Now that we have a real data store, we can simply fetch them all, and return them to the client, like this:

```
public Flux<Image> findAllImages() {
   return imageRepository.findAll();
}
```

In this last bit of code, we leverage `imageRepository` to do all the work with its `findAll()` method. Remember--`findAll` was defined inside `ReactiveCrudRepository`. We didn't have to write it ourselves. And since it already gives us a `Flux<Image>`, there is no need to do anything else.

It's good to remember that the `Flux` of images being returned is *lazy*. That means that only the number of images requested by the client is pulled from the database into memory and through the rest of the system at any given time. In essence, the client can ask for one or as many as possible, and the database, thanks to reactive drivers, will comply.

Let's move on to something a little more complex--storing a `Flux` of images as follows:

```
public Mono<Void> createImage(Flux<FilePart> files) {
   return files
     .flatMap(file -> {
       Mono<Image> saveDatabaseImage = imageRepository.save(
         new Image(
           UUID.randomUUID().toString(),
            file.filename())));

       Mono<Void> copyFile = Mono.just(
         Paths.get(UPLOAD_ROOT, file.filename())
           .toFile())
           .log("createImage-picktarget")
           .map(destFile -> {
             try {
               destFile.createNewFile();
               return destFile;
             } catch (IOException e) {
               throw new RuntimeException(e);
             }
           })
           .log("createImage-newfile")
           .flatMap(file::transferTo)
           .log("createImage-copy");

       return Mono.when(saveDatabaseImage, copyFile);
     })
     .then();
}
```

The preceding code can be described as follows:

- With a `Flux` of multipart files, `flatMap` each one into two independent actions: saving the image and copying the file to the server.
- Using `imageRepository`, put together a `Mono` that stores the image in MongoDB, using `UUID` to create a unique key and the filename.
- Using `FilePart`, WebFlux's reactive multipart API, build another `Mono` that copies the file to the server.
- To ensure both of these operations are completed, join them together using `Mono.when()`. This means that each file won't be completed until the record is written to MongoDB *and* the file is copied to the server.
- The entire flow is terminated with `then()` so we can signal when all the files have been processed.

 Ever worked with promises? They are quite popular in the JavaScript world. Project Reactor's `Mono.when()` is akin to the A+ Promise spec's `promise.all()` API, that waits until all sub-promises are completed before moving forward. Project Reactor can be thought of as promises on steroids with many more operations available. In this case, by stringing several operations together using `then()`, you can avoid *callback hell* while ensuring the flow of how things unfold.

On a fundamental level, we need **creating an image** to involve two things--copying the file's contents to the server, and writing a record of it in MongoDB. That is on par with what we've declared in the code by using `Mono.when()` to combine two separate actions.

`imageRepository.save()` is already a reactive operation, so we can capture it straight up as a `Mono`. Because `MultipartFile` is, inherently, tied to the blocking servlet paradigm, WebFlux has a new interface, `FilePart`, meant to handle file uploads reactively. Its `transferTo()` API returns a `Mono<Void>` letting us signal when to carry out the transfer.

Is this a transaction? Certainly not an **ACID**-style one (**Atomic, Consistent, Isolated, Durable**) traditionally found with relational data stores. Those types of transactions have a long history of not scaling well. When more clients try to alter the same rows of data, traditional transactions block with increasing frequency. And blocking in, and of itself, is not congruent with reactive programming.

However, semantically, perhaps we are engaged in a transaction. After all, we are saying that both of these actions must *complete* from a Reactive Streams perspective before the given `FilePart` is considered to be processed in the middle of the `Flux`. Given the long history of assumptions made regarding **transactions**, it might be best to leave that term behind, and refer to this as a **reactive promise**.

 While it's possible to inline both the `saveDatabaseImage` operation and the `copyFile` operation inside the `Mono.when()`, they were pulled out as separate variables for readability. The more flows you write, the more you may be tempted to streamline things in a single, chained statement. If you're feeling lucky, go for it!

When it comes to order of processing, which goes first? Saving the document in MongoDB, or storing the file on the server? It's actually not specified in the API. All that is declared is that both of these operations must be completed to move on, and Reactor guarantees that if any asynchronous threading is being used, the framework will handle any and all coordination.

This is why `Mono.when()` is the perfect construct when two or more tasks need to be completed, and **the order doesn't matter**. The first time the code is run, perhaps, MongoDB is able to store the record first. It's quite possible that the next time this code is exercised, MongoDB may be slightly delayed due to external factors such as responding to another operation, hence allowing the file to be copied first. And the time after that, other factors may cause the order to swap. But the key point of this construct is to ensure that we use resources with maximum efficiency while still having a consistent result--both are completed before moving on.

 Notice how we used `flatMap` to turn each file into a promise to both copy the file and save a MongoDB record? `flatMap` is kind of like `map` and then, but on steroids. `map` has a signature of `map(T → V) : V`, while `flatMap` has `flatMap(T → Publisher<V>) : V`, meaning, it can unwrap the `Mono` and produce the contained value. If you're writing a reactive flow that isn't clicking, check if one of your `map` or `then` calls needs to be replaced with a `flatMap`.

If we wanted a certain order to happen, the best construct would be `Mono.then()`. We can chain multiple `then` calls together, ensuring that a certain uniform state is achieved at each step before moving forward.

Let's wrap up this section by making adjustments to `deleteImage` as follows:

```
public Mono<Void> deleteImage(String filename) {
  Mono<Void> deleteDatabaseImage = imageRepository
    .findByName(filename)
    .flatMap(imageRepository::delete);

  Mono<Void> deleteFile = Mono.fromRunnable(() -> {
    try {
      Files.deleteIfExists(
        Paths.get(UPLOAD_ROOT, filename));
    } catch (IOException e) {
      throw new RuntimeException(e);
    }
  });

  return Mono.when(deleteDatabaseImage, deleteFile)
    .then();
}
```

The previous code can be explained as follows:

- First we create a `Mono` to delete the MongoDB image record. It uses `imageRepository` to first `findByName`, and then it uses a Java 8 method handle to invoke `imageRepository.delete`.
- Next, we create a `Mono` using `Mono.fromRunnable` to delete the file using `Files.deleteIfExists`. This delays deletion until `Mono` is invoked.
- To have both of these operations completed together, we join them with `Mono.when()`.
- Since we're not interested in the results, we append a `then()`, which will be completed when the combined `Mono` is done.

We repeat the same coding pattern as `createImage()` where we collect operations into multiple `Mono` definitions, and wrap them with a `Mono.when()`. This is the promise pattern, and when coding reactively, we'll use it often.

 Traditionally, `Runnable` objects are started in some multithreaded fashion, and are meant to run in the background. In this situation, Reactor is in full control of how it gets started through the use of its scheduler. Reactor is also able to ensure that the reactive streams **complete** signal is issued when the `Runnable` object is done with its work.

At the end of the day, that is the whole point of these various operations from Project Reactor. We declare the desired state, and offload all the work scheduling and thread management to the framework. We use a toolkit that is designed from the ground up to support asynchronous, non-blocking operations for maximum resource usage. This gives us a consistent, cohesive way to define expected results while getting maximum efficiency.

Creating custom finders

With Spring Data repositories, we are able to create queries to suit any situation. Earlier in this chapter, we saw `findByName`, which merely queries based on the domain object's `name` attribute.

The following table shows a more comprehensive collection of finders we can write with Spring Data MongoDB. To illustrate the breadth of these keywords, it presumes a domain model bigger than the `Image` class we defined earlier:

Finder Method	Description
`findByLastName(...)`	Query based on `lastName`
`findByFirstNameAndLastName(...)`	Query based on `firstName` and `lastName`
`findByFirstNameAndManagerLastName(...)`	Query based on `firstName` and by a related manager's `lastName`
`findTop10ByFirstName(...)` or `findFirst10ByFirstName(...)`	Query based on `firstName`, but only return the first ten entries
`findByFirstNameIgnoreCase(...)`	Query by `firstName`, but ignore the case of the text
`findByFirstNameAndLastNameAllIgnoreCase(...)`	Query by `firstName` and `lastName`, but ignore the case of the text in ALL fields

`findByFirstNameOrderByLastNameAsc(...)`	Query by `firstName`, but order the results based on `lastName` in ascending order (or use `Desc` for descending order)
`findByBirthdateAfter(Date date)`	Query based on `birthdate` being after the `date`
`findByAgeGreaterThan(int age)`	Query based on `age` attribute being greater than `age` parameter.
`findByAgeGreaterThanEqual(int age)`	Query based on `age` attribute being greater than or equal to `age` parameter.
`findByBirthdateBefore(Date date)`	Query based on `birthdate` being before the `date`
`findByAgeLessThan(int age)`	Query based on `age` attribute being less than `age` parameter.
`findByAgeLessThanEqual(int age)`	Query based on `age` attribute being less than or equal to `age` parameter.
`findByAgeBetween(int from, int to)`	Query based on `age` being between `from` and `to`
`findByAgeIn(Collection ages)`	Query based on `age` being found in the supplied collection
`findByAgeNotIn(Collection ages)`	Query based on `age` NOT being found in the supplied collection

`findByFirstNameNotNull()` or `findByFirstNameIsNotNull()`	Query based on `firstName` **not being null**
`findByFirstNameNull()` or `findByFirstNameIsNull()`	Query based on `firstName` **being null**
`findByFirstNameLike(String f)` or `findByFirstNameStartingWith(String f)` or `findByFirstNameEndingWith(String f)`	Query based on input being a regular expression
`findByFirstNameNotLike(String f)` or `findByFirstNameIsNotLike(String f)`	Query based on input being a regex, with a MongoDB `$not` applied
`findByFirstnameContaining(String f)`	For a string input, query just like `Like`; for a collection, query testing membership in the collection
`findByFirstnameNotContaining(String f)`	For a string input, query like like `NotLike`; for a collection, query testing lack of membership in the collection
`findByFirstnameRegex(String pattern)`	Query using `pattern` as a regular expression
`findByLocationNear(Point p)`	Query by geospatial relation using MongoDB's `$near`
`findByLocationNear(Point p, Distance max)`	Query by geospatial relation using MongoDB's `$near` and `$maxDistance`
`findByLocationNear(Point p, Distance min, Distance max)`	Query by geospatial relation using MongoDB's `$near`, `$minDistance`, and `$maxDistance`

`findByLocationWithin(Circle c)`	Query by geospatial relation using MongoDB's `$geoWithin`, `$circle`, and distance
`findByLocationWithin(Box b)`	Query by geospatial relation using MongoDB's `$geoWithin`, `$box`, and square coordinates
`findByActiveIsTrue()`	Query by `active` being true
`findByActiveIsFalse()`	Query by `active` being false
`findByLocationExists(boolean e)`	Query by `location` having the same Boolean value as the input

All of these aforementioned keywords can also be used to construct `deleteBy` methods.

 Many of these operators also work with other supported data stores including JPA, Apache Cassandra, Apache Geode, and GemFire to name a few. However, be sure to check the specific reference guide.

While the previous table shows all the keywords supported for MongoDB repository queries, the following list shows the various supported return types:

- `Image` (or Java primitive types)
- `Iterable<Image>`
- `Iterator<Image>`
- `Collection<Image>`
- `List<Image>`
- `Optional<Image>` (Java 8 or Guava)
- `Option<Image>` (Scala or Vavr)
- `Stream<Image>`
- `Future<Image>`

- CompletableFuture<Image>
- ListenableFuture<Image>
- @Async Future<Image>
- @Async CompletableFuture<Image>
- @Async ListenableFuture<Image>
- Slice<Image>
- Page<Image>
- GeoResult<Image>
- GeoResults<Image>
- GeoPage<Image>
- Mono<Image>
- Flux<Image>

Spring Data blocking APIs support void return types as well. In Reactor-based programming, the equivalent is Mono<Void>, because the caller needs the ability to invoke subscribe().

In a nutshell, just about every container type is covered by Spring Data, which means that we can pick the right solution to suit our needs. Since this book's focus is reactive programming, we'll stick with Mono and Flux, considering they encapsulate asynchronous + non-blocking + lazy, without impacting the client, and regardless of quantity.

Querying by example

So far, we've built up several reactive queries using property navigation. And we've updated ImageService to reactively transform our queried results into operations needed to support our social media platform.

But something that may not be apparent in the design of our data API is the fact that our method signatures are tied to the properties directly. This means that if a domain field changes, we would have to update the queries, or they will break.

There are other issues we might run into, such as offering the ability to put a filter on our web page, and letting the user fetch a subset of images based on their needs.

What if we had a system that listed information about employees. If we imagined writing a finder that lets a user enter `firstName`, `lastName`, and age range, it would probably look like this:

```
interface PersonRepository
  extends ReactiveCrudRepository<Person, Long> {

    List<Person> findByFirstNameAndLastNameAndAgeBetween(
        String firstName, String lastName, int from, int to);
}
```

Yikes! That's ugly. (Even worse, imagine making all the strings case insensitive!)

All of these things lead us toward an alternative Spring Data solution--**Query by Example**.

Query by Example, simply stated, has us assemble a domain object with the criteria provided, and submit them to a query. Let's look at an example. Assume we were storing `Employee` records like this:

```
@Data
@Document
public class Employee {

  @Id private String id;
  private String firstName;
  private String lastName;
  private String role;
}
```

This preceding example is a very simple domain object, and can be explained as follows:

- Lombok's `@Data` annotation provides getters, setters, `equals`, `hashCode`, and `toString` methods
- Spring Data MongoDB's `@Document` annotation indicates this POJO is a target for storage in MongoDB
- Spring Data Commons' `@Id` annotation indicates that the `id` field is the identifier
- The rest of the fields are simple strings

Next, we need to define a repository as we did earlier, but we must also mix in another interface that gives us a standard complement of Query by Example operations. We can do that with the following definition:

```
public interface EmployeeRepository extends
  ReactiveCrudRepository<Employee, String>,
  ReactiveQueryByExampleExecutor<Employee> {

}
```

This last repository definition can be explained as follows:

- It's an interface declaration, meaning, we don't write any implementation code
- `ReactiveCrudRepository` provides the standard CRUD operations with reactive options (`Mono` and `Flux` return types, and more)
- `ReactiveQueryByExampleExecutor` is a **mix-in** interface that introduces the **Query by Example** operations which we'll poke at shortly

Once again, with just a domain object and a Spring Data repository defined, we have all the tools to go forth and query MongoDB!

First things first, we should again use blocking `MongoOperations` to preload some data like this:

```
mongoOperations.dropCollection(Employee.class);

Employee e1 = new Employee();
e1.setId(UUID.randomUUID().toString());
e1.setFirstName("Bilbo");
e1.setLastName("Baggins");
e1.setRole("burglar");

mongoOperations.insert(e1);

Employee e2 = new Employee();
e2.setId(UUID.randomUUID().toString());
e2.setFirstName("Frodo");
e2.setLastName("Baggins");
e2.setRole("ring bearer");

mongoOperations.insert(e2);
```

The preceding setup can be described as follows:

- Start by using `dropCollection` to clean things out
- Next, create a new `Employee`, and insert it into MongoDB
- Create a second `Employee` and insert it as well

Only use `MongoOperations` to preload test data. Do NOT use it for production code, or your efforts at building reactive apps will be for nothing.

With our data preloaded, let's take a closer look at that `ReactiveQueryByExampleExecutor` interface used to define our repository (provided by Spring Data Commons). Digging in, we can find a couple of key query signatures like this:

```
<S extends T> Mono<S> findOne(Example<S> example);
<S extends T> Flux<S> findAll(Example<S> example);
```

Neither of these aforementioned methods have any properties whatsoever in their names compared to finders like `findByLastName`. The big difference is the usage of `Example` as an argument. `Example` is a container provided by Spring Data Commons to define the parameters of a query.

What does such an `Example` object look like? Let's construct one right now!

```
Employee e = new Employee();
e.setFirstName("Bilbo");
Example<Employee> example = Example.of(e);
```

This construction of an `Example` is described as follows:

- We create an `Employee` probe named `e`
- We set the probe's `firstName` to `Bilbo`
- Then we leverage the `Example.of` static helper to turn the probe into an `Example`

In this example, the probe is hard coded, but in production, the value would be pulled from the request whether it was part of a REST route, the body of a web request, or somewhere else.

Before we actually use the `Example` to conduct a query, it pays to understand *what* an `Example` object is. Simply put, an `Example` consists of a probe and a matcher. The probe is the POJO object containing all the values we wish to use as criteria. The matcher is an `ExampleMatcher` that governs how the probe is used. We'll see different types of matching in the following various usages.

Proceeding with our `Example` in hand, we can now solicit a response from the repository as follows:

```
Mono<Employee> singleEmployee = repository.findOne(example);
```

We no longer have to put `firstName` in the query's method signature. Instead, it has become a parameter fed to the query through the `Example` input.

Examples, by default, only query against non-null fields. That's a fancy way of saying that only the fields populated in the probe are considered. Also, the values supplied must match the stored records exactly. This is the default matcher used in the `Example` objects.

Since an exact match isn't always what's needed, let's see how we can adjust things, and come up with a different match criteria, as shown in this code:

```
Employee e = new Employee();
e.setLastName("baggins"); // Lowercase lastName

ExampleMatcher matcher = ExampleMatcher.matching()
  .withIgnoreCase()
  .withMatcher("lastName", startsWith())
  .withIncludeNullValues();

Example<Employee> example = Example.of(e, matcher);
```

This preceding example can be described as follows:

- We create another `Employee` probe
- We deliberately set the `lastName` value as lowercase
- Then we create a custom `ExampleMatcher` using `matching()`
- `withIgnoreCase` says to ignore the case of the values being checked
- `withMatcher` lets us indicate that a given document's `lastName` starts *with* the probe's value
- `withIncludeNullValues` will also match any entries that have nulled-out values
- Finally, we create an `Example` using our probe, but with this custom matcher

With this highly customized example, we can query for ALL employees matching these criteria:

```
Flux<Employee> multipleEmployees = repository.findAll(example);
```

This last code simply uses the `findAll` query, that returns a `Flux` using the same example criteria.

 Remember how we briefly mentioned that Query by Example can lend itself to a form on a web page where various fields are filled out? Based on the fields, the user can decide what to fetch. Notice how we used `withIgnoreCase`? By default, that flag flips to `true`, but it's possible to feed it a Boolean. It means we can put a checkbox on the web page allowing the user to decide whether or not to ignore case in their search.

Simple or complex, Query by Example provides flexible options to query for results. And using Reactor types, we can get just about anything we need with the two queries provided: `findOne` or `findAll`.

Querying with MongoOperations

So far, we have delved into the repository solution using both query by property and Query by Example. There is another angle we can use, `MongoTemplate`.

`MongoTemplate` mimics the Spring Framework's `JdbcTemplate`, the first data access mechanism implemented by Spring. `JdbcTemplate` allows us to focus on writing queries while delegating connection management and error handling to the framework.

`MongoTemplate` brings the same power to bear on crafting MongoDB operations. It's very powerful, but there is a critical tradeoff. All code written using `MongoTemplate` is MongoDB-specific. Porting solutions to another data store is very difficult. Hence, it's not recommended as the first solution, but as a tool to keep in our back pocket for critical operations that require highly tuned MongoDB statements.

To perform reactive `MongoTemplate` operations, there is a corresponding `ReactiveMongoTemplate` that supports Reactor types. The recommended way to interact with `ReactiveMongoTemplate` is through its interface, `ReactiveMongoOperations`.

The tool that actually conducts MongoDB repository operations under the hood is, in fact, a `MongoTemplate` (or a `ReactiveMongoTemplate` depending on the nature of the repository).

Additionally, Spring Boot will automatically scan the classpath, and if it spots Spring Data MongoDB 2.0 on the classpath along with MongoDB itself, it will create a `ReactiveMongoTemplate`. We can simply request a copy autowired into our class, whether by constructor injection or field injection, as follows:

```
@Autowired
ReactiveMongoOperations operations;
```

`@Autowired` in the last code snippet indicates this field will be injected when the class is loaded, and we'll get a copy of the bean that implements `ReactiveMongoOperations`.

For test cases, field injection is fine. But for actual running components, the Spring team recommends constructor injection, as will be shown throughout this book. For more details about the benefits of constructor injection, read Spring Data lead Oliver Gierke's blog post at http://olivergierke.de/2013/11/why-field-injection-is-evil/.

Using `ReactiveMongoOperations` along with `Query byExample`, we can see the previous query rewritten as follows:

```
Employee e = new Employee();
e.setFirstName("Bilbo");
Example<Employee> example = Example.of(e);

Mono<Employee> singleEmployee = operations.findOne(
    new Query(byExample(example)), Employee.class);
```

We can tear apart this latest wrinkle in MongoDB querying as follows:

- The declaration of the probe and its example is the same as shown earlier
- To create a query for one entry, we use `findOne` from `ReactiveMongoOperations`
- For the first parameter, we create a new `Query`, and use the `byExample` static helper to feed it the example
- For the second parameter, we tell it to return an `Employee`

Because this is `ReactiveMongoOperations`, the value is returned wrapped inside a `Mono`.

A similar tune-up can be made to fetch multiple entries with custom criteria, as follows:

```
Employee e = new Employee();
e.setLastName("baggins"); // Lowercase lastName

ExampleMatcher matcher = ExampleMatcher.matching()
  .withIgnoreCase()
  .withMatcher("lastName", startsWith())
  .withIncludeNullValues();

Example<Employee> example = Example.of(e, matcher);

Flux<Employee> multipleEmployees = operations.find(
   new Query(byExample(example)), Employee.class);
```

Now let's check out the details of this preceding query:

- The example is the same as the previous `findAll` query
- This time we use `find`, which accepts the same parameters as `findOne`, but returns a `Flux`

`ReactiveMongoOperations` and its `Query` input opens up a world of powerful operations, like this:

```
reactiveMongoOperations
  .findOne(
    query(
      where("firstName").is("Frodo")), Employee.class)
```

Beyond that, there is support for updating documents, finding-then-updating, and upserting, all supporting the rich, native MongoDB operators through a fluent API.

Delving into more MongoDB operations is beyond the scope of this book, but it's within your grasp should the need arise.

Logging reactive operations

So far, we have crafted a domain object for MongoDB, defined a reactive repository, and updated our `ImageService` to use it. If we fire things up, though, how can we see what's happening? Apart from viewing the web page, what can we expect to see in the console logs?

So far, this appears to be the most we get:

```
org.mongodb.driver.cluster              : Cluster created with settings {hosts=[localhost:27017], mode=SINGLE, requiredCluste
org.mongodb.driver.connection           : Opened connection [connectionId{localValue:1, serverValue:202}] to localhost:27017
org.mongodb.driver.cluster              : Monitor thread successfully connected to server with description ServerDescription{
org.mongodb.driver.cluster              : Cluster created with settings {hosts=[localhost:27017], mode=SINGLE, requiredCluste
org.mongodb.driver.connection           : Opened connection [connectionId{localValue:2, serverValue:203}] to localhost:27017
org.mongodb.driver.cluster              : Monitor thread successfully connected to server with description ServerDescription{
o.s.j.e.a.AnnotationMBeanExporter        : Registering beans for JMX exposure on startup
r.ipc.netty.tcp.BlockingNettyContext     : Started HttpServer on /0:0:0:0:0:0:0:0:8080
o.s.b.web.embedded.netty.NettyWebServer  : Netty started on port(s): 8080
org.mongodb.driver.connection           : Opened connection [connectionId{localValue:3, serverValue:204}] to localhost:27017
```

We see some log messages about connecting to an instance of MongoDB, but that's it! Not much there to debug things, ehh? Never fear, Spring Boot to the rescue.

Spring Boot comes with extensive logging support. Off the cuff, we can create a `logback.xml` file, and add it to our configuration in `src/main/resources`. Spring Boot will read it, and override its default logging policy. That's nice if we want to totally overhaul the log settings.

But often times, we just want to adjust some logging levels for specific packages. Spring Boot grants us a more fine-grained way to alter *what* gets logged.

Simply add this to `src/main/resources/application.properties`:

```
logging.level.com.greglturnquist=DEBUG
logging.level.org.springframework.data=TRACE
logging.level.reactor.core=TRACE
logging.level.reactor.util=TRACE
```

These adjustments can be described as follows:

- `logging.level` tells Spring Boot to adjust log levels with the name of the package tacked on followed by a level
- The application code, `com.greglturnquist`, is set to `DEBUG`
- Spring Data, `org.springframework.data`, is set to `TRACE`
- Project Reactor, `reactor.core` and `reactor.util`, are set to `TRACE`

With these adjustments, if we launch our application, this is part of the output we get:

```
org.mongodb.driver.cluster          : Cluster created with settings {hosts=[localhost:27017], mode=SINGLE, requiredClust
org.mongodb.driver.connection       : Opened connection [connectionId{localValue:1, serverValue:205}] to localhost:27017
org.mongodb.driver.cluster          : Monitor thread successfully connected to server with description ServerDescription
org.mongodb.driver.cluster          : Cluster created with settings {hosts=[localhost:27017], mode=SINGLE, requiredClust
org.mongodb.driver.connection       : Opened connection [connectionId{localValue:2, serverValue:206}] to localhost:27017
org.mongodb.driver.cluster          : Monitor thread successfully connected to server with description ServerDescription
.m.c.i.MongoPersistentEntityIndexCreator : Analyzing class class com.greglturnquist.learningspringboot.Image for index inform
.m.c.i.MongoPersistentEntityIndexCreator : Analyzing class class com.greglturnquist.learningspringboot.Image for index inform
o.s.j.e.a.AnnotationMBeanExporter    : Registering beans for JMX exposure on startup
r.ipc.netty.tcp.BlockingNettyContext : Started HttpServer on /0:0:0:0:0:0:0:0:8080
o.s.b.web.embedded.netty.NettyWebServer : Netty started on port(s): 8080
org.mongodb.driver.connection       : Opened connection [connectionId{localValue:3, serverValue:207}] to localhost:27017
o.s.data.mongodb.core.MongoTemplate  : Dropped collection [image]
o.s.data.mongodb.core.MongoTemplate  : Inserting Document containing fields: [_id, name, _class] in collection: image
o.s.data.mongodb.core.MongoTemplate  : Inserting Document containing fields: [_id, name, _class] in collection: image
o.s.data.mongodb.core.MongoTemplate  : Inserting Document containing fields: [_id, name, _class] in collection: image
```

This preceding output shows some MongoDB activity including cluster configuration, connections, and domain analysis. Toward the end, the effects of `InitDatabase` preloading our data can be seen to some degree, and can be explained as follows:

- `Dropped collection [image]`: This indicates all the entries being deleted by our `dropCollection`
- `Inserting Document containing fields...`: This indicates entries being saved using our `insert`

This is definitely an improvement, but something that's missing is the role that Reactor plays in handling all of this. While we've dialed up the log levels for Reactor, nothing has been output.

If we look at `ImageService`, the question arises, where *can* we add more logging? In traditional imperative programming, we would, typically, write `log.debug("blah blah")` at several spots along the way. But in this reactive flow, there are no "stops" to put them.

Project Reactor comes with a declarative log statement we can add along the way. Here is how we can decorate `findAllImages`:

```java
public Flux<Image> findAllImages() {
  return imageRepository.findAll()
    .log("findAll");
}
```

This preceding service operation has but one reactive step, so we can only slip in a single `log` statement. `ImageService.findOneImage` has the same story, so no need to show that.

However, `createImage` has several steps, which are seen in this code:

```
public Mono<Void> createImage(Flux<FilePart> files) {
  return files
    .log("createImage-files")
    .flatMap(file -> {
      Mono<Image> saveDatabaseImage = imageRepository.save(
        new Image(
          UUID.randomUUID().toString(),
          file.filename()))
          .log("createImage-save");

      Mono<Void> copyFile = Mono.just(
        Paths.get(UPLOAD_ROOT, file.filename())
        .toFile())
        .log("createImage-picktarget")
        .map(destFile -> {
          try {
            destFile.createNewFile();
            return destFile;
          } catch (IOException e) {
            throw new RuntimeException(e);
          }
        })
        .log("createImage-newfile")
        .flatMap(file::transferTo)
        .log("createImage-copy");

      return Mono.when(saveDatabaseImage, copyFile)
        .log("createImage-when");
    })
    .log("createImage-flatMap")
    .then()
    .log("createImage-done");
}
```

This last code is identical to what we had before except that each Reactor operation is tagged with a `log` statement. And each one has a unique tag appended, so, we can tell *exactly* what is happening and where.

If we exercise this code from a unit test that uploads two mock multipart files (a test we'll look closer at in the next chapter, Chapter 4, *Testing with Spring Boot*), we can spot each tag in the console output as follows:

```
createImage-files                    : | onSubscribe([Synchronous Fuseable] FluxArray.ArraySubscription)
createImage-flatMap                  : onSubscribe(FluxFlatMap.FlatMapMain)
createImage-done                     : onSubscribe(MonoIgnoreElements.IgnoreElementsSubscriber)
createImage-done                     : request(unbounded)
createImage-flatMap                  : request(unbounded)
createImage-files                    : | request(256)
createImage-files                    : | onNext(Mock for FilePart, hashCode: 154449199)
createImage-when                     : onSubscribe([Fuseable] MonoWhen.WhenCoordinator)
createImage-when                     : request(32)
o.s.d.m.core.ReactiveMongoTemplate   : Saving Document containing fields: [_id, name, _class]
createImage-save                     : onSubscribe(FluxOnErrorResume.ResumeSubscriber)
createImage-save                     : request(unbounded)
createImage-copy                     : | onSubscribe([Fuseable] MonoFlatMap.FlatMapMain)
createImage-copy                     : | request(unbounded)
createImage-picktarget               : | onSubscribe([Synchronous Fuseable] Operators.ScalarSubscription)
createImage-newfile                  : | onSubscribe([Fuseable] FluxMapFuseable.MapFuseableSubscriber)
createImage-newfile                  : | request(unbounded)
createImage-picktarget               : | request(unbounded)
createImage-picktarget               : | onNext(upload-dir/alpha.jpg)
createImage-newfile                  : | onNext(upload-dir/alpha.jpg)
createImage-copy                     : | onComplete()
createImage-picktarget               : | onComplete()
createImage-newfile                  : | onComplete()
createImage-files                    : | onNext(Mock for FilePart, hashCode: 430329518)
createImage-when                     : onSubscribe([Fuseable] MonoWhen.WhenCoordinator)
createImage-when                     : request(32)
o.s.d.m.core.ReactiveMongoTemplate   : Saving Document containing fields: [_id, name, _class]
createImage-save                     : onSubscribe(FluxOnErrorResume.ResumeSubscriber)
createImage-save                     : request(unbounded)
createImage-copy                     : | onSubscribe([Fuseable] MonoFlatMap.FlatMapMain)
createImage-copy                     : | request(unbounded)
createImage-picktarget               : | onSubscribe([Synchronous Fuseable] Operators.ScalarSubscription)
createImage-newfile                  : | onSubscribe([Fuseable] FluxMapFuseable.MapFuseableSubscriber)
createImage-newfile                  : | request(unbounded)
createImage-picktarget               : | request(unbounded)
createImage-picktarget               : | onNext(upload-dir/bravo.jpg)
org.mongodb.driver.connection        : Opened connection [connectionId{localValue:4, serverValue:220}] to lo
createImage-newfile                  : | onNext(upload-dir/bravo.jpg)
createImage-copy                     : | onComplete()
createImage-picktarget               : | onComplete()
createImage-newfile                  : | onComplete()
createImage-files                    : | onComplete()
org.mongodb.driver.connection        : Opened connection [connectionId{localValue:5, serverValue:221}] to lo
createImage-save                     : onNext(Image(id=85c62c00-c315-4a6b-914b-059e1020ee6b, name=bravo.jpg)
createImage-save                     : onNext(Image(id=7f4fb639-8b0d-4791-b88a-366b2cce0b55, name=alpha.jpg)
createImage-when                     : onComplete()
createImage-when                     : onComplete()
createImage-save                     : onComplete()
createImage-flatMap                  : onComplete()
createImage-done                     : onComplete()
```

This preceding output shows each of the steps, and how they play together in the reactive streams' dance of subscribe, request, next, and complete. Most notably, the outer operations (files, flatMap, and done) are shown at the top when subscriptions are made. Each file causes a filter operation to occur followed by a save and a copy. And at the bottom, the same outer operations (again files, flatMap, and done) issue a reactive streams **complete**.

To mark up deleteImage with logs, let's make these changes:

```
public Mono<Void> deleteImage(String filename) {
  Mono<Void> deleteDatabaseImage = imageRepository
    .findByName(filename)
    .log("deleteImage-find")
    .flatMap(imageRepository::delete)
    .log("deleteImage-record");

  Mono<Object> deleteFile = Mono.fromRunnable(() -> {
    try {
      Files.deleteIfExists(
        Paths.get(UPLOAD_ROOT, filename));
    } catch (IOException e) {
        throw new RuntimeException(e);
    }
  })
  .log("deleteImage-file");

  return Mono.when(deleteDatabaseImage, deleteFile)
    .log("deleteImage-when")
    .then()
    .log("deleteImage-done");
}
```

This is the same deleteImage code we wrote earlier, only, we've sprinkled in log statements everywhere to indicate exactly what is happening.

With everything set up, we should be able to test things out. For starters, we can launch the code by either running the LearningSpringBootApplication class's public static void main() method, or we can run it from the command line using Gradle like this:

```
$ ./gradlew clean bootRun
```

If we launch the application and navigate to `http://localhost:8080`, we can see our preloaded images, as seen in this screenshot:

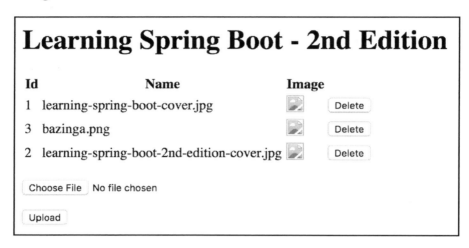

We can click on a single image, and see some comparable log messages like this:

```
findOneImage : | onSubscribe([Fuseable] Operators.MonoSubscriber)
findOneImage : | request(unbounded)
findOneImage : | onNext(URL [file:upload-dir/learning-spring-boot-
  cover.jpg])
findOneImage : | onComplete()
```

This very simple flow illustrates the Reactive Streams pattern. We subscribe for an image. A request is sent--in this case, unbounded (even though we know in advance there is only one result). onNext is the answer, and it's a file-based URL (a Spring `Resource`) being returned. Then the `complete` is issued.

 This logging is confined to `ImageService`, which means we don't see it transformed into an HTTP response. If you wish to explore this further, feel free to add extra `log` statements to `HomeController.oneRawImage`.

If we click on the **Delete** button, it deletes the image and refreshes the page, as follows:

Id	Name	Image	
3	bazinga.png		Delete
2	learning-spring-boot-2nd-edition-cover.jpg		Delete

After completing the deletion, if we look at the console logs and focus on what happened, we will see something like this:

```
o.s.d.m.r.query.MongoQueryCreator      : Created query Query: { "name" : "learning-spring-boot-cover.jpg"}, Fields:
o.s.d.m.core.ReactiveMongoTemplate     : findOne using query: { "name" : "learning-spring-boot-cover.jpg"} fields:
deleteImage-when                       : onSubscribe([Fuseable] MonoWhen.WhenCoordinator)
deleteImage-done                       : onSubscribe(MonoIgnoreElements.IgnoreElementsSubscriber)
deleteImage-done                       : request(unbounded)
deleteImage-when                       : request(unbounded)
deleteImage-record                     : | onSubscribe([Fuseable] MonoFlatMap.FlatMapMain)
deleteImage-record                     : | request(unbounded)
o.s.d.m.core.ReactiveMongoTemplate     : findOne using query: { "name" : "learning-spring-boot-cover.jpg"} fields:
deleteImage-find                       : onSubscribe(FluxOnErrorResume.ResumeSubscriber)
deleteImage-find                       : request(unbounded)
deleteImage-file                       : onSubscribe([Fuseable] Operators.EmptySubscription)
deleteImage-file                       : request(unbounded)
deleteImage-file                       : onComplete()
deleteImage-find                       : onNext(Image(id=1, name=learning-spring-boot-cover.jpg))
o.s.d.m.core.ReactiveMongoTemplate     : Remove using query: { "_id" : "1"} in collection: image.
deleteImage-find                       : onComplete()
deleteImage-record                     : | onComplete()
deleteImage-when                       : onComplete()
deleteImage-done                       : onComplete()
```

At the very top, we can see a MongoDB query issued to find the desired image with the `findOne using query` output. A `Mono.when` is set up, and then, a `Remove using query` is issued to delete the record. The actual deletion of the file is logged with little details except the complete signal. The whole thing is wrapped up when we see `deleteImage-done` issue a complete.

 We haven't begun to mark up the `HomeController` with log messages, but we don't need to at this stage. If you wish to explore that area, feel free to do so. Using these log statements, you can get a real feel for how Reactor arranges tasks, and even spot cases where the order of operations fluctuates at different times. The key thing is we have a real tool for debugging reactive flows.

With this, we have successfully coded a reactive `ImageService` that both copies files to the server and writes records in MongoDB; and we did it letting Spring Boot autoconfigure all the beans needed to make Spring Data MongoDB work seamlessly with Spring WebFlux and MongoDB.

Summary

In this chapter, we wrote several data access operations using a repository-based solution. We explored alternative querying options. Then we showed how to wire that into our controller, and store live data. We wrapped things up by exploring logging options in a functional, reactive nature.

In the next chapter, we will discover all the various ways Spring Boot makes testing super easy, combined with the utilities provided by Project Reactor to test async, non-blocking flows.

4
Testing with Spring Boot

Most innovative contribution to the java ecosystem: spring Boot #jaxlondon

– @JAXenter

If we go back more than 10 years, we would find testing a process mostly conducted by legions of test engineers. But with the rise of JUnit, the adoption of **continuous integration (CI)** servers, a plethora of test assertion libraries, and integrated test coverage services, we can see widespread adoption of automated testing.

In this chapter, we will see how critical Spring Boot views automated testing by providing multiple levels of support. We shall do the following:

- Write some basic unit tests
- Introduce **slice** testing
- Embark upon WebFlux testing
- Leverage complete embedded container testing
- Draft some autoconfiguration tests

Test dependencies

So far, we have used the Spring Initializr (`http://start.spring.io`) to create our social media platform. We picked several dependencies and added others along the way. But we haven't investigated test libraries.

It turns out, Spring Boot takes testing so seriously that it's not an option on the website. All projects created automatically have this test-scoped dependency:

```
testCompile('org.springframework.boot:spring-boot-starter-test')
```

So what's included with that single line?

- **JUnit**: De-facto standard for testing Java apps
- **JSON Path**: XPath for JSON
- **AssertJ**: Fluent assertion library
- **Mockito**: Java mocking library
- **Hamcrest**: Library of matcher objects
- **JSONassert**: Assertion library for JSON
- **Spring Test** and **Spring Boot Test**: Test libraries provided by the Spring Framework and Spring Boot

In addition to these various testing libraries being automatically supplied, many optional dependencies are also included. This means that they can be added to our project's list of dependencies without specifying the version. The optional dependencies are listed as follows:

- **HTMLUnit**: Testing toolkit for HTML outputs
- **Selenium**: Browser automation for UI testing
- **Flapdoodle**: Embedded MongoDB database for testing
- **H2**: Embedded SQL database for testing
- **Spring REST Docs**: Generates REST documentation using automated tests

 Before we dig any deeper, it's important to understand that entire books have been written about testing applications. We'll attempt to get a good cross-section of testing and look at how Spring Boot makes certain types of tests even easier, but don't consider this chapter to be the end-all of what's possible.

Unit testing

The smallest scoped tests we can write are referred to as unit tests. In fact, people have been writing tiny tests for years. A common paradigm is to try and test just one class in a given unit test.

To get going, let's test the smallest unit of code we have: our Lombok-enabled `Image` domain object.

As a reminder, here is what that code looks like:

```
@Data
@Document
public class Image {
    @Id final private String id;
    final private String name;
}
```

This tiny little POJO is flagged with Spring Data MongoDB annotations as well as Lombok's `@Data` annotation providing getters and setters.

A unit test shouldn't be too hard. We can start by creating `ImageTests.java` in `/src/test/java`, and in the same package as the original class (`com.greglturnquist.learningspringboot`), as follows:

```
public class ImageTests {
  @Test
  public void imagesManagedByLombokShouldWork() {
    Image image = new Image("id", "file-name.jpg");
    assertThat(image.getId()).isEqualTo("id");
    assertThat(image.getName()).isEqualTo("file-name.jpg");
  }
}
```

This preceding unit test can easily be explained, as follows:

- `@Test` indicates that `imagesManagedByLombokShouldWork` is a JUnit test case, ensuring it is automatically picked up and run either from our IDE when we choose or from Gradle when we build the system
- The test creates a new `Image` object
- Then it uses AssertJ's `assertThat()` method to prove the values are as expected

Let's run it!

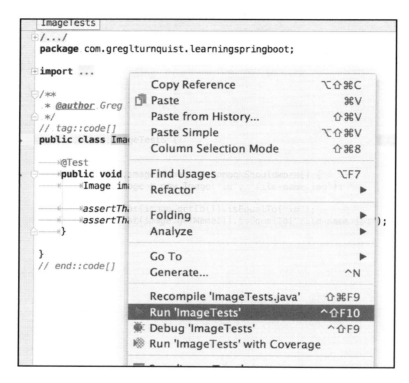

As shown in the preceding screenshot, we merely right-click on the class `ImageTests`, select **Run 'ImageTests'**, and watch for the output (shown next):

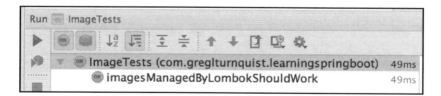

Hooray! There is always a little happiness when our automated tests go green.

 I know that in print, the color green turns to grey. But we can also see the **OK** text in the bubble next to the test case, indicating that it passed.

So far, so good. With our first test written, we have gotten off the ground with a test-based approach to things. But testing can get more complicated, quickly.

Slice-based testing

Across the industry, many express an interest in testing. Yet, when push comes to shove and we run into tricky situations, it's quite easy to throw up our hands and shout, *This is too hard!*

Spring Boot aims to help!

JUnit, all by itself, gives us the power to declare tests and assert pass/fail scenarios. But in reality, not everything works straight out of the box. For example, parts of our code will easily come to rely upon Boot autoconfiguring various beans as well as having that powerful property support.

A keen example is the need to do some MongoDB operations. It would be quite handy if we could ask Spring Boot to autoconfigure just enough beans to support MongoDB for our tests but nothing else.

Well, today's our lucky day.

Spring Boot 1.5 introduced slice testing. This is where a subset of Spring Boot's autoconfiguration power can be switched on, while also having full access to its property support. The following list of test annotations each enable a different slice of code:

- `@DataMongoTest`
- `@DataJpaTest`
- `@JdbcTest`
- `@JsonTest`
- `@RestClientTest`
- `@WebFluxTest`
- `@WebMvcTest`

Each of these annotations enables a different slice of beans to be configured. For example, `@DataJpaTest` will:

- Enable transactions by applying Spring's `@Transactional` annotation to the test class
- Enable caching on the test class, defaulting to a `NoOp` cache instance
- Autoconfigure an embedded test database in place of a real one
- Create a `TestEntityManager` bean and add it to the application context
- Disable the general Spring Boot autoconfiguration, confining things to the autoconfiguration policies found in `spring-boot-test-autoconfigure`

 All of these annotations require additionally annotating our test class with `@RunWith(SpringRunner.class)`.

An important point to understand is that tests work best when confined to a relatively narrow scope. Hence, using more than one of these `@...Test` annotations is not recommended. Instead, break things up into multiple test classes.

Testing with embedded MongoDB

The first annotation listed above for slice testing is `@DataMongoTest`. In this section, we want to write some test methods that involve our MongoDB-specific code.

When it comes to testing MongoDB code, we have the following two options provided by Spring Boot:

- Testing against an embedded MongoDB instance
- Testing against a live MongoDB instance

Spring Boot, by default, will check if Flapdoodle, the embedded MongoDB database, is on the classpath. If so, it will attempt to run the test using it. If Flapdoodle is NOT on our classpath, it will attempt to connect to a real MongoDB instance.

So let's get started by adding `flapdoodle` to our project's list of dependencies as follows:

```
testCompile("de.flapdoodle.embed:de.flapdoodle.embed.mongo")
```

Since we are going to test our Reactor-based APIs, we also want to leverage Reactor Test, a library of utilities provided by Project Reactor. Let's add the following test dependency:

```
testCompile("io.projectreactor:reactor-test")
```

With this last dependency added to our project, we can now start writing `EmbeddedImageRepositoryTests.java` inside `src/test/java`, in the `com.greglturnquist.learningspringboot` package, like this:

```
@RunWith(SpringRunner.class)
@DataMongoTest
public class EmbeddedImageRepositoryTests {

    @Autowired
    ImageRepository repository;

    @Autowired
    MongoOperations operations;
```

The preceding code for the first part of this test class can be described as follows:

- `@RunWith(SpringRunner.java)` is needed to ensure that Spring Boot test annotations run properly within JUnit
- `@DataMongoTest` will disable the general Spring Boot autoconfiguration, and instead, use Spring Boot's test-based autoconfigurations to create a `MongoTemplate`, a MongoDB connection, MongoDB property settings, a `ReactiveMongoTemplate` and an embedded MongoDB instance; it will also enable the MongoDB repositories
- With the Spring Data MongoDB repositories enabled, Spring Boot will automatically instantiate an `ImageRepository`, and inject it into our autowired `repository` field

> In general, it's recommended to use constructor injection for production code. But for test code where constructors are limited due to JUnit, autowiring as we've just done is fine.

With access to a clean MongoDB instance (embedded), we can now perform a little setup work as follows:

```
/**
 * To avoid {@code block()} calls, use blocking
 * {@link MongoOperations} during setup.
 */
@Before
```

```
public void setUp() {
  operations.dropCollection(Image.class);
  operations.insert(new Image("1",
    "learning-spring-boot-cover.jpg"));
  operations.insert(new Image("2",
    "learning-spring-boot-2nd-edition-cover.jpg"));
  operations.insert(new Image("3",
    "bazinga.png"));
  operations.findAll(Image.class).forEach(image -> {
    System.out.println(image.toString());
  });
}
```

This preceding setup method can be described as follows:

- The @Before flags this method to be run before every single @Test method in this class
- The operations is used to dropCollection and then insert three new entries in the database, turn around and fetch them all, and print them to the console

With things preloaded properly, we can start writing our first test case, as shown next:

```
@Test
public void findAllShouldWork() {
  Flux<Image> images = repository.findAll();
  StepVerifier.create(images)
    .recordWith(ArrayList::new)
    .expectNextCount(3)
    .consumeRecordedWith(results -> {
      assertThat(results).hasSize(3);
      assertThat(results)
      .extracting(Image::getName)
      .contains(
        "learning-spring-boot-cover.jpg",
        "learning-spring-boot-2nd-edition-cover.jpg",
        "bazinga.png");
    })
    .expectComplete()
    .verify();
}
```

This preceding test case can be described as follows:

- @Test indicates this is a test method and the method name describes our overall goal.

- We use Reactor Test's `StepVerifier` to subscribe to the `Flux` from the repository and then assert against it.
- Because we want to assert against the whole collection, we need to pipe it through Reactor Test's `recordWith` method, which fetches the entire `Flux` and converts it into an `ArrayList` via a method handle.
- We verify that there were indeed three entries.
- We write a lambda to peek inside the recorded `ArrayList`. In it, we can use AssertJ to verify the size of `ArrayList` as well as extract each image's name with `Image::getName` and verify them.
- Finally, we can verify that `Flux` emitted a **Reactive Streams** complete signal, meaning that it finished correctly.

`StepVerifier` speaks Reactive Streams and will execute all the various signals to talk to the enclosed `Publisher`. In this case, we interrogated a `Flux` but this can also be used on a `Mono`.

To wrap things up, we are going to test our custom finder, `findByName`, as shown here:

```
@Test
public void findByNameShouldWork() {
  Mono<Image> image = repository.findByName("bazinga.png");
  StepVerifier.create(image)
    .expectNextMatches(results -> {
      assertThat(results.getName()).isEqualTo("bazinga.png");
      assertThat(results.getId()).isEqualTo("3");
      return true;
    });
}
```

This last test case can be described as follows:

- `repository.findByName()` is used to fetch one record
- We again use `StepVerifier` to create a subscriber for our `Mono` and then expect the next signal to come through, indicating that it was fetched
- Inside the lambda, we perform a couple of AssertJ assertions to verify the state of this `Image`

 Due to the functional nature of `StepVerifier`, we need to return a Boolean representing pass/fail.

By the way, exactly how many CRUD methods do we need to test? We covered `findAll` and `findByName`. In principle, we could sidestep `findAll` since that can be considered a part of Spring Data MongoDB. But it makes a good example in this book for testing a Reactor `Flux` result.

In general, we shouldn't bite off testing framework code. But verifying our custom finder makes perfect sense. And there's always room for end-to-end testing, which we'll explore further in this chapter.

Testing with a real MongoDB database

Testing against an embedded MongoDB instance is quite handy. But there are times when we need to work with a real instance, and for multiple reasons: security settings, a batch of live data, a customized configuration. Whatever the reason, there is no need for that to derail our testing efforts.

We can write another test class, `LiveImageRepositoryTests`, and make it look like this:

```
@RunWith(SpringRunner.class)
@DataMongoTest(excludeAutoConfiguration =
  EmbeddedMongoAutoConfiguration.class)
  public class LiveImageRepositoryTests {
    @Autowired
    ImageRepository repository;
    @Autowired
    MongoOperations operations;
```

The details for this preceding live test are as follows:

- `@RunWith(SpringRunner.class)` is our familiar annotation to integrate Spring with JUnit.
- `@DataMongoTest` (and the other `@...Test` annotations) lets us exclude explicit autoconfiguration classes. To switch off Flapdoodle, all we need to do is exclude `EmbeddedMongoAutoConfiguration`

The rest of the code in this class is the same as `EmbeddedImageRepositoryTests`, so there's no need to show it here. (In fact, it would be quite nice if the exact same tests ran on both embedded as well as a live MongoDB instance.)

Let's run our latest batch of both embedded and live MongoDB tests:

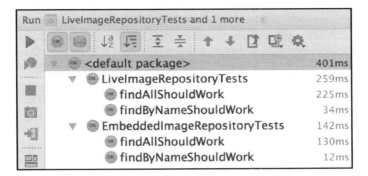

All green (along with the **OK** icon)!

 Keeping identical test code in two different classes violates the **DRY** (**Don't Repeat Yourself**) principle. If we altered one test class, we should presumably alter the matching test case in the other class. But a new teammate may not be aware of this. It's left as an exercise for the reader to extract an abstract set of test methods to be used by both `LiveImageRepositoryTests` and `EmbeddedImageRepositoryTests`.

Testing WebFlux controllers

So far, we've looked at unit testing as well as slice testing for MongoDB. These are good for covering services and backend logic. The last part we need to ensure is whether the web controllers are working properly.

Spring Boot comes with automated support to help us pick the exact type of test that we want to run. Let's start with an example:

```
@RunWith(SpringRunner.class)
@WebFluxTest(controllers = HomeController.class)
@Import({ThymeleafAutoConfiguration.class})
public class HomeControllerTests {
  @Autowired
  WebTestClient webClient;
  @MockBean
  ImageService imageService;
  ...
}
```

This preceding beginning of a controller test case can be described as follows:

- `@RunWith(SpringRunner.class)` ensures all of our Spring Framework and Spring Boot test annotations integrate properly with JUnit.
- `@WebFluxTest(controllers = HomeController.class)` is another slice of testing which focuses on Spring WebFlux. The default configuration enables all `@Controller` beans and `@RestController` beans as well as a mock web environment, but with the rest of the autoconfiguration disabled. However, by using the `controllers` argument, we have confined this test case to ONLY enable `HomeController`.
- `@Import(...)` specifies what additional bits we want configured outside of any Spring WebFlux controllers. In this case, the Thymeleaf autoconfiguration is needed.
- A `WebTestClient` bean is autowired into our test case, giving us the means to make mock web calls.
- `@MockBean` signals that the `ImageService` collaborator bean needed by our `HomeController` will be replaced by a mock, which we'll configure shortly.

 Even though `@WebFluxTest` is another slice similar to `@DataMongoTest`, we broke it out of the previous section, Slice Testing, because WebFlux testing comes with an extensive range of configuration options, which we will explore later in more detail.

Let's look at a test case where we get the base URL /:

```
@Test
public void baseRouteShouldListAllImages() {
  // given
  Image alphaImage = new Image("1", "alpha.png");
  Image bravoImage = new Image("2", "bravo.png");
  given(imageService.findAllImages())
    .willReturn(Flux.just(alphaImage, bravoImage));

  // when
  EntityExchangeResult<String> result = webClient
    .get().uri("/")
    .exchange()
    .expectStatus().isOk()
    .expectBody(String.class).returnResult();

  // then
  verify(imageService).findAllImages();
  verifyNoMoreInteractions(imageService);
  assertThat(result.getResponseBody())
```

```
    .contains(
      "<title>Learning Spring Boot: Spring-a-Gram</title>")
    .contains("<a href=\"/images/alpha.png/raw\">")
    .contains("<a href=\"/images/bravo.png/raw\">");
}
```

We can cover the details of this last test case as follows:

- `@Test` marks this method as a JUnit test case.
- The method name, `baseRouteShouldListAllImages`, gives us a quick summary of what this method should verify.
- The first three lines mock up the `ImageService` bean to return a `Flux` of two images when `findAllImages` gets called.
- `webClient` is then used to perform a `GET` / using its fluent API.
- We verify the HTTP status to be a 200 OK, and extract the body of the result into a string.
- We use Mockito's `verify` to prove that our `ImageService` bean's `findAllImages` was indeed called.
- We use Mockito's `verifyNoMoreInteractions` to prove that no other calls are made to our mock `ImageService`.
- Finally, we use AssertJ to inspect some key parts of the HTML page that was rendered.

This test method gives us a pretty good shake out of `GET` /. We are able to verify that the web page was rendered with the right content. We can also verify that our `ImageService` bean was called as expected. And both were done without involving a real MongoDB engine and without a fully running web container.

Spring's WebFlux machinery is verified since it still includes the bits that take an incoming request for / and routes it to `HomeController.index()`, yielding a Thymeleaf-generated HTML page. This way, we know our controller has been wired properly. And oftentimes, this is enough to prove the web call works.

A key scenario to explore is actually fetching a file, mockingly. It's what our app does when requesting a single image. Check out the following test case:

```
@Test
public void fetchingImageShouldWork() {
  given(imageService.findOneImage(any()))
    .willReturn(Mono.just(
      new ByteArrayResource("data".getBytes())));

  webClient
```

```
        .get().uri("/images/alpha.png/raw")
        .exchange()
        .expectStatus().isOk()
        .expectBody(String.class).isEqualTo("data");
    verify(imageService).findOneImage("alpha.png");
    verifyNoMoreInteractions(imageService);
}
```

This preceding test case can be described as follows:

- `@Test` flags this method as a JUnit test case.
- The method name, `fetchingImageShouldWork`, hints that this tests successful file fetching.
- The `ImageService.findOneImage` method returns a `Mono<Resource>`, so we need to assemble a mock resource. That can be achieved using Spring's `ByteArrayResource`, which takes a `byte[]`. Since all Java strings can be turned into byte arrays, it's a piece of cake to plug it in.
- `webClient` calls `GET /images/alpha.png/raw`.
- After the `exchange()` method, we verify the HTTP status is `OK`.
- We can even check the data content in the body of the HTTP response given that the bytes can be curried back into a Java string.
- Lastly, we use Mockito's `verify` to make sure our mock was called once and in no other way.

Since we're coding against a very simple interface, `Resource`, we don't have to go through any complicated ceremony of staging a fake test file and having it served up. While that's possible, Mockito makes it easy to stand up stubs and mocks. Additionally, Spring's assortment of `Resource` implementations lets us pick the right one. This reinforces the benefit of coding services against interfaces and not implementations when possible.

The other side of the coin when testing file retrieval is to verify that we properly handle file errors. What if we attempted to fetch an image but for some reason the file on the server was corrupted? Check it out in the following test code:

```
@Test
public void fetchingNullImageShouldFail() throws IOException {
    Resource resource = mock(Resource.class);
    given(resource.getInputStream())
        .willThrow(new IOException("Bad file"));
    given(imageService.findOneImage(any()))
        .willReturn(Mono.just(resource));

    webClient
```

```
.get().uri("/images/alpha.png/raw")
.exchange()
.expectStatus().isBadRequest()
.expectBody(String.class)
.isEqualTo("Couldn't find alpha.png => Bad file");

verify(imageService).findOneImage("alpha.png");
verifyNoMoreInteractions(imageService);
}
```

This preceding test of a failure can be described as follows:

- @Test flags this method as a JUnit test case.
- The method name, fetchingNullImageShouldFail, hints that this test is aimed at a failure scenario.
- We need to mock out the file on the server, which is represented as a Spring Resource. That way, we can force it to throw an IOException when getInputStream is invoked.
- That mock is returned when ImageService.findOneImage is called. Notice how we use Mockito's any() to simplify inputs?
- webClient is again used to make the call.
- After the exchange() method is made, we verify that the HTTP status is a 400 Bad Request.
- We also check the response body and ensure it matches the expected body from our controller's exception handler.
- Finally, we use Mockito to verify that our mock ImageService.findOneImage() was called once (and only once!) and that no other calls were made to this mock bean.

This test case shows a critical skill we all need to polish: verifying that the path of failure is handled properly. When a manager asks *what if the file isn't there?*, we can show them a test case indicating that we have covered it. Say we write a try...catch clause in the our code, like this one in HomeController.oneRawImage():

```
return imageService.findOneImage(filename)
.map(resource -> {
  try {
    return ResponseEntity.ok()
    .contentLength(resource.contentLength())
    .body(new InputStreamResource(
      resource.getInputStream())));
  } catch (IOException e) {
    return ResponseEntity.badRequest()
```

```
            .body("Couldn't find " + filename +
                " => " + e.getMessage());
        }
    });
```

We should immediately start thinking of two test cases: one test case for the try part when we can find the file and return an OK, and another test case for the catch part when `IOException` gets thrown and we return a Bad Request.

While it's not hard to think up all the successful scenarios, capturing the failure scenarios and testing them is important. And Mockito makes it quite easy to mock failing behavior. In fact, it's a common pattern to have one mock return another, as we did in this test case.

 Mockito makes it easy to mock things left and right. Just keep sight of what you're really trying to test. One can get so caught up in mocking so that all that gets tested are the mocks. We must be sure to verify the actual behavior of the code, or the test will be meaningless.

Another webish behavior that happens all the time is processing a call and then redirecting the client to another web location. This is exactly the behavior when we issue an HTTP `DELETE` to our site. The URL is expected to carry the resource that must be deleted. Once completed, we need to instruct the browser to go back to the home page.

Check out the following test case:

```
@Test
public void deleteImageShouldWork() {
    Image alphaImage = new Image("1", "alpha.png");
    given(imageService.deleteImage(any())).willReturn(Mono.empty());

    webClient
        .delete().uri("/images/alpha.png")
        .exchange()
        .expectStatus().isSeeOther()
        .expectHeader().valueEquals(HttpHeaders.LOCATION, "/");

    verify(imageService).deleteImage("alpha.png");
    verifyNoMoreInteractions(imageService);
}
```

We can describe this preceding redirecting web call as follows:

- The `@Test` flags this method as a JUnit test case.
- We prep our `ImageService` mock bean to handle a `deleteImage` by returning `Mono.empty()`. This is the way to construct a `Mono<Void>` object, which represents the promise that our service hands us when deletion of the file and its corresponding MongoDB record are both completed.
- `webClient` performs a `DELETE /images/alpha.png`.
- After the `exchange()` is complete, we verify the HTTP status is `303 See Other`, the outcome of a Spring WebFlux `redirect:/` directive.
- As part of the HTTP redirect, there should also be a `Location` header containing the new URL, `/`.
- Finally, we confirm that our `ImageService` mock bean's `deleteImage` method was called and nothing else.

This proves that we have properly invoked our service and then followed it up with a redirect back to the home page. It's actually possible to grab that Location header and issue another `webClient` call, but there is no point in this test case. We have already verified that behavior.

However, imagine that the redirect included some contextual thing like `redirect:/?msg=Deleted` showing a desire to bounce back to the home page but with extra data to be shown. That would be a great time to issue a second call and prove that this special message was rendered properly.

Now we can run the entire test case and see green bubbles all the way down:

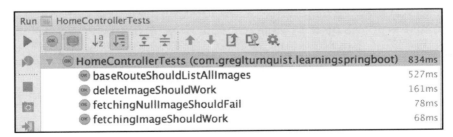

 We have used Mockito quite a bit but we aren't going to delve into all its features. For that, I recommend reading *Mockito Cookbook* written by Spring teammate Marcin Grzejszczak (`@MGrzejszczak`).

Fully embedded Spring Boot app tests

We did some nice testing of the web controller and verified that it behaves properly. But that was just another slice. At some point, it's good to test the whole thing, end-to-end. And with today's modern suite of test tools, it's totally doable.

Spring Boot doesn't always support every tool. For example, Selenium WebDriver, a popular browser automation toolkit, is not yet supported outside of servlets.

No problem! What we really need is for Spring Boot to launch our application, preferably on an unoccupied port, and get out of the way while we do some testing. So let's do just that.

We can start by crafting a new test case like this:

```
@RunWith(SpringRunner.class)
@SpringBootTest(
  webEnvironment = SpringBootTest.WebEnvironment.RANDOM_PORT)
  public class EndToEndTests {
```

This preceding test class can be described as follows:

- `@RunWith(SpringRunner.class)` ensures the Spring Boot annotations integrate with JUnit.
- `@SpringBootTest` is the test annotation where we can activate all of Spring Boot in a controlled fashion. With `webEnvironment` switched from the default setting of a mocked web environment to `SpringBootTest.WebEnvironment.RANDOM_PORT`, a real embedded version of the app will launch on a random available port.

This configuration will spin up a copy of our application on an open port, with a full-blown autoconfiguration, and all of our `CommandLineRunners` will run. That means our `InitDatabase` class that pre-loads MongoDB will kick in.

 By the way, Flapdoodle will also run an embedded MongoDB instance because we are in the test scope.

First of all, we need a handful of test objects declared as fields of our test class. These are obtained as follows:

```
static ChromeDriverService service;
static ChromeDriver driver;
@LocalServerPort
int port;
```

These attributes of `EndToEndTests` can be described as follows:

- `ChromeDriverService`: This gives us a handle on the bridge between Selenium and the Chrome handling library
- `ChromeDriver`: This is an implementation of the `WebDriver` interface, giving us all the operations to drive a test browser
- `@LocalServerPort`: This is a Spring Boot annotation that instructs Boot to autowire the port number of the web container into `port`

 To use `ChromeDriver`, not only do we need the browser Chrome downloaded and installed in its default location, we also need a separate executable: `chromedriver`. Assuming you have visited `https://sites.google.com/a/chromium.org/chromedriver/downloads`, downloaded the bundle (macOS in my case), unzipped it, and put the executable in a folder named `ext`, you can proceed.

With `chromedriver` installed in `ext`, we can configure it to start and stop as follows:

```
@BeforeClass
public static void setUp() throws IOException {
  System.setProperty("webdriver.chrome.driver",
    "ext/chromedriver");
  service = createDefaultService();
  driver = new ChromeDriver(service);
  Path testResults = Paths.get("build", "test-results");
  if (!Files.exists(testResults)) {
    Files.createDirectory(testResults);
  }
}

@AfterClass
public static void tearDown() {
  service.stop();
}
```

This setup/teardown behavior can be described as follows:

- `@BeforeClass` directs JUnit to run this method before any test method inside this class runs and to only run this method once
- Inside the `setUp` method, it sets the `webdriver.chrome.driver` property to the relative path of `chromedriver`
- Next, it creates a default service
- Then it creates a new `ChromeDriver` to be used by all the test methods
- Finally, it creates a test directory to capture screenshots (as we'll soon see)
- `@AfterClass` directs JUnit to run the `tearDown` method after ALL tests have run in this class
- It commands `ChromeDriverService` to shut down. Otherwise, the server process will stay up and running

Is this starting to sound a bit convoluted? We'll explore options to simplify this later on in this chapter.

For now, let's focus on writing this test case:

```java
@Test
public void homePageShouldWork() throws IOException {
    driver.get("http://localhost:" + port);

    takeScreenshot("homePageShouldWork-1");

    assertThat(driver.getTitle())
        .isEqualTo("Learning Spring Boot: Spring-a-Gram");

    String pageContent = driver.getPageSource();

    assertThat(pageContent)
        .contains("<a href=\"/images/bazinga.png/raw\">");
    WebElement element = driver.findElement(
        By.cssSelector("a[href*=\"bazinga.png\"]"));
    Actions actions = new Actions(driver);
    actions.moveToElement(element).click().perform();

    takeScreenshot("homePageShouldWork-2");
    driver.navigate().back();
}
```

This preceding test case can be detailed as follows:

- `@Test` indicates this is a JUnit test case
- `driver` navigates to the home page using the injected `port`
- It takes a screenshot so we can inspect things after the fact
- We verify the title of the page is as expected
- Next, we grab the entire page's HTML content and verify one of the links
- Then we hunt down that link using a W3C CSS selector (there are other options as well), move to it, and click on it
- We grab another snapshot and then click on the back button

This is a pretty basic test. It doesn't do a lot apart from verifying the home page and checking out one link. However, it demonstrates that we can automatically test the entire system. Remember, we have the whole system up, including a live MongoDB database (if you count an embedded one as being real). This verifies not only our own code, but our assumptions regarding what gets autoconfigured, autowired, and initialized.

As a culmination of testing nirvana, we can even grab screen snapshots to prove we were here. Or at least that our test case was here. That code is shown here:

```
private void takeScreenshot(String name) throws IOException {
  FileCopyUtils.copy(
    driver.getScreenshotAs(OutputType.FILE),
    new File("build/test-results/TEST-" + name + ".png"));
}
```

Snapping a screenshot can be explained as follows:

- `driver.getScreenshotAs(OutputType.FILE)` taps the `TakesScreenshot` subinterface to grab a snapshot of the screen and put it into a `temp` file
- Spring's `FileCopyUtils` utility method is used to copy that `temp` file into the project's `build/test-results` folder using the input argument to give it a custom name

Taking screenshots is a key reason to use either `ChromeDriver`, `FirefoxDriver`, or `SafariDriver`. All of these real-world browser integrations support this feature. And thanks to that, we have the following snapshot results:

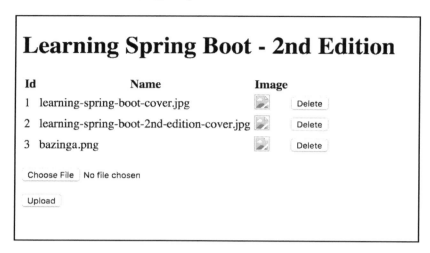

That first shot shows the whole web page. The following screenshot shows a single image after being clicked:

The screenshot of this image may look a little awkward, but remember; these images aren't real JPGs. Instead, they are strings stuffed into the filesystem.

If we run our entire suite of test cases, we can see the whole thing takes just shy of 2.5 seconds:

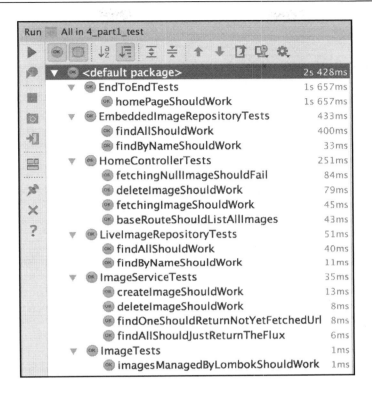

Impressive, huh?

How good a test suite is that? Using the IDE, we can run the same test suite but with coverage analysis turned on:

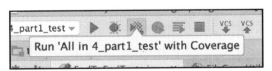

After running the same test suite but with the IDE's coverage tools enabled, we can get a read out in the source code listing, as seen in this screenshot:

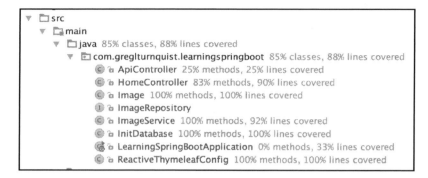

That's quite handy. We can even drill into each class and see what's missing. As deft as this is, we aren't going to delve any more into test coverage. That's something best left to a more test-oriented book.

Don't let test coverage consume you. As mentioned in my other book, *Python Testing Cookbook*, in *Chapter 9* under the *Coverage isn't everything* section, the test coverage should be used to identify new, reasonable scenarios that should be checked out, not gaming the system to squeeze out another percentage point or two. And coverage reports should never be used to compare one system or test regimen against another, let alone be used as a gate for release. We should all seek to increase test coverage over time as the means to increase confidence and reduce risk, not as a gate to make releases.

We just mentioned all the ceremony invested into getting Chrome to operate. Why did we do that? Because the one `WebDriver` implementation that requires no such effort to bring online *doesn't support taking screenshots*. There is also no way of knowing if the person checking out your code has the same browser installed.

If we coded everything around Chrome because we don't like Firefox but another teammate doesn't have Chrome, we've got a problem.

On one hand, if screenshots aren't important, then `HtmlUnitDriver` is the way to go. It comes out of the box, works as good as any other `WebDriver`, and doesn't require any third-party executables or drivers. But that is the penalty of going by the least common denominator.

Wouldn't it be preferable to have *whatever* WebDriver we can get based on whatever we have installed on our system and automatically load that into our test case? After all, Spring Boot is about reducing Java complexity when building apps.

If you sense a slow walk toward a Spring Boot-oriented solution to this craziness, you're right. In the next section, we'll explore how to autoconfigure a WebDriver based on what's available and then we'll unit test that autoconfiguration policy.

Testing your custom Spring Boot autoconfiguration

If picking between several WebDriver implementations sounds hokey and unnecessarily complicated, then let's do what Spring Boot does best: autoconfigure it!

Okay, if we're going to autoconfigure something, we sure as heck want to *test* what we're doing. That way, we can make sure it performs as expected. To do so requires a little bit of test setup. Check it out:

```
public class WebDriverAutoConfigurationTests {
  private AnnotationConfigApplicationContext context;
  @After
  public void close() {
    if (this.context != null) {
      this.context.close();
    }
  }

  private void load(Class<?>[] configs, String... environment) {
    AnnotationConfigApplicationContext applicationContext =
      new AnnotationConfigApplicationContext();
    applicationContext
      .register(WebDriverAutoConfiguration.class);
    if (configs.length > 0) {
      applicationContext.register(configs);
    }
    EnvironmentTestUtils
      .addEnvironment(applicationContext, environment);
    applicationContext.refresh();
    this.context = applicationContext;
  }

  ...more coming later...

}
```

This preceding test case is set up as follows:

- It starts off very different from what we've seen up until now. Instead of using various Spring Boot test annotations, this one starts with nothing. That way, we can add only the bits of Boot that we want in a very fine-grained fashion.
- We'll use Spring's `AnnotationConfigApplicationContext` as the DI container of choice to programmatically register beans.
- The `@After` annotation flags the `close()` method to run after every test case and close the application context, ensuring the next test case has a clean start.
- `load()` will be invoked by each test method as part of its setup, accepting a list of Spring configuration classes as well as optional property settings, as it creates a new application context.
- `load()` then registers a `WebDriverAutoConfiguration` class (which we haven't written yet).
- After that, it registers any additional test configuration classes we wish.
- It then uses Spring Boot's `EnvironmentTestUtils` to add any configuration property settings we need to the application context. This is a convenient way to programmatically set properties without mucking around with files or system settings.
- It then uses the application context's `refresh()` function to create all the beans.
- Lastly, it assigns the application context to the test class's `context` field.

In this bit of code, we programmatically build up a Spring application context from scratch. In this test class, we register our brand new `WebDriverAutoConfiguration` class to be at the heart of all of our tests. Then we are free to run all kinds of test cases, ensuring it acts properly. We can even register different configuration classes to override any of the autoconfiguration beans.

Now let's noodle out our first test case. What's a good place to start? What if we were to disable all the browser-based `WebDriver` instances (like Firefox and Chrome), and instead, expect the thing to fall back to the universal `HtmlUnitDriver`? Let's try it:

```
@Test
public void fallbackToNonGuiModeWhenAllBrowsersDisabled() {
  load(new Class[]{},
    "com.greglturnquist.webdriver.firefox.enabled:false",
    "com.greglturnquist.webdriver.safari.enabled:false",
    "com.greglturnquist.webdriver.chrome.enabled:false");
  WebDriver driver = context.getBean(WebDriver.class);
  assertThat(ClassUtils.isAssignable(TakesScreenshot.class,
    driver.getClass())).isFalse();
  assertThat(ClassUtils.isAssignable(HtmlUnitDriver.class,
```

```
    driver.getClass())).isTrue();
}
```

This test case can be explained as follows:

- `@Test` **marks** `fallbackToNonGuiModeWhenAllBrowsersDisabled` as a JUnit test method.
- To start things, it uses the `load()` method. Since we don't have any custom overrides, we supply it with an empty array of configuration classes. We also include a slew of properties, the first one being `com.greglturnquist.webdriver.firefox.enabled:false`. From a design perspective, it's nice to optionally exclude certain types, so having a well-qualified property (using a domain we own) and setting them all to false sounds like a good start.
- Now we can ask the application context to give us a `WebDriver` bean.
- If it bypassed all those browser-specific ones and landed on `HtmlUnitDriver`, then it shouldn't support the `TakesScreenshot` interface. We can verify that with the AssertJ `assertThat()` check, using Spring's `ClassUtils.isAssignable` check.
- To make it crystal clear that we're getting an `HtmlUnitDriver`, we can also write another check verifying that.

Since we aren't actually testing the guts of Selenium WebDriver, there is no need to examine the object anymore. We have what we want, an autoconfigured `WebDriver` that should operate well.

Having captured our first expected set of conditions, it's time to roll up our sleeves and get to work. We'll start by creating `WebDriverAutoConfiguration.java` as follows:

```
@Configuration
@ConditionalOnClass(WebDriver.class)
@EnableConfigurationProperties(
  WebDriverConfigurationProperties.class)
@Import({ChromeDriverFactory.class,
  FirefoxDriverFactory.class, SafariDriverFactory.class})
public class WebDriverAutoConfiguration {
  ...
}
```

This preceding Spring Boot autoconfiguration class can be described as follows:

- `@Configuration`: This indicates that this class is a source of beans' definitions. After all, that's what autoconfiguration classes do--create beans.
- `@ConditionalOnClass(WebDriver.class)`: This indicates that this configuration class will only be evaluated by Spring Boot if it detects `WebDriver` on the classpath, a telltale sign of Selenium WebDriver being part of the project.
- `@EnableConfigurationProperties(WebDriverConfigurationProperties.class)`: This activates a set of properties to support what we put into our test case. We'll soon see how to easily define a set of properties that get the rich support Spring Boot provides of overriding through multiple means.
- `@Import(...)`: This is used to pull in extra bean definition classes.

This class is now geared up for us to actually define some beans pursuant to creating a `WebDriver` instance. To get an instance, we can imagine going down a list and trying one such as Firefox. If it fails, move on to the next. If they all fail, resort to using `HtmlUnitDriver`.

The following class shows this perfectly:

```
@Primary
@Bean(destroyMethod = "quit")
@ConditionalOnMissingBean(WebDriver.class)
public WebDriver webDriver(
  FirefoxDriverFactory firefoxDriverFactory,
  SafariDriverFactory safariDriverFactory,
  ChromeDriverFactory chromeDriverFactory) {
    WebDriver driver = firefoxDriverFactory.getObject();

    if (driver == null) {
      driver = safariDriverFactory.getObject();
    }

    if (driver == null) {
      driver = chromeDriverFactory.getObject();
    }

    if (driver == null) {
      driver = new HtmlUnitDriver();
    }

    return driver;
}
```

This `WebDriver` creating code can be described as follows:

- `@Primary`: This indicates that this method should be given priority when someone is trying to autowire a `WebDriver` bean over any other method (as we'll soon see).
- `@Bean(destroyMethod = "quit")`: This flags the method as a Spring bean definition, but with the extra feature of invoking `WebDriver.quit()` when the application context shuts down.
- `@ConditionalOnMissingBean(WebDriver.class)`: This is a classic Spring Boot technique. It says to skip this method if there is already a defined `WebDriver` bean. HINT: There should be a test case to verify that Boot backs off properly!
- `webDriver()`: This expects three input arguments to be supplied by the application context--a `FirefoxDriver` factory, a `SafariDriver` factory, and a `ChromeDriver` factory. What is this for? It allows us to swap out `FirefoxDriver` with a mock for various test purposes. Since this doesn't affect the end user, this form of indirection is suitable.
- The code starts by invoking `firefoxDriver` using the `FirefoxDriver` factory. If null, it will try the next one. It will continue doing so until it reaches the bottom, with `HtmlUnitDriver` as the last choice. If it got a hit, these `if` clauses will be skipped and the `WebDriver` instance returned.

This laundry list of browsers to try out makes it easy to add new ones down the road should we wish to do so. But before we investigate, say `firefoxDriver()`, let's first look at `FirefoxDriverFactory`, the input parameter to that method:

```
class FirefoxDriverFactory implements ObjectFactory<FirefoxDriver>
{
  private WebDriverConfigurationProperties properties;

  FirefoxDriverFactory(WebDriverConfigurationProperties properties)
  {
    this.properties = properties;
  }

  @Override
  public FirefoxDriver getObject() throws BeansException {
    if (properties.getFirefox().isEnabled()) {
      try {
        return new FirefoxDriver();
      } catch (WebDriverException e) {
        e.printStackTrace();
        // swallow the exception
```

```
        }
      }
    return null;
    }
  }
```

This preceding driver factory can be described as follows:

- This class implements Spring's `ObjectFactory` for the type of `FirefoxDriver`. It provides the means to create the named type.
- With constructor injection, we load a copy of `WebDriverConfigurationProperties`.
- It implements the single method, `getObject()`, yielding a new `FirefoxDriver`.
- If the `firefox` property is enabled, it attempts to create a `FirefoxDriver`. If not, it skips the whole thing and returns null.

This factory uses the *old trick of try to create the object* to see if it exists. If successful, it returns it. If not, it swallows the exception and returns a null. This same tactic is used to implement a `SafariDriver` bean and a `ChromeDriver` bean. Since the code is almost identical, it's not shown here.

Why do we need this factory again? Because later in this chapter when we wish to prove it will create such an item, we don't want the test case to require installing Firefox to work properly. Thus, we'll supply a mocked solution. Since this doesn't impact the end user receiving the autoconfigured `WebDriver`, it's perfectly fine to use such machinery.

Notice how we used `properties.getFirefox().isEnabled()` to decide whether or not we would try? That was provided by our `com.greglturnquist.webdriver.firefox.enabled` property setting. To create a set of properties that Spring Boot will let consumers override as needed, we need to create a `WebDriverConfigurationProperties` class like this:

```
@Data
@ConfigurationProperties("com.greglturnquist.webdriver")
public class WebDriverConfigurationProperties {

  private Firefox firefox = new Firefox();
  private Safari safari = new Safari();
  private Chrome chrome = new Chrome();

  @Data
  static class Firefox {
    private boolean enabled = true;
  }
```

```
@Data
static class Safari {
  private boolean enabled = true;
}

@Data
static class Chrome {
  private boolean enabled = true;
}
}
```

This last property-based class can be described as follows:

- `@Data` is the Lombok annotation that saves us from creating getters and setters.
- `@ConfigurationProperties("com.greglturnquist.webdriver")` marks this class as a source for property values with `com.greglturnquist.webdriver` as the prefix.
- Every field (`firefox`, `safari`, and `chrome`) is turned into a separately named property.
- Because we want to nest subproperties, we have `Firefox`, `Safari`, and `Chrome`, each with an `enabled` Boolean property defaulted to `True`.
- Each of these subproperty classes again uses Lombok's `@Data` annotation to simplify their definition.

It's important to point out that the name of the property class, `WebDriverConfigurationProperties`, and the names of the subclasses such as `Firefox` are not important. The prefix is set by `@ConfigurationProperties`, and the individual properties use the field's name to define themselves.

With this class, it's easy to inject this strongly typed POJO into any Spring-managed bean and access the settings.

At this stage, our first test case, `fallbackToNonGuiModeWhenAllBrowsersDisabled`, should be operational. We can test it out.

Assuming we verified it, we can now code another test, verifying that `FirefoxDriver` is created under the right circumstances. Let's start by defining our test case. We can start by deliberately disabling the other choices:

```
@Test
public void testWithMockedFirefox() {
  load(new Class[]{MockFirefoxConfiguration.class},
    "com.greglturnquist.webdriver.safari.enabled:false",
```

```
            "com.greglturnquist.webdriver.chrome.enabled:false");
        WebDriver driver = context.getBean(WebDriver.class);
        assertThat(ClassUtils.isAssignable(TakesScreenshot.class,
            driver.getClass())).isTrue();
        assertThat(ClassUtils.isAssignable(FirefoxDriver.class,
            driver.getClass())).isTrue();
    }
```

This preceding test case is easily described as follows:

- @Test marks testWithMockedFirefox as a JUnit test method
- load is used to add MockFirefoxConfiguration, a configuration class we'll soon write to help us mock out the creation of a real FirefoxDriver
- We also disable Chrome and Safari using the property settings
- Fetching a WebDriver from the application context, we verify that it implements the TakesScreenshot interface and is actually a FirefoxDriver class

As one can imagine, this is tricky. We can't assume the developer has the Firefox browser installed. Hence, we can never create a real FirefoxDriver. To make this possible, we need to introduce a little indirection. When Spring encounters multiple bean definition methods, the last one wins. So, by adding another config class, MockFirefoxConfiguration, we can sneak in and change how our default factory works.

The following class shows how to do this:

```
@Configuration
protected static class MockFirefoxConfiguration {
    @Bean
    FirefoxDriverFactory firefoxDriverFactory() {
        FirefoxDriverFactory factory =
            mock(FirefoxDriverFactory.class);
        given(factory.getObject())
            .willReturn(mock(FirefoxDriver.class));
        return factory;
    }
}
```

The previous class can be described as follows:

- @Configuration marks this class as a source of bean definitions.
- @Bean shows that we are creating a FirefoxDriverFactory bean, the same type pulled into the top of our WebDriverAutoConfiguration class via the @Import annotation. This means that this bean definition will overrule the one we saw earlier.

- We use Mockito to create a mock `FirefoxDriverFactory`.
- We instruct this mock factory to create a mock `FirefoxDriver` when it's factory method is invoked.
- We return the factory, so it can be used to run the actual test case.

With this code, we are able to verify things work pretty well. There is a slight bit of hand waving. The alternative would be to figure out the means to *ensure* every browser was installed. Including the executables in our test code for every platform and running them all, may yield a little more confidence. But at what price? It could possibly violate the browser's license. Ensuring that every platform is covered, just for a test case, is a bit extreme. So, all in all, this test case hedges such a risk adequately by avoiding all that extra ceremony.

It's left as an exercise for the reader to explore creating Safari and Chrome factories along with their corresponding test cases.

If we run all the test cases in `WebDriverAutoConfigurationTests`, what can we hope to find?

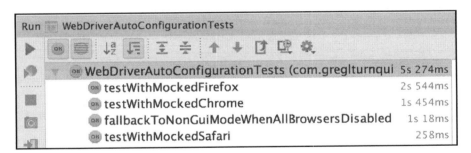

Using Spring Boot and Spring Framework test modules along with JUnit and Flapdoodle, we have managed to craft an autoconfiguration policy for Selenium WebDriver with a complete suite of test methods. This makes it possible for us to release our own third-party autoconfiguration module that autoconfigures Selenium WebDriver.

So what have we covered? Unit tests, MongoDB-oriented slice tests, WebFlux-oriented slice tests, full container end-to-end tests, and even autoconfiguration tests.

This is a nice collection of tests that should deliver confidence to any team. And Spring Boot made it quite easy to execute.

Summary

In this chapter, we crafted unit tests using JUnit and AssertJ. Then we performed slice-based tests against MongoDB using Spring Boot's `@DataMongoTest` annotation, with and without embedded MongoDB. We tested WebFlux controllers, ensuring they operated correctly. We also wrote end-to-end tests with Spring Boot spinning up an entire embedded web container so that Selenium WebDriver could drive it from the browser. Finally, we put together an autoconfiguration policy for Selenium WebDriver using test-first practices to verify that it worked.

In the next chapter, we will explore the developer tools provided by Spring Boot to ease the tasks we all must deal with.

5

Developer Tools for Spring Boot Apps

*I owe @springboot a lot. #productivity #engineering #sota #minimalist #microservices
#performance #quality #bestpractises*

– Amir Sedighi @amirsedighi

In the previous chapter, you learned how to use Spring Boot's various testing features. We saw how to craft simple unit tests, slice tests, mock WebFlux tests, and even fully spun-up embedded Netty integration tests.

When we get into the swing of things, anything that can bend the curve of time spent building an app is appreciated. We will explore the various tools Spring Boot brings to the table to help us hack away at our applications.

In this chapter, we will do the following:

- Using Spring Boot's DevTools for hot code reloading and decaching
- Glean what Spring Boot did with its autoconfiguration report
- Make local changes and see them on the target system
- Write a custom health check
- Add build data to the `/application/info` endpoint
- Create custom metrics

Using Spring Boot's DevTools for hot code reloading

Developers are *always* looking for ways to speed things up. Long ago, one of the biggest speedups was incremental compilers and having them run every time we saved a file. Now that it's permeated modern tools, no one thinks twice about such a feature.

Something critically needed when it comes to building Spring Boot apps is the ability to detect a change in our code and relaunch the embedded container.

Thankfully, we just need one addition to our code we built in the previous chapter:

```
compile("org.springframework.boot:spring-boot-devtools")
```

 If you happen to be using Maven, you would want to include the `optional` flag.

So, this tiny module performs the following activities:

- Disables cache settings for autoconfigured components
- When it detects a change in code, it restarts the application, holding onto third-party classes and simply throwing away and reloading custom classes
- Activates an embedded **LiveReload** (http://livereload.com/) server that can trigger the browser to refresh the page automatically

For a listing of all the disabled components, look at the following code snippet:

```
properties.put("spring.thymeleaf.cache", "false");
properties.put("spring.freemarker.cache", "false");
properties.put("spring.groovy.template.cache", "false");
properties.put("spring.mustache.cache", "false");
properties.put("server.session.persistent", "true");
properties.put("spring.h2.console.enabled", "true");
properties.put("spring.resources.cache-period", "0");
properties.put("spring.resources.chain.cache", "false");
properties.put("spring.template.provider.cache", "false");
properties.put("spring.mvc.log-resolved-exception", "true");
properties.put("server.servlet.jsp.init-parameters.development",
  "true");
properties.put("spring.reactor.stacktrace-mode.enabled", "true");
```

Many IDEs also come with additional reloading support when apps are run in the debug mode, a highly recommended option to use in conjunction with Spring Boot DevTools.

What is the net benefit, you ask?

When we make a change to our code and either issue a **Save** or a **Make Project**, DevTools will throw away the class loader holding our custom code and launch a new application context. This makes for a relatively speedy restart.

Save or Make Project? Spring Boot DevTools listens for file updates. For certain IDEs, such as Eclipse, ⌘-S is used to perform a **Save** operation. IntelliJ IDEA autosaves, so an alternative signal is Make Project, ⌘-F9, which refreshes the environment.

With the LiveReload server running and a LiveReload plugin (`http://livereload.com/extensions/`) installed in our browser, we can enable LiveReloading upon visiting the site. Anytime we update the code, the plugin will essentially click the browser's refresh button for us.

Restarting versus **reloading**: DevTools provides the ability to restart the application quickly, but it is limited in various ways. For example, updating the classpath by adding new dependencies is not picked up. Adding new classes isn't supported. For more sophisticated tools that handle these complex use cases, you may wish to investigate something such as Spring Loaded (`https://github.com/spring-projects/spring-loaded`) or JRebel (`http://zeroturnaround.com/software/jrebel/`).

With all these caches cleared out, we can see changes propagate much faster. Let's test it out by launching `LearningSpringBootApplication` in the debug mode. If we visit the site, things look as expected:

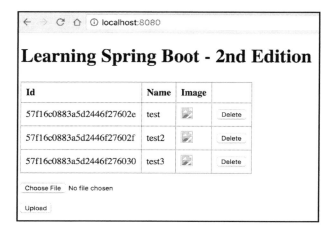

The site starts off with our pre-loaded test data. To have the browser listen for updates, we need to click the LiveReload icon:

At first, the dot in the center is hollow. When enabled, the dot turns solid, as shown in the preceding screenshot.

Let's make some edits to our template:

```
<body>

    <h1>Learning Spring Boot - 2nd Edition</h1>
    <h3>Using the LiveReload plugin in your browser will speed up efforts.</h3>
```

With this extra sub-header, we just need to hit Save or Make Project in our IDE. Switching to the browser will show the results instantly:

Learning Spring Boot - 2nd Edition

Using the LiveReload plugin in your browser will speed up efforts.

Let's make some tweaks to `HomeController` as shown here:

```
@GetMapping("/")
public Mono<String> index(Model model) {
  model.addAttribute("images",
    imageService.findAllImages());
  model.addAttribute("extra",
    "DevTools can also detect code changes too");
  return Mono.just("index");
}
```

This is the same as the previous chapter, except that we have added a new attribute, `extra`, to the model. We can display it with an adjustment to our template:

```
<h4 th:text="${extra}"></h4>
```

This displays the new `extra` model attribute as an H4 header, all without clicking a thing in our browser:

Learning Spring Boot - 2nd Edition

Using the LiveReload plugin in your browser will speed up efforts.

DevTools can also detect code changes too

There is one key side effect when using Spring Boot DevTools for restarts-- any in-memory data or state will be lost.

That can be good or bad. It certainly encourages you to create a pre-loader, perhaps with a `@Profile("dev")` annotation such that it only runs when `spring.profiles.active=dev` is switched on.

This can become an issue if our use case takes a lot of steps to set up, and restarting the app makes us repeat these steps again and again. This is amplified by in-memory database solutions such as H2. In our situation, the start-up code that cleans out the uploaded files will cause a similar refresh of data.

Another reason to consider NOT switching on LiveReload in the browser (yet let the app restart) is if we are working on a JavaScript-heavy frontend and don't want every change to force a reload. For example, we might have a page with a lot of fields filled out. A triggered restart may clean out our form and force us to re-enter the data.

Nevertheless, this is a good problem to have. Having the option to refresh the browser and stay in sync with code changes is a powerful tool.

Using Spring Boot's autoconfiguration report

As we've seen in this book so far, Spring Boot autoconfigures beans to help us avoid configuring infrastructure and instead focus on coding business requirements. However, sometimes, we may want to know *what* Spring Boot did (or didn't) do for us.

That's why it has an **autoconfiguration report**. Essentially, every time a bean is selected based on some conditional check, Spring Boot logs the decision (yea or nay) and offers it to us in many different ways.

The simplest approach is to add --debug to the run configuration. In the following screenshot, we can see how to set it in IntelliJ:

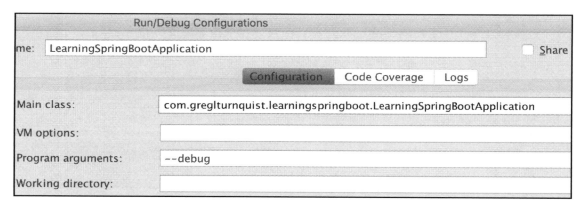

If we launch our app with --debug as a program argument, an autoconfiguration report is printed out to the console:

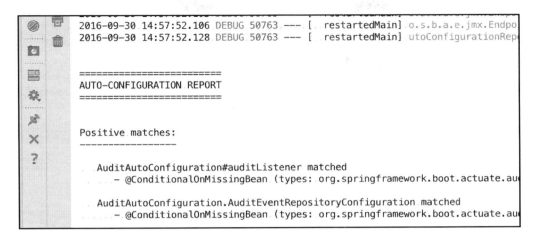

```
2016-09-30 14:57:52.106 DEBUG 50763 --- [ restartedMain] o.s.b.a.e.jmx.Endpo
2016-09-30 14:57:52.128 DEBUG 50763 --- [ restartedMain] utoConfigurationRep

=============================
AUTO-CONFIGURATION REPORT
=============================


Positive matches:
-----------------

   AuditAutoConfiguration#auditListener matched
      - @ConditionalOnMissingBean (types: org.springframework.boot.actuate.au

   AuditAutoConfiguration.AuditEventRepositoryConfiguration matched
      - @ConditionalOnMissingBean (types: org.springframework.boot.actuate.au
```

That's nice, and during certain failure scenarios, the report will print out automatically to help with postmortem analysis. However, scraping the console for a report isn't very effective.

If we use **Spring Boot Actuator**, we can consume this report in a nicer JSON structure. If you'll recall, we included **Actuator** in our list of dependencies back in `Chapter 1`, *Quick Start with Java*:

```
compile('org.springframework.boot:spring-boot-starter-actuator')
```

> If you're building a new application and *didn't* pick it on `http://start.spring.io`, this dependency is quite valuable.

In addition to adding Spring Boot's Actuator module, we have to *opt in* or rather enable its features. In Spring Boot 2.0, Actuator supports many technologies including Spring MVC, Spring WebFlux, and JMX. We have to signal what platforms we wish to enable instead of expecting Spring Boot to guess. To do so, we need to add the following line of code to our `application.properties` file:

endpoints.default.web.enabled=true

This will make Actuator's endpoints active from an HTTP perspective; (to enable Actuator for JMX, we would want to set `endpoints.default.jmx.enabled` to `true`).

When we launch our application, several Spring WebFlux endpoints are added, providing additional information. To get a quick glance at all the available endpoints, we can visit `http://localhost:8080/application`, as shown in the following screenshot:

his screenshot doesn't capture them all, but there is a long list of endpoints serving up detailed information about our application. (By the way, earlier in the book, we enabled just one actuator endpoint, `/application/health`. This flag lets us switch on all the default endpoints.)

From there, we can easily find the autoconfiguration report at `http://localhost:8080/application/autoconfig`, click on it, and thanks to JSON Viewer (`https://github.com/tulios/json-viewer`), see this nicely formatted report:

Okay, so we've seen a couple ways to generate this report. But what does it *say*?

If we zoom into one fragment, we can figure something out:

```
"ReactiveWebServerConfiguration.ReactorNettyAutoConfiguration": [
  {
    "condition": "OnClassCondition",
    "message": "@ConditionalOnClass found required class
    'reactor.ipc.netty.http.server.HttpServer';
    @ConditionalOnMissingClass did not find unwanted class"
  },
  {
    "condition": "OnBeanCondition",
    "message": "@ConditionalOnMissingBean (types:
      org.springframework.boot.web.reactive
```

```
          .server.ReactiveWebServerFactory; SearchStrategy: all) did
          not find any beans"
   }
   ]
```

This fragment of JSON in the autoconfiguration report can be described as follows:

- `ReactiveWebServerConfiguration.ReactorNettyAutoConfiguration` is a Spring Boot autoconfiguration policy that was evaluated, specifically on the subject of Netty.
- `@ConditionalOnClass` matched on spotting Reactor's `HttpServer` class, glue code used by Reactor to embed the Netty container. This shows that Netty was on the classpath.
- `@ConditionalOnMissingBean` is the second condition, and was negative, indicating there is no overriding, user-defined `ReactiveWebServerFactory` defined. Therefore, Spring Boot is activating its default policy for Reactor Netty.

To divine exactly what this autoconfiguration policy was, we can open the code and inspect it ourselves. Using our IDE, we merely need to look for the parent class, `ReactiveWebServerConfiguration`:

```
abstract class ReactiveWebServerConfiguration {

   @ConditionalOnMissingBean(ReactiveWebServerFactory.class)
   @ConditionalOnClass({ HttpServer.class })
   static class ReactorNettyAutoConfiguration {

     @Bean
     public NettyReactiveWebServerFactory
      NettyReactiveWebServerFactory() {
         return new NettyReactiveWebServerFactory();
     }

   }
   ...
}
```

This fragment from Spring Boot's Reactive web server configuration code can be explained as follows:

- `ReactiveWebServerConfiguration` is an abstract class that is merely used as a container for other policies

- `@ConditionalOnMissingBean(ReactiveWebServerFactory.class)` tells Spring Boot to back off and not use this if the user has declared such a bean elsewhere
- `@ConditionalOnClass({HttpServer.class})` tells Spring Boot to only consider this if Reactor Netty is on the classpath
- `static class ReactorNettyAutoConfiguration` names this rule used to autoconfigure Reactor Netty
- `@Bean` flags the code as a Spring bean
- `return new NettyReactiveWebServerFactory()` actually creates the Spring bean for Reactor Netty

All this comes together to allow Reactor Netty to be configured automatically when put on the classpath. And we spotted it in the autoconfiguration report.

 There are other bean definitions in `ReactiveWebServerConfiguration`, including support for Jetty, Apache Tomcat, and Undertow, but aren't shown due to space constraints.

What is this good for?

If we are attempting to use some feature of Spring Boot and it's not going as desired, one thing to debug is whether or not the expected beans are being created. Another usage is if we are working on our own autoconfiguration module for a given project and need to see if the right beans are being created.

You see, the autoconfiguration report isn't confined to what is released by the Spring team. It looks at *everything*.

Speaking of making a change, notice how we have Netty running under the hood. We can tell both from the console output as well as the autoconfiguration report we just looked at.

What if we wanted to change containers? It's quite easy with Spring Boot. We simply have to tweak the build file.

By default, Spring Boot uses Netty for Reactive apps, but it's not hard to switch:

```
compile('org.springframework.boot:spring-boot-starter-webflux') {
    exclude module: 'spring-boot-starter-reactor-netty'
}
compile('org.springframework.boot:spring-boot-starter-undertow')
```

The changes to `build.gradle` are as follows:

- Excludes `spring-boot-starter-reactor-netty` from the reactive web dependency
- Introduces `spring-boot-starter-undertow` as an alternative container

If we relaunch our application and look at the autoconfiguration report again and look for the `ReactorNettyAutoConfiguration` entry, we will find this:

```
"ReactiveWebServerConfiguration.ReactorNettyAutoConfiguration": {
  "notMatched": [
  {
    "condition": "OnClassCondition",
    "message": "@ConditionalOnClass did not find required class
    'reactor.ipc.netty.http.server.HttpServer'"
  }
  ],
  "matched": [

  ]
}
```

The new fragment of JSON from the autoconfiguration report shows that the same policy we just looked at has now switched to `notMatched`. In the details, it failed because `@ConditionalOnClass` didn't spot `HttpServer` on the classpath.

In light of switching from Reactor Netty to Undertow, searching for `Undertow` in the autoconfiguration report will lead us to this:

```
"ReactiveWebServerConfiguration.UndertowAutoConfiguration": [
{
  "condition": "OnClassCondition",
  "message": "@ConditionalOnClass found required class
  'io.undertow.Undertow'; @ConditionalOnMissingClass did not
  find unwanted class"
},
{
  "condition": "OnBeanCondition",
  "message": "@ConditionalOnMissingBean (types:
  org.springframework.boot.web.reactive.server
  .ReactiveWebServerFactory; SearchStrategy: all) did not
  find any beans"
}
]
```

This fragment of JSON reveals that `UndertowAutoConfiguration` is now in effect as follows:

- `@ConditionalOnClass` has found `Undertow` on the classpath
- `@ConditionalOnMissingBean` has not found a user-defined `ReactiveWebServerFactory` bean; hence, Spring Boot did not back off with its autoconfiguration of Undertow.

On further digging into `UndertowReactiveWebServerFactory`, we will find all the details needed to run Undertow for a Reactor-based application.

Making local changes and seeing them on the target system

So far, we've seen how to speed up developer time by using automatic restarts, and we have gathered information on what Spring Boot is up to, courtesy of its autoconfiguration report.

The next step for developers is often using the debugger of their IDE. We won't go into profuse detail about that because it's highly specific to which IDE you use. However, something of extended value offered by Spring Boot is the opportunity to remotely connect to an application and make changes.

Imagine we have built up our application and pushed it to the cloud. We test a key feature in this environment because it's the only way to tie it to a particular resource or in a certain configuration. Well, the process for making changes is much more expensive. We would have to bundle things up, redeploy, restart, and re-navigate. All for a few lines of code!

Spring Boot's DevTools provide the means to connect our IDE to our remotely running application and push code changes over the wire, allowing us to automatically make mods and test them immediately.

To get geared up, we must execute the following steps:

1. Add `spring.devtools.remote.secret=learning-spring-boot` to `application.properties`.
2. Build the application using `./gradlew build`.
3. Push the application to the cloud (Pivotal Web Services in this case with `cf push learning-spring-boot -p build/libs/learning-spring-boot-0.0.1-SNAPSHOT.jar`).

4. Instead of running the app locally in our IDE, run Spring Boot's `RemoteSpringApplication` class instead.

5. Add `https://learning-spring-boot.cfapps.io` (or whatever the app's remote URL is) as a program argument.

6. Launch the `RemoteSpringApplication` configured runner.

The following screenshot shows how to configure it in IntelliJ IDEA:

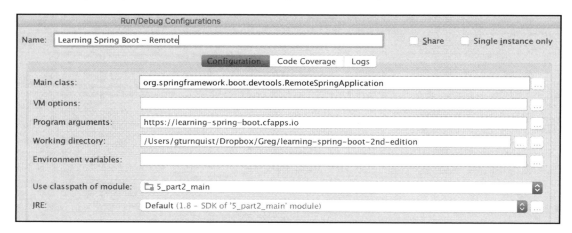

After it launches, the console in our IDE shows a remote banner:

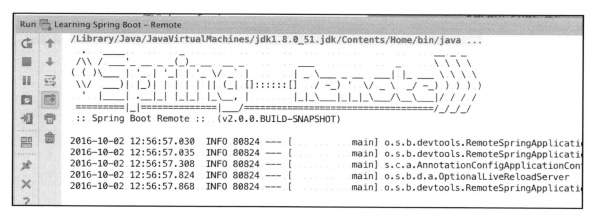

Now, we are free to make changes in our IDE, Save/Make Project, and watch them propagate to our cloud-based app running at `https://learning-spring-boot.cfapps.io`.

First of all, let's tweak our template at `src/main/resources/templates/index.html`. We can add a sub-header below the main header similar to what we did earlier in this chapter:

```html
<h1>Learning Spring Boot - 2nd Edition</h1>

<h2>It's really handy to make local edits and watch them go out
to the cloud automatically</h2>

<h4 th:text="${extra}"></h4>
```

Hitting Save or Make Project, the code change will be uploaded to the cloud and trigger a restart (this is a great opportunity to use the LiveReload server and automatically refresh the page):

```
←  →  C  ⌂  ⓘ  learning-spring-boot.cfapps.io

Learning Spring Boot - 2nd Edition

It's really handy to make local edits and watch them go out to the cloud automatically.
```

With this flow, we can make all sorts of changes. When ready, we can commit them locally, build a newer JAR file, push to the cloud, and continue forward.

It's *always* recommended to use `https://` when connecting to a remote application. It prevents other users from snooping the network for secrets.

Enabling Spring Boot DevTools on a remote application is a risk. The only thing protecting the application from code updates is the simple secret the two share. You should never enable this on a production deployment.

Writing a custom health check

Another critical feature needed when we take our application to production is monitoring it. In the olden days, people would set up a CRON job to ping a server and see if it was up. More intricate systems would track disk usage, memory usage, and ideally page someone when the database was at 95%, so it could be saved before falling over.

Spring Boot provides a new era in health check monitoring. To kick things off, launch the application and visit /application/health:

```
{
    status: "UP",
    diskSpace: {
        status: "UP",
        total: 498937626624,
        free: 96519303168,
        threshold: 10485760
    },
    mongo: {
        status: "UP",
        version: "3.4.6"
    }
}
```

Out of the box, this provides us with an endpoint we can ping and additionally, gives us some information regarding disk space. It also includes an automatically included MongoDB health check.

But what if we needed to write our own health check? Perhaps, there is a system we are dependent upon. Knowing if this upstream service is unavailable could prove valuable.

To write our own health check, we merely need to write a Spring component that implements Spring Boot's HealthIndicator interface:

```
@Component
public class LearningSpringBootHealthIndicator
 implements HealthIndicator {

    @Override
    public Health health() {
      try {
        URL url =
          new URL("http://greglturnquist.com/books/learning-spring-
            boot");
        HttpURLConnection conn =
          (HttpURLConnection) url.openConnection();
        int statusCode = conn.getResponseCode();
        if (statusCode >= 200 && statusCode < 300) {
          return Health.up().build();
        } else {
            return Health.down()
              .withDetail("HTTP Status Code", statusCode)
              .build();
        }
```

```
        } catch (IOException e) {
            return Health.down(e).build();
        }
    }
}
```

Let's dissect this custom health indicator:

- @Component marks this class so that Spring Boot picks it up and registers it automatically.
- By implementing the HealthIndicator interface, Spring Boot will include it along with the pre-built health checks when we hit /application/health.
- The name LearningSpringBootHealthIndicator is used to create the indicator. HealthIndicator will be trimmed off, and the remaining text will be formatted with lazy camel style.
- There is but one method in this interface (meaning you *could* implement it using a Java 8 lambda), health(). It uses some plain old Java APIs to open a connection to a remote URL and fetch a status code. If the status code is good, it will build a Health status code of UP. Otherwise, it will build a Health status code of DOWN while also giving us the failed HTTP status code.
- Finally, if any other exceptions occur, we will also get a Health status code of DOWN but with the information from the exception instead of a commonly coded error path.

Let's relaunch the application and see what our /application/health endpoint reports:

```
{
  "status": "UP",
  "details": {
    "mongo": {
      "status": "UP",
      "details": {
        "version": "3.4.6"
      }
    },
    "diskSpace": {
      "status": "UP",
      "details": {
        "total": 498937626624,
        "free": 43632435200,
        "threshold": 10485760
      }
    },
    "learningSpringBoot": {
```

```
        "status": "UP"
      }
    }
  }
```

We can see our new health indicator, `learningSpringBoot`, listed with its status of `UP`.

To simulate a failure, let's alter the URL by switching the domain in the code to `greglturnquist.io` and see what happens:

```
URL url = new URL("http://greglturnquist.io/books/learning-spring-
    boot");
```

When we restart and ping `/application/health`, this is the outcome:

```
{
  "status": "DOWN",
  "details": {
    "mongo": {
      "status": "UP",
      "details": {
        "version": "3.4.6"
      }
    },
    "diskSpace": {
      "status": "UP",
      "details": {
        "total": 498937626624,
        "free": 43629961216,
        "threshold": 10485760
      }
    },
    "learningSpringBoot": {
      "status": "DOWN",
      "details": {
        "error": "java.net.UnknownHostException: greglturnquist.io"
      }
    }
  }
}
```

A few things have happened:

- Our `learningSpringBoot` indicator now reports `DOWN`. It's not due to some HTTP status code, but instead `ConnectionException` caused by not being able to form a connection.
- While `diskSpace` and `mongo` are `UP`, the `DOWN` status of this indicator percolates to the top-level status, switching it to `DOWN`.

If we change the URL to simply `http://greglturnquist.com/foo` and restart, we can see a different status:

```
// 20170912234318
// http://localhost:8080/application/health

{
  "status": "DOWN",
  "details": {
    "mongo": {
      "status": "UP",
      "details": {
        "version": "3.4.6"
      }
    },
    "diskSpace": {
      "status": "UP",
      "details": {
        "total": 498937626624,
        "free": 43624402944,
        "threshold": 10485760
      }
    },
    "learningSpringBoot": {
      "status": "DOWN",
      "details": {
        "HTTP Status Code": 404
      }
    }
  }
}
```

In this situation, we still have a DOWN status, but the HTTP status code 404 is reported. Both of these indicators can be quite informative for the DevOps team watching our application.

Adding build data to /application/info

One of the biggest issues in getting to the heart of problems is knowing what version is running! Have you ever gotten a 3:00 a.m. call from a customer reporting that the system is broken? In a half-awake state, it's easy to start trying to solve the problem only to discover two hours later, the customer is running an older version and that their issue was patched last week.

The solution is embedding precise versions in every release so that the customer can relay this over the phone. Then, we can quickly figure out if this issue is new, fixed, or a regression. Interested?

Just add this to the build.gradle file, right below the buildscripts section:

```
id "com.gorylenko.gradle-git-properties" version "1.4.17"
```

This will add a new task, generateGitProperties, to our system. Anytime we engage Gradle to build the app, whether it's to package up a runnable JAR or simply to bootRun it, a new build/resources/main/git.properties file will be generated and served up via Spring Boot Actuator's /application/info endpoint:

```
{
    git: {
        commit: {
            time: 1474434957000,
            id: "3ac9c1c"
        },
        branch: "master"
    }
}
```

This report gives us the timestamp, git commit hash, and branch. That tiny nugget of knowledge has the potential to save us *hours* of effort over the long haul.

Using Maven? There is a similar plugin:

```
<build>
    <plugins>
        <plugin>
            <groupId>pl.project13.maven</groupId>
            <artifactId>git-commit-id-plugin</artifactId>
```

```
            </plugin>
         </plugins>
      </build>
```

It works the same.

One extra tidbit--Spring Boot has two different modes of git information. The format shown is the **SIMPLE** mode. To get more details, add this to `application.properties`:

```
management.info.git.mode=full
```

This will produce a much more detailed report:

```
{
    git: {
        commit: {
            message: {
                full: "Move images back to 1/image",
                short: "Move images back to 1/image"
            },
            time: 1474434957000,
            id: "3ac9c1c7875d7378d6fbd607d0af5ef206e21ede",
            id.abbrev: "3ac9c1c",
            user: {
                email: "gturnquist@pivotal.io",
                name: "Greg Turnquist"
            }
        },
        branch: "master"
    }
}
```

It's up to each team to decide which version is the most useful and which version doesn't leak out unnecessary details.

Additionally, we can grab more details about the build by adding this to our `build.gradle` file:

```
springBoot {
  buildInfo()
}
```

This little addition, when we run Gradle's `build` task, will add a `build-info.properties` file to our JAR file, showing content like this:

```
#Properties
#Tue Sep 12 23:53:05 CDT 2017
build.time=2017-09-12T23\:53\:05-0500
```

```
build.artifact=5/part2
build.group=learning-spring-boot
build.name=5/part2
build.version=unspecified
```

Both of these reports (a simple git report + build info details) would give us this nice bit of information useful to start debugging an issue by visiting `localhost:8080/application/info`.

Creating custom metrics

Every program manager loves metrics. In fact, a popular company (Netflix) is so well known in this arena that people describe it as a metrics-gathering company that happens to stream video.

When it comes to Spring Boot, metrics are a prime piece of **Spring Boot Actuator** functionality. If we visit `/application/metrics`, we can see a list of metrics:

```
{
  "names": [
    "jvm.buffer.memory.used",
    "jvm.memory.used",
    "jvm.buffer.count",
    "logback.events",
    "process.uptime",
    "jvm.memory.committed",
    "http.server.requests",
    "jvm.buffer.total.capacity",
    "jvm.memory.max",
    "process.starttime"
  ]
}
```

This lists all sorts of stuff--memory, garbage collection, heap versus nonheap, threads, and more. That's nice, but what's usually needed is the ability to create our own metrics.

Spring Boot provides an interface to register our own metrics and have them appear on the same page. Supplied immediately is the ability to grab a `MeterRegistry`.

To make use of this three meter registry, we need to inject it into `ImageService` we built in `Chapter 3`, *Reactive Data Access with Spring Boot*:

```
@Service
public class ImageService {
```

```
...

private final MeterRegistry meterRegistry;

public ImageService(ResourceLoader resourceLoader,
   ImageRepository imageRepository,
   MeterRegistry meterRegistry) {

   this.resourceLoader = resourceLoader;
   this.imageRepository = imageRepository;
   this.meterRegistry = meterRegistry;
}
...
```

This code shows the following:

- Three metric services, CounterService, GaugeService, and
  InMemoryMetricRepository declared as final attributes
- These three fields are populated by **constructor injection**, ensuring they are
  supplied when the service is created

With that in place, further down inside createImage, we can define custom metrics:

```
public Mono<Void> createImage(Flux<FilePart> files) {
  return files
    .log("createImage-files")
    .flatMap(file -> {
      Mono<Image> saveDatabaseImage = imageRepository.save(
        new Image(
          UUID.randomUUID().toString(),
          file.filename()))
          .log("createImage-save");

      Mono<Void> copyFile = Mono.just(Paths.get(UPLOAD_ROOT,
        file.filename()).toFile())
        .log("createImage-picktarget")
        .map(destFile -> {
          try {
            destFile.createNewFile();
            return destFile;
          } catch (IOException e) {
            throw new RuntimeException(e);
          }
        })
        .log("createImage-newfile")
        .flatMap(file::transferTo)
        .log("createImage-copy");
```

```
            Mono<Void> countFile = Mono.fromRunnable(() -> {
                meterRegistry
                    .summary("files.uploaded.bytes")
                    .record(Paths.get(UPLOAD_ROOT,
                    file.filename()).toFile().length())
            });

            return Mono.when(saveDatabaseImage, copyFile, countFile)
                .log("createImage-when");
        })
        .log("createImage-flatMap")
        .then()
        .log("createImage-done");
}
```

The first part of the code where a new image is created is the same, but following that is `meterRegistry.summary("files.uploaded.bytes").record(... )`, which creates a new **distribution summary** named `files.uploaded.bytes`. A distribution summary includes both a name, optional tags, and a value. What is registered is both a value and an occurrence. Each time a meter is added, it counts it, and the running total is tabulated.

With these adjustments, we can refresh the application, wait for it to reload, and then upload a few images, as shown here:

Learning Spring Boot - 2nd Edition

Id	Name	Image	
57f07b6c8dd1b00a1c3cee4a	B05771_MockupCover_Normal.jpg		Delete
57f07b788dd1b00a1c3cee4b	spring-boot-project-logo.png		Delete
57f07ba48dd1b00a1c3cee4d	bazinga.png		Delete

Choose File   No file chosen

Upload

After uploading these images, if we revisit `/application/metrics`, we can see our new metric at the bottom of the list:

```
{
  "names": [
    "jvm.buffer.memory.used",
    "jvm.memory.used",
    "jvm.buffer.count",
    "logback.events",
    "process.uptime",
    "jvm.memory.committed",
    "http.server.requests",
    "jvm.buffer.total.capacity",
    "jvm.memory.max",
    "process.starttime",
    "files.uploaded.bytes"
  ]
}
```

If we navigate to
`http://localhost:8080/application/metrics/files.uploaded.bytes`, we can view it:

```
{
  "name": "files.uploaded.bytes",
  "measurements": [
    {
      "statistic": "Count",
      "value": 3.0
    },
    {
      "statistic": "Total",
      "value": 208020.0
    }
  ],
  "availableTags": [

  ]
}
```

This JSON shows that **three** measurements have been registered with `files.uploaded.bytes`, totaling `208020` bytes. What's not immediately shown is also the time when these metrics were posted. It's possible to calculate upload trends using the new Micrometer module (`http://micrometer.io`).

Micrometer is a new project at Pivotal. It's a facade for metrics gathering. Think SLF4J, but for metrics instead. It is designed to integrate with lots of metric-gathering systems, including Atlas, Prometheus, Datadog, Influx, Graphite, and more. In this case, it's using a memory-based solution. Since it's currently under development and could warrant its *own* book, we will not delve too deep.

This is but a sampling of the possible metrics that can be defined. Feel free to dig in and experiment with the data.

Working with additional Actuator endpoints

Spring Boot Actuator provides *lots* of extra data. The following table is a quick summary:

Actuator Endpoint	Description
auditevents	Exposes audit events for the current application
autoconfig	Reports what Spring Boot did and didn't autoconfigure and why
beans	Reports all the beans configured in the application context (including ours as well as the ones autoconfigured by Boot)
configprops	Exposes all configuration properties
env	Reports on the current system environment
health	A simple endpoint to check the life of the app
heapdump	Returns a GZip-compressed **hprof** heap dump file (hprof is a tool by every JDK)
info	Serves up custom content from the app
logfile	Returns the contents of the logfile (assuming `logging.file` or `logging.path` has been set)
loggers	Lists all configured loggers and their levels. Also supports updating log levels through `POST` operations.
metrics	Shows counters and gauges on web usage
mappings	Gives us details about all Spring WebFlux routes
status	threaddump

Creates thread dump report	trace

 Every one of these is prefixed (by default) with `/application/`. For example, `health` is found at `/application/health`. To override this prefix, just add `management.context-path` to `application.properties` and swap out your preferred prefix (such as `/manager`). Also, `management.context-path` is relative to `server.context-path`.

It's possible to adjust the port that Actuator endpoints are served on. Setting the `management.port` property to `8081` will change the port for all these endpoints to `8081`. We can even adjust the network address used by setting `management.address=127.0.0.1`. This setting would make these information-rich endpoints only visible to the local box and curtail visibility to outside connections.

Summary

In this chapter, we hooked up Spring Boot's DevTools module. This made it possible to use an embedded LiveReload server as well as decache the templates. We used Spring Boot's autoconfiguration report to glean information about the embedded container. Then, we swapped out Netty with Undertow and verified it through the same report. We dabbled with writing a custom health check and a custom metric. Then, we buttoned things up by embedding our build information into the application to spot the version in operations should we get a late night phone call from our Ops center.

In the next chapter, we'll learn how to communicate between processes using fault-tolerant **Advanced Message Queuing Protocol (AMQP)** messaging.

6

AMQP Messaging with Spring Boot

I should add that we are @springboot / @SpringCloudOSS from top to bottom.

– DaShaun Carter @dashaun

In the previous chapter, we added some tools to our social media application to speed up developer time as well as to provide basic operational support features.

But nothing stands still. In various social media platforms, there is some form of messaging between the users. Why not create one for ours?

In this chapter, we will learn the following topics:

- Getting started with RabbitMQ, an AMQP broker
- Creating a message-based module for our social media app
- Adding customized metrics to track message flow
- Creating dynamically routed messages
- Taking a peek at Spring Cloud Stream and its RabbitMQ bindings

Getting started with RabbitMQ

RabbitMQ is an open source AMQP broker. **Advanced Message Queuing Protocol (AMQP)** is an open protocol that includes the format of messages sent over the wire. This has risen in popularity compared to other messaging solutions like JMS. Why?

JMS is an API, whereas AMQP is a protocol. JMS defines how to talk to the broker but not the format of its messages. And it's confined to Java apps. AMQP doesn't speak about how to talk to a broker but about how messages are put on the wire and how they are pulled down.

To illustrate this point, imagine two different applications. If they were both Java, they could communicate via JMS. But if one of them were Ruby, JMS would be off the table.

To further demonstrate the differences between JMS and AMQP, a JMS-speaking broker can actually use AMQP under the hood to transport the messages.

 In fact, I have contributed to the RabbitMQ JMS Client developed by Pivotal Software found at `https://github.com/rabbitmq/rabbitmq-jms-client`.

For this chapter, we will explore using RabbitMQ in the spirit of maximum options.

Installing RabbitMQ broker

To do this, we need to install the RabbitMQ broker.

On a macOS, if we are using Homebrew (`http://brew.sh/`), it's as simple as this:

```
$ brew install rabbitmq
==> Installing dependencies for rabbitmq: openssl, libpng, libtiff,
    wx...
==> Pouring openssl-1.0.2j.el_capitan.bottle.tar.gz
    /usr/local/Cellar/openssl/1.0.2j: 1,695 files, 12M
==> Pouring libpng-1.6.25.el_capitan.bottle.tar.gz
    /usr/local/Cellar/libpng/1.6.25: 25 files, 1.2M
==> Pouring libtiff-4.0.6_2.el_capitan.bottle.tar.gz
    /usr/local/Cellar/libtiff/4.0.6_2: 261 files, 3.4M
==> Pouring wxmac-3.0.2_3.el_capitan.bottle.tar.gz
    /usr/local/Cellar/wxmac/3.0.2_3: 809 files, 23.6M
==> Pouring erlang-19.1.el_capitan.bottle.tar.gz
    /usr/local/Cellar/erlang/19.1: 7,297 files, 279.8M
==> Installing rabbitmq
    /usr/local/Cellar/rabbitmq/3.6.4: 187 files, 5.8M, built in 6
    seco...
```

On Debian Linux, you can use the following command:

```
$ sudo apt-get install rabbitmq-server
```

On any of the Red Hat Linux systems, the following command can be run:

```
$ yum install erlang
$ yum install rabbitmq-server-<version>.rpm
```

On various cloud solutions, including Cloud Foundry, RabbitMQ can be found as a service (including Pivotal's RabbitMQ for PCF at `https://network.pivotal.io/products/p-rabbitmq`), something we'll explore in `Chapter 10`, *Taking Your App to Production with Spring Boot*.

For more details on downloading and installing, visit `https://www.rabbitmq.com/download.html`.

Launching the RabbitMQ broker

With the RabbitMQ broker installed, we just need to launch it. There are these two approaches to doing that:

- Starting it in our current shell
- Having it start when the machine boots

To start in our current shell, we can execute the following command:

```
$ rabbitmq-server
RabbitMQ 3.6.4. Copyright (C) 2007-2016 Pivotal Software...
##  ##        Licensed under the MPL.  See http://www.rabbitmq.com/
##  ##
##########  Logs: /usr/local/var/log/rabbitmq/rabbit@localhost.log
######  ##        /usr/local/var/log/rabbitmq/rabbit@localhost-sasl....
##########
Starting broker...
completed with 10 plugins.
```

On a macOS with Homebrew, use the following to launch as a daemon process and relaunch when we reboot:

```
$ brew services start rabbitmq
==> Tapping homebrew/services
Cloning into '/usr/local/Homebrew/Library/Taps/homebrew/homebrew-
services'...
remote: Counting objects: 10, done.
```

```
remote: Compressing objects: 100% (7/7), done.
remote: Total 10 (delta 0), reused 6 (delta 0), pack-reused 0
Unpacking objects: 100% (10/10), done.
Checking connectivity... done.
Tapped 0 formulae (36 files, 46K)
==> Successfully started `rabbitmq` (label: homebrew.mxcl.rabbitmq)
```

If you are using Homebrew, there is a feature to manage various *services*. Type `homebrew services` to see the commands available. For example, `brew services list` will list all services and their state:

```
$ brew services list
Name      Status  User       Plist
activemq  stopped
mongodb   started gturnquist
/Users/gturnquist/Library/LaunchAgents/hom...
mysql     stopped
neo4j     stopped
rabbitmq  started gturnquist
/Users/gturnquist/Library/LaunchAgents/hom...
redis     stopped
tor       stopped
```

Now we can see that RabbitMQ has joined MongoDB (which we installed in `Chapter 3`, *Reactive Data Access with Spring Boot*).

This, essentially, leverages macOS X's `launchctl` system with a Homebrew-supplied daemon control file.

For Windows, check out `https://www.rabbitmq.com/install-windows.html`. It has links to download the broker. Upon installation, it will configure it with various defaults and also start it up.

To control the broker, check out the `rabbitmqctl.bat` script found in the `sbin` folder (as administrator). Use the following commands:

- `rabbitmqctl start`
- `rabbitmqctl stop`
- `rabbitmqctl status`

Want to poke around with the RabbitMQ broker in a more visual way? Run `rabbitmq-plugins enable rabbitmq_managment`, and visit `http://localhost:15672`. The default username/password for RabbitMQ is `guest/guest`. I suggest looking at *Exchanges* and *Queues* first.

With the RabbitMQ broker up and running, we can now shift focus to our application efforts.

Adding messaging as a new component to an existing application

What have we built so far for our social media platform? We have the ability to upload and delete pictures. However, a key piece of any social media platform is to allow users to interact with each other. This is commonly done by either commenting on the social media content or chatting directly with each other.

Let's start by adding the ability to comment on images. But before we get going, let's stop and discuss the architecture.

For years, people have used the layer approach to split up applications. Fundamentally, we don't want a big application with all the classes in one package because it's too hard to keep up with everything.

So far, we have everything located in `com.greglturnquist.learningspringboot`. Historically, the pattern has been to split things up in a domain layer, a services layer, and a controllers layer, as shown in the following screenshot:

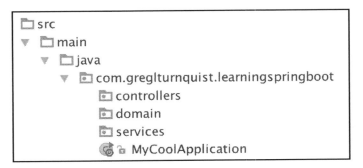

In this structure, we would put every service into the `services` subpackage and create further sub-subpackages if need be. We'd put all the domain objects in `domain` and all the controllers would go into `controllers`.

The idea was that controllers call services and services return domain objects. It prevented entanglements such as services invoking controllers, which made sense at the time.

But with the rise of microservices (something we'll dig into in *Chapter 7, Microservices with Spring Boot*), these layer-based approaches become an issue when the application gets really big. When refactoring is in order, services found in the same package that are functionally unrelated can get tricky due to needless coupling we may have created.

A more slim and trim approach is to break things up using vertical **slices** instead of horizontal **layers**:

With the structure shown in the preceding screenshot, we have split things up into `images` and `comments`, a more function-based nature.

We would put everything related to handling images in the former and everything related to comments in the latter. If the need arises, either of these packages can be further split up into subpackages, as follows:

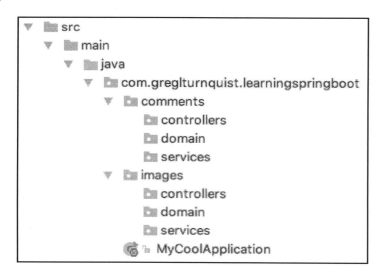

Worried that this will cause an explosion of the `domain/services/controllers` trio all over our code? Don't panic! We only do this as needed, and given that each `domain` subpackage will be relatively small in scope as compared to the old layer approach, the functionality should be highly cohesive, that is, have much in common with each other.

Since we are about to create a separate piece of functionality (comments), it would make sense to go ahead and break up our application into `images` and `comments`. So let's do that!

First, let's create the `images` and `comments` subpackages. With that in place, the most obvious change is to move `Image`, `ImageRepository`, and `ImageService` into the `image` subpackage. Easy enough.

That leaves us with the following:

- `LearningSpringBootApplication`
- `HomeController`
- `LearningSpringBootHealthIndicator`

`LearningSpringBootApplication` embodies the entire app, so it should stay at the top level. This isn't just a semantic statement. That class contains our `SpringBootApplication` annotation, which enables the application's autoconfigured behaviors like component scanning. Component scanning should start at the top level and search all subpackages.

`HomeController` represents an interesting concept. Even though it calls into `ImageService`, since it serves the application's top-level view, let's leave it at the top level as well.

As for `LearningSpringBootHealthIndicator`, a similar case could be made to keep it at the root. Since we are shooting to keep things light at the top, why don't we create a separate module to encompass all Ops-based features that aren't specific to any one module, `ops`.

Given all these decisions, our new structure now looks like this:

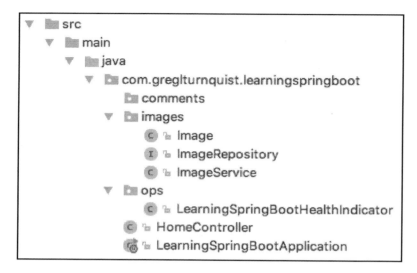

Is spending this amount of time debating package structure worth it? In any agile environment, it's okay to try something if it doesn't cost two weeks of effort. Stopping to spend ten minutes thinking about a maintainable structure is an acceptable investment, especially if we're willing to change it later should the need arise.

Creating a message producer/message consumer

Having restructured our application to make room for comments, let's get to it!

First of all, we need to add a new dependency to our build file, which is done with the following code:

```
compile('org.springframework.boot:spring-boot-starter-amqp')
```

That will give us access to Spring AMQP, which includes RabbitMQ support.

Adding messaging technology to our application may make us clamor to, well, write some code that talks to RabbitMQ. But that isn't really a good flow. Instead, we should start from one of two perspectives--writing a unit test or writing some UI.

Either approach is aimed at figuring out the use case we are trying to solve. Before *solving* the problem at hand, we need to noodle out what our exact problem is. In this case, let's start from the UI perspective.

To do that, we can take advantage of **Spring Boot DevTools** from the last chapter and launch our application in the **Debug** mode with the LiveReload feature enabled. That way, as we make changes, we can see them right away:

```
 o.s.b.d.a.OptionalLiveReloadServer        : LiveReload server is running on port 35729
 o.s.j.e.a.AnnotationMBeanExporter         : Registering beans for JMX exposure on startup
 o.s.j.e.a.AnnotationMBeanExporter         : Bean with name 'rabbitConnectionFactory' has been a
 o.s.j.e.a.AnnotationMBeanExporter         : Located managed bean 'rabbitConnectionFactory': reg
 o.s.c.support.DefaultLifecycleProcessor   : Starting beans in phase -2147482648
 o.s.c.support.DefaultLifecycleProcessor   : Starting beans in phase 0
 o.s.c.support.DefaultLifecycleProcessor   : Starting beans in phase 2147483647
 o.s.a.r.c.CachingConnectionFactory        : Created new connection: rabbitConnectionFactory#168
 o.s.amqp.rabbit.core.RabbitAdmin          : Auto-declaring a non-durable, auto-delete, or exclu
 r.ipc.netty.tcp.BlockingNettyContext      : Started HttpServer on /0:0:0:0:0:0:0:0:8080
 o.s.b.web.embedded.netty.NettyWebServer   : Netty started on port(s): 8080
 org.mongodb.driver.connection             : Opened connection [connectionId{localValue:3, serve
boot-cover.jpg)
boot-2nd-edition-cover.jpg)

 c.g.l.LearningSpringBootApplication       : Started LearningSpringBootApplication in 6.655 seco
```

With this preceding screenshot, we can see our application up and running with the LiveReload server enabled (and some sample data preloaded).

Displaying comments

Now we can make edits to our Thymeleaf template and create input fields for people to write comments:

```
<td>
    <ul>
        <li th:each="comment : ${image.comments}"
            th:text="${comment.comment}"></li>
    </ul>
</td>
<td>
    <form th:method="post" th:action="@{'/comments'}">
        <input name="comment" value="" type="text" />
        <input name="imageId" th:value="${image.id}"
         type="hidden" />
        <input type="submit" />
    </form>
</td>
```

The section of our preceding template where each row is rendered can be explained as follows:

- There is a new column containing an HTML unordered list to display each comment
- The unordered list consists of an HTML line item for each comment via Thymeleaf's th:each construct
- There is also a new column containing an HTML form to post a new comment
- The form contains an HTML text input for the comment itself
- The form also contains a hidden HTML element specifying the ID of the image that the comment will be associated with

To support this, we need to update HomeController as follows:

```
private final ImageService imageService;
private final CommentReaderRepository repository;

public HomeController(ImageService imageService,
  CommentReaderRepository repository) {
    this.imageService = imageService;
    this.repository = repository;
}
```

We have updated the class definition as follows:

- A new repository field is created for CommentReaderRepository (which we'll define further ahead in the chapter)
- This field is initialized by **constructor injection**

We need to look up the comments. To do that, we need a Spring Data repository that can read comments. And reading comments is ALL this repository needs to do at this stage of our social media app.

Let's take this new repository and use it inside the Spring WebFlux handler for GET /, like this:

```
@GetMapping("/")
public Mono<String> index(Model model) {
  model.addAttribute("images",
    imageService
    .findAllImages()
    .flatMap(image ->
      Mono.just(image)
        .zipWith(repository.findByImageId(
```

```
            image.getId()).collectList()))
    .map(imageAndComments -> new HashMap<String, Object>(){{
        put("id", imageAndComments.getT1().getId());
        put("name", imageAndComments.getT1().getName());
        put("comments",
            imageAndComments.getT2());
    }})
);
model.addAttribute("extra",
    "DevTools can also detect code changes too");
return Mono.just("index");
}
```

This last code contains a slight adjustment to the model's `images` attribute:

- The code takes the `Flux` returned from our `ImageService.findAll()` method and flatMaps each entry from an Image into a call to find related comments.
- `repository.findByImageId(image.getId()).collectList()` actually fetches all `Comment` objects related to a given `Image`, but turns it into `Mono<List<Comment>>`. This waits for all of the entries to arrive and bundles them into a single object.
- The collection of comments and it's related image are bundled together via `Mono.zipWith(Mono)`, creating a tuple-2 or a pair. (This is the way to gather multiple bits of data and pass them on to the next step of any Reactor flow. Reactor has additional tuple types all the way up to `Tuple8`.)
- After flatMapping `Flux<Image>` into `Flux<Tuple2<Image, List<Comment>>>`, we then map each entry into a classic Java `Map` to service our Thymeleaf template.
- Reactor's `Tuple2` has a strongly typed `getT1()` and `getT2()`, with `T1` being the `Image` and `T2` being the list of comments, which is suitable for our needs since it's just a temporary construct used to assemble details for the web template.
- The image's `id` and `name` attributes are copied into the target map from `T1`.
- The `comments` attribute of our map is populated with the complete `List<Comment>` extracted from `T2`.

Since Thymeleaf templates operate on key-value semantics, there is no need to define a new domain object to capture this construct. A Java `Map` will work just fine.

As we continue working with Reactor types, these sorts of flows are, hopefully, becoming familiar. Having an IDE that offers code completion is a key asset when putting flows like this. And the more we work with these types of transformations the easier they become.

 If you'll notice, `ImageService` is fully reactive given that we use MongoDB's reactive drivers. The operation to retrieve comments is *also* reactive. Chaining reactive calls together, using Reactor's operators and hitching them to Thymeleaf's reactive solution, ensures that everything is being fetched as efficiently as possible and only when necessary. Writing reactive apps hinges on having a fully reactive stack.

To round out our feature of **reading comments**, we need to define `CommentReaderRepository` as follows:

```
public interface CommentReaderRepository
  extends Repository<Comment, String> {

    Flux<Comment> findByImageId(String imageId);
}
```

The preceding code can be described as follows:

- It's a declarative interface, similar to how we created `ImageRepository` earlier in this book.
- It extends Spring Data Commons' `Repository` interface, which contains no operations. We are left to define them all. This lets us create a read-only repository.
- It has a `findByImageId(String imageId)` method that returns a `Flux` of `Comment` objects.

This repository gives us a read-only readout on comments. This is handy because it lets us fetch comments and does not accidentally let people write through it. Instead, we intend to implement something different further in this chapter.

Our `CommentReaderRepository` needs one thing: a `Comment` domain object:

```
package com.greglturnquist.learningspringboot.images;

import lombok.Data;

import org.springframework.data.annotation.Id;

@Data
public class Comment {
```

```
@Id private String id;
private String imageId;
private String comment;

}
```

This preceding domain object contains the following:

- The `@Data` annotation tells Lombok to generate getters, setters, `toString()`, `equals()`, and `hashCode()` methods
- The `id` field is marked with Spring Data Commons' `@Id` annotation so we know it's the key for mapping objects
- The `imageId` field is meant to hold an `Image.id` field, linking comments to images
- The `comment` field is the place to store an actual comment

> For both `CommentReaderRepository` and `Comment`, the entire class is shown including the package. That's to show that it's located in the `images` subpackage we defined earlier in this chapter. This domain object provides the comment information **pertinent to images**. And this information is read-only, which means that this is not where updates regarding comments are made.

Producing comments

Having written the code to display comments, it's now time to craft the bits to create them.

We've already seen the changes to our template adding an HTML form to write a comment. Let's code the corresponding controller **in the comments subpackage**, as follows:

```
@Controller
public class CommentController {

  private final RabbitTemplate rabbitTemplate;

  public CommentController(RabbitTemplate rabbitTemplate) {
    this.rabbitTemplate = rabbitTemplate;
  }

  @PostMapping("/comments")
  public Mono<String> addComment(Mono<Comment> newComment) {
    return newComment.flatMap(comment ->
     Mono.fromRunnable(() -> rabbitTemplate
```

```
        .convertAndSend(
          "learning-spring-boot",
          "comments.new",
          comment)))
        .log("commentService-publish")
        .then(Mono.just("redirect:/"));
    }

  }
```

The code can be explained as follows:

- It's the first class we have put in the new `comments` subpackage.
- The `@Controller` annotation marks this as another Spring controller.
- It contains a `RabbitTemplate` initialized by constructor injection. This `RabbitTemplate` is created automatically by Spring Boot when it spots `spring-amqp` on the classpath.
- The `@PostMapping("/comments")` annotation registers this method to respond to the form submissions that we added earlier in the template with `th:action="@{'/comments'}"`.
- Spring will automatically convert the body of the POST into a `Comment` domain object. Additionally, since we are using WebFlux, deserializing the request body is wrapped in a `Mono`, hence that process will only occur once the framework subscribes to the flow.
- The incoming `Mono<Comment>` is unpacked using `flatMap` and then turned into a `rabbitTemplate.convertAndSend()` operation, which itself is wrapped in `Mono.fromRunnable`.
- The comment is published to RabbitMQ's `learning-spring-boot` exchange with a routing key of `comments.new`.
- We wait for this to complete with `then()`, and when done, return a Spring WebFlux **redirect** to send the webpage back to the home page.

Time out. That bullet point about the RabbitMQ exchange and routing key may have sounded a bit complex.

The comment is published to RabbitMQ's `learning-spring-boot` exchange with a routing key of `comments.new`.

We need to take this apart to understand the basics of AMQP a little better.

AMQP fundamentals

If you've already used JMS, then you're aware that it has queues and topics. AMQP has queues as well but the semantics are different.

Each message sent by a JMS-based producer is consumed by just one of the clients of that queue. AMQP-based producers don't publish directly to queues but to **exchanges** instead. When queues are declared, they must be bound to an exchange. Multiple queues can be bound to the same exchange, emulating the concept of topics.

JMS has message selectors which allow consumers to be selective about the messages they receive from either queues or topics. AMQP has **routing keys** that behave differently based on the type of the exchange, as listed next.

A **direct exchange** routes messages based on a fixed routing key, often the name of the queue. For example, the last code that we just looked at mentioned `learning-spring-boot` as the name of exchange and `comments.new` as the routing key. Any consumer that binds their own queue to that exchange with a routing key of `comments.new` will receive a copy of each message posted earlier.

A **topic exchange** allows routing keys to have wildcards like `comments.*`. This situation best suits clients where the actual routing key isn't known until a user provides the criteria. For example, imagine a stock-trading application where the user must provide a list of ticker symbols he or she is interested in monitoring.

A **fanout exchange** blindly broadcasts every message to every queue that is bound to it, regardless of the routing key.

Regarding the semantics of AMQP, let's explore that further by looking at the `CommentService` (also in `comments` subpackage) in chunks:

```
@Service
public class CommentService {

  private CommentWriterRepository repository;

  public CommentService(CommentWriterRepository repository) {
    this.repository = repository;
  }
  ... more to come below...
}
```

This preceding code can be described as follows:

- The `@Service` annotation marks it as a Spring service to be registered with the application context on startup
- `CommentWriterRepository` is a Spring Data repository used to write new comments and is initialized by the constructor injection

Which brings us to the meat of this service, which is as follows:

```
@RabbitListener(bindings = @QueueBinding(
    value = @Queue,
    exchange = @Exchange(value = "learning-spring-boot"),
    key = "comments.new"
))
public void save(Comment newComment) {
    repository
        .save(newComment)
        .log("commentService-save")
        .subscribe();
}
```

This last little function packs a punch, so let's take it apart:

- The `@RabbitListener` annotation is the easiest way to register methods to consume messages.
- The `@QueueBinding` annotation is the easiest way to declare the queue *and* the exchange it's bound to on-the-fly. In this case, it creates an anonymous queue for this method and binds to the `learning-spring-boot` exchange.
- The routing key for this method is `comments.new`, meaning any message posted to the `learning-spring-boot` exchange with that exact routing key will cause this method to be invoked.
- It's possible for the `@RabbitListener` methods to receive a Spring AMQP `Message`, a Spring Messaging `Message`, various message headers, as well as a plain old Java object (which is what we have here).
- The method itself invokes our `CommentWriterRepository` to actually save the comment in the data store.

To use RabbitMQ, we would normally need `@EnableRabbit`, but thanks to Spring Boot, it's automatically activated when `spring-boot-starter-amqp` is on the classpath. Once again, Boot knows what we want and just does it.

An important thing to understand is that `@RabbitListener` makes it possible to dynamically create all the exchanges and queues needed to operate. However, it only works if an instance of `AmqpAdmin` is in the application context. Without it, ALL exchanges and queues must be declared as separate Spring beans. But Spring Boot's RabbitMQ autoconfiguration policy provides one, so no sweat!

There is one slight issue with this method that will cause it to not operate--object serialization. If we had declared the method signature to provide us with a Spring AMQP `Message` object, we would pull down a byte array. However, out of the box, Spring AMQP has limited functionality in serializing custom domain objects. With no effort, it can handle simple strings and serializables.

But for custom domain objects, there is a more preferred solution--a Spring AMQP message converter, as shown next:

```
@Bean
Jackson2JsonMessageConverter jackson2JsonMessageConverter() {
  return new Jackson2JsonMessageConverter();
}
```

This preceding bean, listed right below the `save(Comment newComment)` method, can be described as follows:

- `@Bean` registers this as a bean definition.
- It creates `Jackson2JsonMessageConverter`, an implementation of Spring AMQP's `MessageConverter`, used to serialize and deserialize Spring AMQP `Message` objects. In this case, is uses Jackson to convert POJOs to/from JSON strings.

Spring Boot's RabbitMQ autoconfiguration policy will look for any implementation of Spring AMQP's `MessageConverter` instances and register them with both the `RabbitTemplate` we used earlier as well as the `SimpleMessageListenerContainer` that it creates when it spots `@RabbitListener` in our code.

To start our application with a clean slate, we have this code at the bottom of `CommentService`:

```
@Bean
CommandLineRunner setUp(MongoOperations operations) {
  return args -> {
    operations.dropCollection(Comment.class);
  };
}
```

The last code can be described as follows:

- The `@Bean` annotation will register this chunk of code automatically
- By implementing Spring Boot's `CommandLineRunner` interface, the Java 8 lambda expression will run itself when all beans have been created
- It receives a copy of `MongoOperations`, the blocking MongoDB object we can use to drop the entire collection based on `Comment`

 This code is handy for development, but should be either removed in production or wrapped in a `@Profile("dev")` annotation such that it ONLY runs when `spring.profiles.active=dev` is present.

To persist comments in our data store, we have the following Spring Data repository:

```
public interface CommentWriterRepository
  extends Repository<Comment, String> {

  Mono<Comment> save(Comment newComment);

  // Needed to support save()
  Mono<Comment> findById(String id);
}
```

This preceding repository isn't too difficult to dissect, and that can be done as follows:

- It's an interface, which means that we don't have to write any code. We just declare the semantics and Spring Data does the rest.
- By extending Spring Data Commons' `Repository` interface, it will be picked up as a repository. Being an empty interface, it comes with no predefined operations.
- It contains a `save()` operation to store a new comment (and return it after it gets saved). If the ID value is null, Spring Data MongoDB will automatically generate a unique string value for us.
- Spring Data requires a `findOne()` operation in order to perform saves because that's what it uses to fetch what we just saved in order to return it.
- All of these method signatures use Reactor `Mono` types.

This repository is focused on writing data into MongoDB and nothing more. Even though it has a `findOne()`, it's not built for reading data. That has been kept over in the `images` subpackage.

To finish things up in our `comments` subpackage, let's look at the core domain object:

```
package com.greglturnquist.learningspringboot.comments;

import lombok.Data;

import org.springframework.data.annotation.Id;
import org.springframework.data.mongodb.core.mapping.Document;

@Data
@Document
public class Comment {

  @Id private String id;
  private String imageId;
  private String comment;
}
```

This previous domain object contains the following:

- The `@Data` annotation tells Lombok to generate getters, setters, `toString()`, `equals()`, and `hashCode()` methods
- The `id` field is marked with Spring Data Common's `@Id` annotation so we know it's the key for mapping objects
- The `imageId` field is meant to hold an `Image.id` field linking comments to images
- The `comment` field is the place to store an actual comment

Wait a second! Isn't this the *exact same code* found in `com.greglturnquist.learningspringboot.images.Comment`? It is right now. But it's important to recognize that different *slices* may need different attributes in the future. By keeping a slice-specific domain object, we can change one without the risk of changing the other. In fact, it's possible that we can (spoiler alert!), later in this book, move this entire comments system into a separate microservice. By keeping things in nicely divided slices, the risk of tight coupling can be reduced.

Another factor is that RabbitMQ is *not reactive*. Invoking `rabbitTemplate.convertAndSend()` is blocking. That may sound awkward given AMQP is a pub/sub technology. But the whole process of publishing the message to the RabbitMQ broker holds up our thread, and is, by definition, blocking.

So our code wraps that inside a Java `Runnable` and converts it into a `Mono` via Reactor's `Mono.fromRunnable`. That makes it possible to invoke this blocking task only when we're ready at the right time. It's important to know that a Mono-wrapped-Runnable doesn't act like a traditional Java `Runnable` and doesn't get launched in a separate thread. Instead, the `Runnable` interface provides a convenient wrapper where Reactor controls precisely when the `run()` method is invoked inside its scheduler.

If we refresh our code in the IDE and let it restart, we can now start creating comments. Check out the following screenshot:

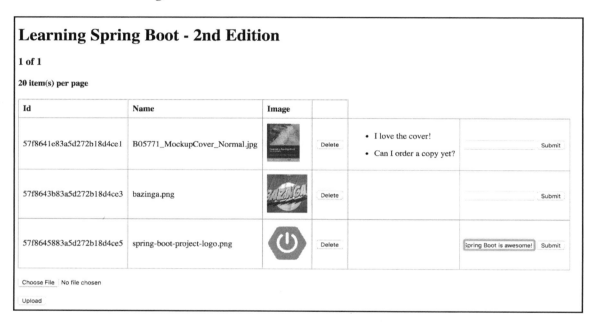

The preceding screenshot shows a couple of comments added to the first image and a third being written. Cool, ehh?

But perhaps, you're wondering why we spent all that effort splitting up reading and writing comments? After all, Spring Data appears to make it easy enough to define a single repository that could handle both. That may even imply we didn't need RabbitMQ and could let `HomeController` and `CommentController` use the repository directly instead.

The reason to use messaging is to provide a reliable way to offload work to another system. A real system that grows to thousands, if not millions, of users will see a huge flow of traffic. Think about it. Are there any other social media platforms where people write comments constantly but only view a handful at a time?

This facet of our application is designed with scalability in mind. If we had one million users, they may be writing tens of millions of messages a day. Hitching our controller directly to MongoDB may cause it to keel over. But if we push all the writes to a separate service, we can tune suitably.

The number of reads is much smaller.

Adding customized metrics to track message flow

Having added the ability to comment on other people's posted images, it would be nice to start gathering metrics.

To do so, we can introduce metrics similar to those shown in Chapter 5, *Developer Tools for Spring Boot Apps*, as follows:

```
@Controller
public class CommentController {

  private final RabbitTemplate rabbitTemplate;

  private final MeterRegistry meterRegistry;

  public CommentController(RabbitTemplate rabbitTemplate,
   MeterRegistry meterRegistry) {
    this.rabbitTemplate = rabbitTemplate;
    this.meterRegistry = meterRegistry;
  }

  @PostMapping("/comments")
  public Mono<String> addComment(Mono<Comment> newComment) {
    return newComment.flatMap(comment ->
    Mono.fromRunnable(() ->
     rabbitTemplate
      .convertAndSend(
        "learning-spring-boot",
        "comments.new",
      comment))
```

```
          .then(Mono.just(comment)))
        .log("commentService-publish")
        .flatMap(comment -> {
          meterRegistry
            .counter("comments.produced", "imageId",
comment.getImageId())
              .increment();
          return Mono.just("redirect:/");
        });
    }
  }
```

This last code has these few changes compared to what we wrote earlier in this chapter:

- A `MeterRegistry` is injected through the constructor and captured as a field.
- It's used to increment a `comments.produced` metric with every comment.
- Each metric is also "tagged" with the related **imageId**.
- We have to tune the `Mono` wrapping our `rabbitTemplate.convertAndSend()`, and ensure that the **comment** is passed via `then()`. Then it must be unpacked via `flatMap` in the part of the flow that writes metrics.

 Should the code talking to the `meterRegistry` *also* be wrapped in `Mono.fromRunnable()`? Perhaps. The code blocks when writing, but in this incarnation, the metrics are stored in memory, so the cost is low. Nevertheless, the cost could rise, meaning it should be properly managed. If the service became external, the odds would increase quickly in favor of wrapping with a separate `Mono`.

In a similar vein, if we inject `MeterRegistry` into `CommentService`, we can then use it there as well:

```
@RabbitListener(bindings = @QueueBinding(
  value = @Queue,
  exchange = @Exchange(value = "learning-spring-boot"),
  key = "comments.new"
))
public void save(Comment newComment) {
  repository
    .save(newComment)
    .log("commentService-save")
    .subscribe(comment -> {
      meterRegistry
        .counter("comments.consumed", "imageId", comment.getImageId())
        .increment();
    });
```

```
    }
```

This lines up with what we added to `CommentController`. The preceding code can be explained as follows:

- Using the injected `MeterRegistry`, we increment a `comments.consumed` metric with every comment.
- It's also tagged with the comment's related **imageId**.
- The metrics are handled after the save is completed inside the `subscribe` method. This method grants us the ability to execute some code once the flow is complete.

 Spring AMQP doesn't yet support Reactive Streams. That is why `rabbitTemplate.convertAndSend()` must be wrapped in `Mono.fromRunnable`. Blocking calls such as this `subscribe()` method should be red flags, but in this situation, it's a necessary evil until Spring AMQP is able to add support. There is no other way to signal for this Reactor flow to execute without it.

The thought of relaunching our app and manually entering a slew of comments doesn't sound very exciting. So why not write a simulator to do it for us!

```
@Profile("simulator")
@Component
public class CommentSimulator {

  private final CommentController controller;
  private final ImageRepository repository;

  private final AtomicInteger counter;

  public CommentSimulator(CommentController controller,
            ImageRepository repository) {
    this.controller = controller;
    this.repository = repository;
    this.counter = new AtomicInteger(1);
  }

  @EventListener
  public void onApplicationReadyEvent(ApplicationReadyEvent event) {
    Flux
      .interval(Duration.ofMillis(1000))
      .flatMap(tick -> repository.findAll())
      .map(image -> {
        Comment comment = new Comment();
```

```
            comment.setImageId(image.getId());
            comment.setComment(
               "Comment #" + counter.getAndIncrement());
            return Mono.just(comment);
         })
         .flatMap(newComment ->
           Mono.defer(() ->
             controller.addComment(newComment)))
         .subscribe();
    }
  }
```

Let's take this simulator apart:

- The @Profile annotation indicates that this only operates if spring.profiles.active=simulator is present when the app starts
- The @Component annotation will allow this class to get picked up by Spring Boot automatically and activated
- The class itself is located in the root package, com.greglturnquist.learningspring, given that it pulls bits from both subpackages
- The @EventListener annotation signals Spring to pipe application events issued to the app context. In this case, the method is interested in ApplicationReadyEvents, fired when the application is up and operational
- Flux.interval(Duration.ofMillis(1000)) causes a stream of lazy ticks to get fired every 1000 ms, lazily
- By flatMapping over this Flux, each tick is transformed into all images using the ImageRepository
- Each image is used to generate a new, related comment
- Using the injected CommentController, it simulates the newly minted comment being sent in from the web

If we reconfigure our runner with `spring.profiles.active=simulator`, we can see it run. IntelliJ IDEA provides the means to set Spring profiles easily:

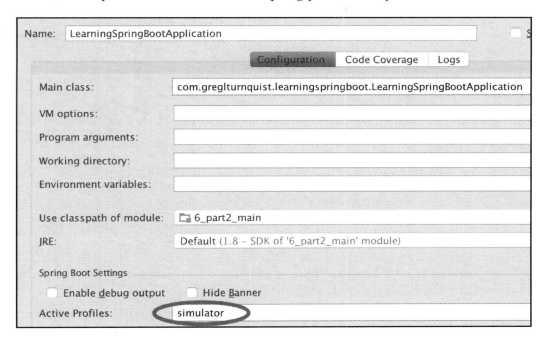

You can see the entry highlighted at the bottom of the previous screenshot.

If we kick things off after hearing our machine's fan move into high gear, we can check the metrics at `http://localhost:8080/application/metrics/comments.consumed` and `http://localhost:8080/application/metrics/comments.produced`, and expect to see tallies.

In this last screenshot, we can clearly see `counter.comments.produced` and `counter.comments.consumed`, and they happen to be the same, which means that none were lost.

We can also see the unique image IDs with an equal number of messages spread between them (as expected with our simulator).

Peeking at Spring Cloud Stream (with RabbitMQ)

Linking lots of small services together via messaging is a very common pattern. It increases in popularity with the rise of microservices. Coding the same pattern over and over using `RabbitTemplate` or some other transport template (`KafkaTemplate` and others) is another level of complexity we shouldn't be saddled with.

Spring Cloud Stream (`http://cloud.spring.io/spring-cloud-stream/`) to the rescue!

Spring Cloud Stream takes the concept of **inputs**, **outputs**, and **transformers** from Spring Integration and makes it super easy to chain them together.

To alter our social media platform to do this, we can remove `spring-boot-starter-amqp` from our build file and add this instead:

```
compile(
  'org.springframework.cloud:spring-cloud-starter-stream-rabbit')
compile(
  'org.springframework.cloud:spring-cloud-stream-reactive')
```

This preceding dependency brings in the following:

- `spring-cloud-stream-binder-rabbit-core`
- `spring-cloud-stream-codec`
- `spring-cloud-stream`
- `spring-cloud-stream-reactive`
- `spring-boot-starter-amqp`
- `spring-integration-amqp`

Spring Cloud Stream has many starters. In essence, we must pick the underlying transport technology, but we don't have to interact with the transport technology directly.

Introduction to Spring Cloud

Spring Cloud? What is that?

Spring Cloud is an extension of Spring Boot provided through various libraries and aimed at addressing different cloud-native patterns. In this case, Spring Cloud Stream aims to simplify the chaining together of services via messaging.

To use any Spring Cloud library, we need to add the following chunk to the bottom of our `build.gradle` file:

```
dependencyManagement {
  imports {
    mavenBom "org.springframework.cloud:spring-cloud-
    dependencies:${springCloudVersion}"
  }
}
```

This preceding fragment of code is part of Spring's Dependency Management gradle plugin, pulling in Spring Cloud **BOM (Bill of Materials)**. In this case, it has a variable, `springCloudVersion`, which we need to select.

Spring Cloud has release trains, which means that each library has a version but all the versions are coordinated. By picking one train, we get a fleet of tools to pick from (and we will throughout the rest of this book!).

The Spring Cloud release train tied to Spring Boot 2.0 is `Finchley`, so let's put that right next to our version of Boot at the top:

```
buildscript {
  ext {
    springBootVersion = '2.0.0.M5'
    springCloudVersion = 'Finchley.M3'
  }
  ...
}
```

If you're curious about the various release trains of Spring Cloud, check out its project page at http://projects.spring.io/spring-cloud/.

With Spring Cloud's BOM and Spring Cloud Stream added to our build, let's return to configuring messaging using Spring Cloud Stream's core interfaces, as follows:

```
@Controller
@EnableBinding(Source.class)
public class CommentController {

  private final CounterService counterService;
  private FluxSink<Message<Comment>> commentSink;
  private Flux<Message<Comment>> flux;

  public CommentController(CounterService counterService) {
    this.counterService = counterService;
    this.flux = Flux.<Message<Comment>>create(
      emitter -> this.commentSink = emitter,
      FluxSink.OverflowStrategy.IGNORE)
      .publish()
      .autoConnect();
  }

  @PostMapping("/comments")
  public Mono<String> addComment(Mono<Comment> newComment) {
    if (commentSink != null) {
      return newComment
        .map(comment -> commentSink.next(MessageBuilder
        .withPayload(comment)
        .build()))
        .then(Mono.just("redirect:/"));
    } else {
        return Mono.just("redirect:/");
    }
  }

  @StreamEmitter
  public void emit(@Output(Source.OUTPUT) FluxSender output) {
    output.send(this.flux);
  }

}
```

This last code is very similar to the `CommentController` that we created earlier in this chapter, but with the following differences:

- `@EnableBinding(Source.class)` flags this app as a **source** for new events. Spring Cloud Stream uses this annotation to signal the creation of **channels**, which, in RabbitMQ, translates to **exchanges** and **queues**.
- The constructor proceeds to set up a `FluxSink`, the mechanism to emit new messages into a downstream `Flux`. This sink is configured to ignore downstream backpressure events. It starts publishing right away, autoconnecting to its upstream source upon subscription.
- The objects being emitted are `Message<Comment>`, which is Spring's abstraction for a POJO wrapped as a transportable message. This includes the ability to add headers and other information.
- Inside `addComments`, if the sink has been established, it maps `newComment` into a `Message<Comment>` using Spring Messaging APIs. Finally, it transmits the message into the sink.
- When the message is successfully emitted to `Flux`, a redirect is issued.
- To transmit `Flux` of `Message<Comment>` objects, a separate method, `emit`, is wired up with an `@StreamEmitter` annotation. This method is fed a `FluxSender`, which provides us with a Reactor-friendly means to transmit messages into a channel. It lets us hook up the `Flux` tied to our `FluxSink`.
- The `@Output(Source.OUTPUT)` annotation marks up *which* channel it gets piped to (visiting `Source.OUTPUT` reveals the channel name as **output**).

That's a lot of stuff packed into this controller. To better understand it, there are some fundamental concepts to realize.

First of all, it's not common practice to create a `Flux` and then add to it. The paradigm is to wrap it around something else. To drive this point home, `Flux` itself is an abstract class. You can't instantiate it. Instead, you must use its various static helper methods to craft one. So, when we want to take a behavior that is tied to users clicking on a site and link it to a `Flux` that was created when the application started, we need something like `FluxSink` to bridge these two things together.

Spring Cloud Stream focuses on chaining together streams of messages with source/sink semantics. When it comes to Reactor, this means adapting a `Flux` of messages onto a channel, a concept curated for several years by Spring Integration. Given that the concrete nature of the channel is abstracted away, it doesn't matter what transport technology we use. Thanks to the power of Spring Boot, this is defined by dependencies on the classpath. Nevertheless, we'll continue using RabbitMQ because it's darn simple and powerful at the same time.

By the way, we'll see this concept of connecting a sink to `Flux` again when we visit Chapter 8, *WebSockets with Spring Boot*. It's a common Reactor pattern when connecting one-off objects to established flows.

To declare a Spring Cloud Stream consumer, we merely need to update our `CommentService` as follows:

```
@Service
@EnableBinding(CustomProcessor.class)
public class CommentService {
```

At the top of `CommentService`, we need to add `@EnableBinding(CustomProcessor.class)`. If this was the only Spring Cloud Stream component, we could have used `@EnableBinding(Processor.class)`, however, we can't share the same channel, output, with the `CommentController`. So we need to code a custom set of channels, `CustomProcessor` as shown below:

```
public interface CustomProcessor {

    String INPUT = "input";
    String OUTPUT = "emptyOutput";

    @Input(CustomProcessor.INPUT)
    SubscribableChannel input();

    @Output(CustomProcessor.OUTPUT)
    MessageChannel output();

}
```

This custom processor is quite similar to Spring Cloud Stream's `Processor`:

- It's a declarative interface.
- It has two channel names, `INPUT` and `OUTPUT`. The `INPUT` channel uses the same as `Processor`. To avoid colliding with the `OUTPUT` channel of `Source`, we create a different channel name, `emptyOutput`. (Why call it `emptyOutput`? We'll see in a moment!)
- The is a `SubscribableChannel` for inputs and a `MessageChannel` for outputs.

This flags our application as both a `Sink` as well as a `Source` for events. Remember how we had to `subscribe` earlier when consuming with `RabbitTemplate`?

Thankfully, Spring Cloud Stream is Reactor-friendly. When dealing with Reactive Streams, our code shouldn't be the termination point for processing. So, receiving an incoming `Flux` of `Comment` objects must result in an outgoing `Flux` that the framework can invoke as we'll soon see.

Further down in `CommentService`, we need to update our `save` method as follows:

```
@StreamListener
@Output (CustomProcessor.OUTPUT)
public Flux<Void> save(@Input(CustomProcessor.INPUT)
 Flux<Comment> newComments) {
    return repository
      .saveAll(newComments)
      .flatMap(comment -> {
        meterRegistry
          .counter("comments.consumed", "imageId", comment.getImageId())
          .increment();
        return Mono.empty();
      });
}
```

Let's tear apart this preceding updated version of `save`:

- The `@RabbitListener` annotation has been replaced with `@StreamListener`, indicating that it's transport-agnostic.
- The argument `newComments` is tied to the **input** channel via the `@Input()` annotation.
- Since we've marked it as `Flux`, we can immediately consume it with our MongoDB repository.

- Since we have to hand a stream back to the framework, we have marked up the whole method with `@Output`.
- From there, we can flatMap it to generate metrics and then transform it into a `Flux` of `Mono<Void>` s with `Mono.empty()`. This ensures that no more processing is done by the framework.

This method has the same concept as all Spring `@*Listener` annotations--invoke the method with optional domain objects. But this time, it receives them from whatever underlying technology we have configured Spring Cloud Stream to use. The benefit is that this is slim and easy to manage and our code is no longer bound to RabbitMQ directly.

That being said, we need to express to Spring Cloud Stream that our source and sink need to communicate through the same RabbitMQ exchange. To do so, we need to provide settings in `application.yml`:

```
spring:
  cloud:
    stream:
      bindings:
        input:
          destination: learning-spring-boot-comments
          group: learning-spring-boot
        output:
          destination: learning-spring-boot-comments
          group: learning-spring-boot
```

This last application configuration contains the following details:

- `spring.cloud.stream.bindings` is configured for both the `input` and the `output` channel's destination to be `learning-spring-boot`. When using RabbitMQ bindings, this is the name of the **exchange** and Spring Cloud Stream uses topic exchanges by default.

- We take advantage of Spring Cloud Streams' support for **consumer groups** by *also* setting the `group` property. This ensures that even if there are multiple stream listeners to a given channel, only one listener will consume any one message. This type of guarantee is required in cloud-native environments when we can expect to run multiple instances.

 As stated early in this book, you can use either `application.properties` or `application.yml`. If you find yourself configuring many settings with the same prefix, use YAML to make it easier to read and avoid repetition.

By the way, remember having to define a `Jackson2JsonMessageConverter` bean earlier in this chapter to handle serialization? No longer needed. Spring Cloud Stream uses Esoteric Software's Kryo library for serialization/deserialization (`https://github.com/EsotericSoftware/kryo`). That means, we can chuck that bean definition. Talk about thinning out the code!

If we run the simulator again (`spring.profiles.active=simulator`) and check `http://localhost:8080/application/metrics`, we can see our custom metrics tabulating everything.

With this, we have managed to change the **comments** solution and yet retain the same set of metrics.

However, by switching to Spring Cloud Stream, we have gathered a whole new fleet of metrics, as seen in this screenshot:

```
integration.channel.output.errorRate.mean: 0,
integration.channel.output.errorRate.max: 0,
integration.channel.output.errorRate.min: 0,
integration.channel.output.errorRate.stdev: 0,
integration.channel.output.errorRate.count: 0,
integration.channel.output.sendCount: 1080,
integration.channel.output.sendRate.mean: 33.2953175275134,
integration.channel.output.sendRate.max: 0.10356745398044587,
integration.channel.output.sendRate.min: 0.00007268595695495606,
integration.channel.output.sendRate.stdev: 127.44592804513556,
integration.channel.output.sendRate.count: 1080,
integration.channel.output.receiveCount: -1,
integration.channel.input.errorRate.mean: 0,
integration.channel.input.errorRate.max: 0,
integration.channel.input.errorRate.min: 0,
integration.channel.input.errorRate.stdev: 0,
integration.channel.input.errorRate.count: 0,
integration.channel.input.sendCount: 1080,
integration.channel.input.sendRate.mean: 30.60592083415993,
integration.channel.input.sendRate.max: 0.10221006900072098,
integration.channel.input.sendRate.min: 0.000672169029712677,
integration.channel.input.sendRate.stdev: 20.733646866079425,
integration.channel.input.sendRate.count: 1080,
integration.channel.input.receiveCount: -1,
```

This is a subset (too many to fill a book) covering the input and output channels.

Remember how we wrote a custom health check in the last chapter? It would be handy to have one for RabbitMQ and its bindings. Guess what? It's already done. Check it out:

```
{
    status: "UP",
  - learningSpringBoot: {
        status: "UP"
    },
  - diskSpace: {
        status: "UP",
        total: 498937626624,
        free: 89344151552,
        threshold: 10485760
    },
  - rabbit: {
        status: "UP",
        version: "3.6.4"
    },
  - mongo: {
        status: "UP",
        version: "3.2.6"
    },
  - binders: {
        status: "UP",
      - rabbit: {
            status: "UP",
          - binderHealthIndicator: {
                status: "UP",
                version: "3.6.4"
            }
        }
    }
}
```

In this last screenshot, we can see the following:

- The RabbitMQ broker is up and operational
- Our RabbitMQ binders are operational as well

With this in place, we have a nicely working **comment** system.

Logging with Spring Cloud Stream

To wrap things up, it would be nice to actually see how Spring Cloud Stream is handling things. To do so, we can dial up the log levels in `application.yml` like this:

```yaml
logging:
  level:
    org:
      springframework:
        cloud: DEBUG
        integration: DEBUG
```

This last code dials up the log levels for both Spring Cloud Stream and its underlying technology, Spring Integration. It's left as an exercise for the reader to change `RabbitTemplate` log levels by setting `org.springframework.amqp=DEBUG` and see what happens.

With these levels dialed up, if we run our application, we can see a little of this:

```
o.s.a.r.c.CachingConnectionFactory         : Created new connection: rabbitConnectionFactory#1470a7b3:0/SimpleConnection@31792aa
o.s.integration.channel.DirectChannel      : Channel 'unknown.channel.name' has 1 subscriber(s).
o.s.c.s.binding.BindableProxyFactory       : Binding outputs for :interface org.springframework.cloud.stream.messaging.Processo
o.s.c.s.binding.BindableProxyFactory       : Binding :interface org.springframework.cloud.stream.messaging.Processor:output
o.s.integration.channel.DirectChannel      : Channel 'application.output' has 1 subscriber(s).
o.s.c.support.DefaultLifecycleProcessor    : Starting beans in phase 0
o.s.i.endpoint.EventDrivenConsumer         : Adding {logging-channel-adapter:_org.springframework.integration.errorLogger} as a
o.s.i.channel.PublishSubscribeChannel      : Channel 'application.errorChannel' has 1 subscriber(s).
o.s.i.endpoint.EventDrivenConsumer         : started _org.springframework.integration.errorLogger
o.s.c.support.DefaultLifecycleProcessor    : Starting beans in phase 2147482647
o.s.c.s.binding.BindableProxyFactory       : Binding inputs for :interface org.springframework.cloud.stream.messaging.Source
o.s.c.s.binding.BindableProxyFactory       : Binding inputs for :interface org.springframework.cloud.stream.messaging.Processor
o.s.c.s.binding.BindableProxyFactory       : Binding :interface org.springframework.cloud.stream.messaging.Processor:input
c.s.b.r.p.RabbitExchangeQueueProvisioner   : declaring queue for inbound: learning-spring-boot-comments.learning-spring-boot, b
c.s.b.r.p.RabbitExchangeQueueProvisioner   : autoBindDLQ=false for: learning-spring-boot-comments.learning-spring-boot
o.s.i.a.i.AmqpInboundChannelAdapter        : started inbound.learning-spring-boot
o.s.i.endpoint.EventDrivenConsumer         : Adding {message-handler:inbound.learning-spring-boot-comments.learning-spring-boot}
o.s.i.endpoint.EventDrivenConsumer         : started inbound.learning-spring-boot-comments.learning-spring-boot
```

This previous screenshot shows a clear separation between Spring Cloud Stream involved in binding compared to Spring Integration dealing with channel settings as well as setting up AMQP exchanges and queues.

It's also nice to observe that the logging prefix `o.s.c.s` is short for `org.springframework.cloud.stream` or Spring Cloud Stream.

If we add a new comment on the web page, we can see the outcome, as seen here:

```
o.s.integration.channel.DirectChannel    : preSend on channel 'output', message: GenericMessage [payload=Comment(id=null, ima
tractMessageChannelBinder$SendingHandler : org.springframework.cloud.stream.binder.AbstractMessageChannelBinder$SendingHandle
o.s.i.codec.kryo.CompositeKryoRegistrar  : registering [40, java.io.File] with serializer org.springframework.integration.cod
o.s.i.a.outbound.AmqpOutboundEndpoint    : org.springframework.integration.amqp.outbound.AmqpOutboundEndpoint@52038bac receiv
s.i.m.AbstractHeaderMapper$HeaderMatcher : headerName=[contentType] WILL be mapped, matched pattern=*
o.s.i.a.outbound.AmqpOutboundEndpoint    : handler 'org.springframework.integration.amqp.outbound.AmqpOutboundEndpoint@52038b
o.s.integration.channel.DirectChannel    : postSend (sent=true) on channel 'output', message: GenericMessage [payload=Comment
s.i.m.AbstractHeaderMapper$HeaderMatcher : headerName=[amqp_receivedDeliveryMode] WILL be mapped, matched pattern=*
s.i.m.AbstractHeaderMapper$HeaderMatcher : headerName=[amqp_receivedRoutingKey] WILL be mapped, matched pattern=*
s.i.m.AbstractHeaderMapper$HeaderMatcher : headerName=[amqp_receivedExchange] WILL be mapped, matched pattern=*
s.i.m.AbstractHeaderMapper$HeaderMatcher : headerName=[amqp_deliveryTag] WILL be mapped, matched pattern=*
s.i.m.AbstractHeaderMapper$HeaderMatcher : headerName=[amqp_correlationId] WILL be mapped, matched pattern=*
s.i.m.AbstractHeaderMapper$HeaderMatcher : headerName=[amqp_redelivered] WILL be mapped, matched pattern=*
s.i.m.AbstractHeaderMapper$HeaderMatcher : headerName=[contentType] WILL be mapped, matched pattern=*
s.i.m.AbstractHeaderMapper$HeaderMatcher : headerName=[contentType] WILL be mapped, matched pattern=*
actMessageChannelBinder$ReceivingHandler : org.springframework.cloud.stream.binder.AbstractMessageChannelBinder$ReceivingHand
findAll                                  : | onSubscribe([Fuseable] FluxOnAssembly.OnAssemblySubscriber)
findAll                                  : | request(256)
o.s.integration.channel.DirectChannel    : preSend on channel 'input', message: GenericMessage [payload=Comment(id=null, imag
findAll                                  : | onNext(Image(id=59894898c4d956e34025dacc, name=learning-spring-boot-cover.jpg))
findAll                                  : | request(1)
findAll                                  : | onNext(Image(id=59894898c4d956e34025dacd, name=learning-spring-boot-2nd-edition-
findAll                                  : | request(1)
findAll                                  : | onNext(Image(id=59894899c4d956e34025dace, name=bazinga.png))
findAll                                  : | onComplete()
o.s.integration.channel.DirectChannel    : postSend (sent=true) on channel 'input', message: GenericMessage [payload=Comment(
```

This screenshot nicely shows **Comment** being transmitted to the **output** channel and then received on the **input** channel later.

Also notice that the logging prefix `o.s.i` indicates Spring Integration, with `s.i.m` being Spring Integration's Message API.

Summary

In this chapter, we created a message-based solution for users to comment on images. We first used Spring AMQP and `RabbitTemplate` to dispatch writes to a separate *slice*. Then we replaced that with Spring Cloud Stream with RabbitMQ bindings. That let us solve the comments situation with messaging, but without our code being bound to a specific transport technology.

In the next chapter, we'll break up our quickly growing, monolithic application into smaller microservices and use Spring Cloud to simplify integration between these distributed components.

7
Microservices with Spring Boot

@SpringBoot and @SpringCloudOSS are making it way too easy to build advanced distributed systems. Shame on you! #ComplimentarySarcasm

– InSource Software @InSourceOmaha

In the previous chapter, we learned how to communicate between different systems using AMQP messaging with RabbitMQ as our broker.

In this day and age, teams around the world are discovering that constantly tacking on more and more functionality is no longer effective after a certain point. Domains become blurred, coupling between various systems makes things resistant to change, and different teams are forced to hold more and more meetings to avoid breaking various parts of the system, sometimes, for the tiniest of changes.

Emerging from all this malaise are **microservices**. The term microservice is meant to connote a piece of software that doesn't attempt to solve too many problems, but a targeted situation instead. Its scope is microscopic when compared with the existing behemoth monoliths that litter the horizon.

And that's where Spring Cloud steps in. By continuing the paradigm of autoconfiguration, Spring Cloud extends Spring Boot into the realm of cloud-native microservices, making the development of distributed microservices quite practical.

In this chapter, we will cover the following topics:

- A quick primer on microservices
- Dynamically registering and finding services with Eureka
- Introducing `@SpringCloudApplication`

- Calling one microservice from another with client-side load balancing
- Implementing microservice circuit breakers
- Monitoring circuits
- Offloading microservice settings to a configuration server

A quick primer on microservices

As we said, a microservice focuses on solving a problem and solving it right, much like the UNIX philosophy of *make each program do one thing well* [Doug McIlroy].

That said, too many people describe microservices as being less than a certain number of lines of code, or less than a certain number of megabytes in total size. Nothing could be further from the truth. In fact, microservices are more closely tied to **bounded contexts** as defined by Eric Evans in *Domain Driven Design*, a worthwhile read despite having been written in 2003.

In essence, a microservice should focus on solving a particular problem, and only use enough domain knowledge to tackle that specific problem. If other parts of the system wish to interact with the same domain, their own context might be different.

 In case you missed it, we introduced Spring Cloud (http://projects.spring.io/spring-cloud/) in the previous chapter using Spring Cloud Stream. Spring Cloud is a collection of Spring projects that are aimed at solving cloud-native problems. These are problems observed time and again when systems grow in size and scope, and are often relegated to cloud platforms. Solving cloud-native problems with microservices has seen a high rate of success, hence making many of their tools a perfect fit for this chapter.

Suffice it to say, entire books have been written on the subject of microservices, so, to further explore this realm, feel free to look about. For the rest of this chapter, we'll see how Spring Boot and Spring Cloud make it super simple to engage in microservice development without paying a huge cost.

 There are *hundreds* of books written on the subject of microservices. For more details, check out the free book, *Migrating to Cloud Native Application Architectures* by cloud native polymath Matt Stine (http://mattstine.com). It covers many concepts that underpin microservices.

Dynamically registering and finding services with Eureka

At a fundamental level, taking one big application (like we've built so far) and splitting it up into two or more microservices requires that the two systems communicate with each other. And to communicate, these systems need to find each other. This is known as **service discovery**.

The Netflix engineering team built a tool for this called **Eureka**, and open sourced it. Eureka provides the means for microservices to power up, advertise their existence, and shutdown as well. It supports multiple copies of the same service registering themselves, and allows multiple instances of Eureka to register with each other to develop a highly available service registry.

Standing up a Eureka Server is quite simple. We simply have to create a new application at `http://start.spring.io`:

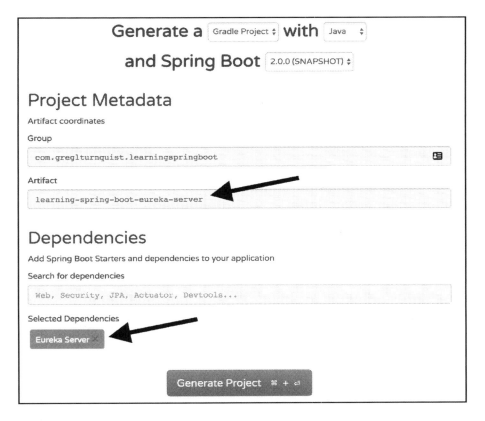

Yes, that's correct. We create an entirely *separate* Spring Boot application using the Spring Initializr, apart from our functional application. And in the preceding screenshot, the arrows point out that we are calling it `learning-spring-boot-eureka-server` while also adding a single dependency, **Eureka Server**. This application will be dedicated to providing our microservices with a **service registry**.

If we peek at our Eureka Server's build file, we'll find a slim list of dependencies toward the bottom:

```
dependencies {
  compile('org.springframework.cloud:spring-cloud-starter-eureka-
    server')
}

dependencyManagement {
  imports {
    mavenBom "org.springframework.cloud:spring-cloud-
      dependencies:${springCloudVersion}"
  }
}
```

This short list has but one dependency--`spring-cloud-starter-eureka-server`. Following it is the same Spring Cloud **Bill of Materials (BOM)** used to provide the proper versions of the Spring Cloud components.

Toward the top of the build file, we can see the exact versions of both Spring Boot and Spring Cloud:

```
buildscript {
  ext {
    springBootVersion = '2.0.0.M5'
    springCloudVersion = 'Finchley.M3'
  }
  ...
}
```

Spring Cloud's `Finchley` release train, also mentioned in the previous chapter, is the version compatible with Spring Boot 2.0.

With that in place, the only code we must write is shown here:

```
@SpringBootApplication
@EnableEurekaServer
public class LearningSpringBootEurekaServerApplication {
```

```
public static void main(String[] args) {
  SpringApplication.run(
    LearningSpringBootEurekaServerApplication.class);
  }
}
```

This preceding simple application can be described as follows:

- @SpringBootApplication marks this app as a Spring Boot application, which means that it will autoconfigure beans based on the classpath, and load properties as well.
- @EnableEurekaServer tells Spring Cloud Eureka that we want to run a Eureka Server. It proceeds to configure all the necessary beans to host a service registry.
- The code inside public static void main is the same as the previous chapters, simply loading the surrounding class.

Before we can launch our Eureka service registry, there are some key settings that must be plugged in. To do so, we need to create a src/main/resources/application.yml file as follows:

```
server:
  port: 8761

eureka:
  instance:
    hostname: localhost
  client:
    registerWithEureka: false
    fetchRegistry: false
    serviceUrl:
      defaultZone:
        http://${eureka.instance.hostname}:${server.port}/eureka/
```

The previous configuration file can be explained in detail as follows:

- server.port lets us run it on Eureka's standard port of 8761.
- For a standalone Eureka Server, we have to configure it with a eureka.instance.hostname and a eureka.client.serviceUrl.defaultZone setting. This resolves to http://localhost:8761/eureka, the URI for this standalone version of Eureka. For a multi-node Eureka Server configuration, we would alter this configuration.

Eureka servers are also clients, which means that with multiple instances running, they will send heartbeats to each other, and also registry data. With a standalone instance, we would get bombarded with log messages about failing to reach peers unless we disable the Eureka server from being a client via `eureka.client.registerWithEureka=false` and `eureka.client.fetchRegistry=false` (as we just did).

To run things in a more resilient mode, we could run two instances, each with a different Spring profile (`peer1` and `peer2`) with the following configuration:

```
---
spring:
  profiles: peer1
eureka:
  instance:
    hostname: peer1
  client:
    serviceUrl:
      defaultZone: http://peer2/eureka/

---
spring:
  profiles: peer2
eureka:
  instance:
    hostname: peer2
  client:
    serviceUrl:
      defaultZone: http://peer1/eureka/
```

`spring.profiles`, in a YAML file with the triple-dash separators, lets us put multiple profiles in the same `application.yml` configuration file. To launch an application with a given profile, we merely need to run it with `spring.profiles.active=peer1` or `SPRING_PROFILES_ACTIVE=peer1`. As stated, this configuration file has two profiles, `peer1` and `peer2`.

Assuming we launched two separate copies of our Eureka Server, each on a different port running each profile, they would seek each other out, register as clients to each other, send heartbeats, and synchronize their registry data. It's left as an exercise for the reader to spin up a pair of Eureka Servers.

Going back to the original configuration file we wrote, we can now run `LearningSpringBootEurekaServerApplication`. With this service running in the background, we can now embark on converting our previous monolith into a set of microservices.

Introducing @SpringCloudApplication

If you haven't caught on by now, we plan to split up the system we've built so far so that one microservice focuses on images, and the other on comments. That way, in the future, we can scale each service with the appropriate number of instances based on traffic.

To make this break, let's basically grab all the code from the `comments` subpackage, and move it into an entirely different project. We'll call one project `images` and the other one `comments`.

Before we can copy all that code, we need a project for each. To do so, simply create two new folders, `learning-spring-boot-comments` and `learning-spring-boot-images`. We could go back to Spring Initializr to create them from scratch, but that's unnecessary. It's much easier to simply copy the existing build file of our monolith into both of our new microservices, and customize the name of the artifact. Since the `build.gradle` file is almost identical to the monolith, there's no need to inspect it here.

The new `comments` microservice file layout should look something like this:

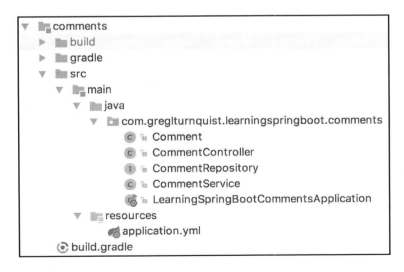

And the new `images` microservice file layout should appear something like this:

```
▼  images
   ►  build
   ►  gradle
   ▼  src
      ▼  main
         ▼  java
            ▼  com.greglturnquist.learningspringboot
               ▼  images
                     C  Comment
                     C  CommentController
                     C  Config
                     C  Image
                     I  ImageRepository
                     C  ImageService
                     C  InitDatabase
                     C  UploadController
               ▼  ops
                     C  CustomMetrics
                     C  LearningSpringBootHealthIndicator
                  C  CommentSimulator
                  C  HomeController
                  C  LearningSpringBootImagesApplication
         ▼  resources
            ►  static
            ▼  templates
                  index.html
               application.yml
      ►  test
   ►  upload-dir
      build.gradle
```

With that completed, we now need to tweak the launcher for our `comments` microservice like this:

```java
@SpringCloudApplication
public class LearningSpringBootCommentsApplication {

    public static void main(String[] args) {
        SpringApplication.run(
            LearningSpringBootCommentsApplication.class);
    }
}
```

This last bit of code is, virtually, identical to what we have seen in previous chapters except for the following:

- `@SpringCloudApplication` replaces the previous `@SpringBootApplication`. This new annotation extends `@SpringBootApplication`, giving us the same autoconfiguration, component scanning, and property support (among other things) that we have come to love. Additionally, it adds `@EnableDiscoveryClient` to register with Eureka and `@EnableCircuitBreaker` so we can create fallback commands if a remote service is down (something we'll see explored later in this chapter).
- The name of the class has been changed to better describe its job.

There are both `@EnableEurekaClient` and `@EnableDiscoveryClient` annotations available. `DiscoveryClient` is the abstract interface that Spring Cloud Netflix puts above `EurekaClient` in the event that future service registry tools are built. At this point in time, there is little difference in our code, except the convenient usage of a single annotation,`@SpringCloudApplication`, to turn our component into a microservice.

Having split up `images` and `comments`, we should make a similar adjustment to the top-level class for `images`:

```
@SpringCloudApplication
public class LearningSpringBootImagesApplication {

  public static void main(String[] args) {
    SpringApplication.run(
      LearningSpringBootImagesApplication.class, args);
  }
}
```

In the preceding code, we have applied the same type to the `images` microservice as we did to the `comments` microservice (`@SpringBootApplication` → `@SpringCloudApplication`).

For each of our microservices to talk to Eureka, we need to add the following code to `src/main/resources/application.yml` (in both `images` and `comments`):

```
eureka:
  client:
    serviceUrl:
      defaultZone: http://localhost:8761/eureka/
```

This single-property configuration file can be described as follows:

- `eureka.client.serviceUrl.defaultZone` instructs our `DiscoveryClient`-powered application to look for Eureka at `http://localhost:8761/eureka`.

 There are many more options for configuring Eureka and its clients. See `http://cloud.spring.io/spring-cloud-netflix/spring-cloud-netflix.html` for more details.

We can now move forward with splitting up our system.

Calling one microservice from another with client-side load balancing

Remember how we configured our Eureka Server earlier to run on a separate port? Every microservice has to run on a distinct port. If we assume the `images` service is our frontend (it has the Thymeleaf template, and is closest to consumers for serving up image data), then we can let it continue to run on Netty's default port of `8080`.

That leaves one decision: what port to run the `comments` service on? Let's add this to the `comments` service's `application.yml`:

```
server:
  port: 9000
```

This setting instructs Spring Boot to run `comments` on port `9000`. With that in place, let's go back to `images`, and make some adjustments.

For starters (Spring Boot starters), we need to add some extra things to the `images` `build.gradle` file:

```
compile('org.springframework.cloud:spring-cloud-starter-eureka')
compile('org.springframework.cloud:spring-cloud-starter-hystrix')
```

These changes include the following:

- `spring-cloud-starter-eureka` is the dependency needed to register our microservice as a Eureka client. It brings in several transitive dependencies, the most important one for this section being **Ribbon**.
- `spring-cloud-starter-hystrix` is the dependency for the circuit-breaker pattern, which we will dig into later in this chapter.

The Spring Framework has had, for a long time, the powerful `RestTemplate` utility. To make a remote call, we just do something like this:

```
List<Comment> comments = restTemplate.exchange(
  "http://localhost:9000/comments/{imageId}",
  HttpMethod.GET,
  null,
  new ParameterizedTypeReference<List<Comment>>() {},
  image.getId()).getBody();
```

There's a lot going on here, so let's take it apart:

- `restTemplate.exchange()` is the generic method for making remote calls. There are shortcuts such as `getForObject()` and `getForEntity()`, but when dealing with generics (such as `List<Comment>`), we need to switch to `exchange()`.
- The first argument is the URL to the `comments` service that we just picked. It has the port number we selected along with the route (`/comments/{imageId}`, a template) where we can serve up a list of comments based on the image's ID.
- The second argument is the HTTP verb we wish to use--GET.
- The third argument is for headers and any body. Since this is a GET, there are none.
- The fourth argument is the return type of the data. Due to limitations of Java's generics and type erasure, we have created a dedicated anonymous class to capture the type details for `List<Comment>`, which Spring can use to interact with Jackson to properly deserialize.
- The final argument is the parameter (`image.getId()`) that will be used to expand our URI template's `{imageId}` field.
- Since `exchange()` returns a Spring `ResponseEntity<T>`, we need to invoke the `body()` method to extract the response body.

There is a big limitation in this code when dealing with microservices--the URL of our target service can change.

Getting locked into a fixed location is never good. What if the comments service changes ports? What if we need to scale up multiple copies in the future?

Frankly, that's unacceptable.

The solution? We should tie in with Netflix's Ribbon service, a software load balancer that also integrates with Eureka. To do so, we only need some small additions to our images service.

First, we should create a RestTemplate object. To do so, let's add a Config class as follows:

```
@Configuration
public class Config {

  @Bean
  @LoadBalanced
  RestTemplate restTemplate() {
    return new RestTemplate();
  }
}
```

We can describe the preceding code as follows:

- @Configuration marks this as a configuration class containing bean definitions. Since it's located underneath LearningSpringBootImagesApplication, it will be automatically picked up by component scanning.
- @Bean marks the restTemplate() method as a bean definition.
- The restTemplate() method returns a plain old Spring RestTemplate instance.
- @LoadBalanced instructs Netflix Ribbon to wrap this RestTemplate bean with load balancing advice.

We can next inject our `RestTemplate` bean into the `HomeController` like this:

```
private final RestTemplate restTemplate;

public HomeController(ImageService imageService,
  RestTemplate restTemplate) {
    this.imageService = imageService;
    this.restTemplate = restTemplate;
}
```

This uses constructor injection to set the controller's final copy of `restTemplate`.

With a **load-balanced, Eureka-aware** `restTemplate`, we can now update our `index()` method to populate the `comments` model attribute like this:

```
restTemplate.exchange(
  "http://COMMENTS/comments/{imageId}",
  HttpMethod.GET,
  null,
  new ParameterizedTypeReference<List<Comment>>() {},
  image.getId()).getBody());
```

This code is almost identical to what we typed out earlier except for one difference--the URL has been revamped into `http://COMMENTS/comments/{imageId}`. COMMENTS is the logical name that our `comments` microservice registered itself with in Eureka.

The logical name for a microservice used by Eureka and Ribbon is set using `spring.application.name` inside its `src/main/resources/application.yml` file:

- comments: spring.application.name: comments
- images: spring.application.name: images

The logical name is case insensitive, so you can use either `http://COMMENTS/comments/{imageId}` or `http://comments/comments/{imageId}`. Uppercase helps make it clear that this is a logical hostname, not a physical one.

With this in place, it doesn't matter where we deploy our system nor how many instances are running. Eureka will dynamically update things, and also support multiple copies registered under the same name. Ribbon will handle routing between all instances.

That's nice except that we still need to move the `CommentReadRepository` we built in the previous chapter to the `comments` microservice!

In the previous chapter, we differentiated between reading comments with a
`CommentReadRepository` and writing comments with a `CommentWriteRepository`.
Since we are concentrating all MongoDB operations in one microservice, it makes sense to
merge both of these into one `CommentRepository` like this:

```
public interface CommentRepository
  extends Repository<Comment, String> {

    Flux<Comment> findByImageId(String imageId);

    Flux<Comment> saveAll(Flux<Comment> newComment);

    // Required to support save()
    Mono<Comment> findById(String id);

    Mono<Void> deleteAll();
}
```

Our newly built repository can be described as follows:

- We've renamed it as `CommentRepository`
- It still extends `Repository<Comment, String>`, indicating it only has the
  methods we need
- The `findByImageId()`, `save()`, `findOne()`, and `deleteAll()` methods are all
  simply copied into this one interface

> It's generally recommended to avoid sharing databases between
> microservices, or at least avoid sharing the same tables. The temptation to
> couple in the database is strong, and can even lead to integrating through
> the database. Hence, the reason to move ALL MongoDB comment
> operations to one place nicely isolates things.

Using this repository, we need to build a REST controller to serve up lists of comments from
`/comments/{imageId}`:

```
@RestController
public class CommentController {

    private final CommentRepository repository;

    public CommentController(CommentRepository repository) {
        this.repository = repository;
    }

    @GetMapping("/comments/{imageId}")
```

```
    public Flux<Comment> comments(@PathVariable String imageId) {
      return repository.findByImageId(imageId);
    }
  }
```

This previous tiny controller can be easily described as follows:

- `@RestController` indicates this is a Spring WebFlux controller where all results are written directly into the HTTP response body
- `CommentRepository` is injected into a field using constructor injection
- `@GetMapping()` configures this method to respond to GET `/comments/{imageId}` requests.
- `@PathVariable String imageId` gives us access to the `{imageId}` piece of the route
- The method returns a `Flux` of comments by invoking our repository's `findByImage()` using the `imageId`

Having coded things all the way from populating the UI with comments in our `images` service, going through Ribbon and Eureka, to our `comments` service, we are fetching comments from the system responsible for managing them.

 `RestTemplate` doesn't speak Reactive Streams. It's a bit too old for that. But there is a new remote calling library in Spring Framework 5 called `WebClient`. Why aren't we using it? Because it doesn't (yet) support Eureka logical hostname resolution. Hence, the part of our application making `RestTemplate` calls is blocking. In the future, when that becomes available, I highly recommend migrating to it, based on its fluent API and support for Reactor types.

In addition to linking two microservices together with remote calls, we have decoupled comment management from image management, allowing us to scale things for efficiency and without the two systems being bound together too tightly.

With all these changes in place, let's test things out. First of all, we must ensure our Eureka Server is running:

```
  /\\ / ___'_ _ _ _(_)_ _ _ _ \ \ \ \
 ( ( )\___ | '_ | '_| | '_ \/ _` | \ \ \ \
  \\/  ___)| |_)| | | | | || (_| |  ) ) ) )
   '  |____| .__|_| |_|_| |_\__, | / / / /
 =========|_|==============|___/=/_/_/_/
 :: Spring Boot ::                (v2.0.0.M5)
2017-08-12 09:48:47.966: Setting initial instance status as:
 STARTING
2017-08-12 09:48:47.993: Initializing Eureka in region us-east-1
2017-08-12 09:48:47.993: Client configured to neither register nor
 que...
2017-08-12 09:48:47.998: Discovery Client initialized at timestamp
 150...
2017-08-12 09:48:48.042: Initializing ...
2017-08-12 09:48:48.044: The replica size seems to be empty.
 Check the...
2017-08-12 09:48:48.051: Finished initializing remote region
 registrie...
2017-08-12 09:48:48.051: Initialized
2017-08-12 09:48:48.261: Registering application unknown with
 eureka w...
2017-08-12 09:48:48.294: Setting the eureka configuration..
2017-08-12 09:48:48.294: Eureka data center value eureka.datacenter
 is...
2017-08-12 09:48:48.294: Eureka environment value
 eureka.environment i...
2017-08-12 09:48:48.302: isAws returned false
2017-08-12 09:48:48.303: Initialized server context
2017-08-12 09:48:48.303: Got 1 instances from neighboring DS node
2017-08-12 09:48:48.303: Renew threshold is: 1
2017-08-12 09:48:48.303: Changing status to UP
2017-08-12 09:48:48.307: Started Eureka Server
2017-08-12 09:48:48.343: Tomcat started on port(s): 8761 (http)
2017-08-12 09:48:48.343: Updating port to 8761
2017-08-12 09:48:48.347: Started
LearningSpringBootEurekaServerApplica...
```

In this preceding subset of console output, bits of Eureka can be seen as it starts up on port 8761 and switches to a state of UP. It may seem quirky to see messages about **Amazon Web Services (AWS)**, but that's not surprising given Eureka's creators (Netflix) run all their systems there. However, isAws returned false clearly shows the system knows it is NOT running on AWS.

 If you look closely, you can spot that the Eureka Server is running on Apache Tomcat. So far, we've run everything on Netty, right? Since Eureka is a separate process not involved in direct operations, it's okay for it not to be a Reactive Streams-based application.

Next, we can fire up the images service:

```
  .   ____          _            __ _ _
 /\\ / ___'_ __ _ _(_)_ __  __ _ \ \ \ \
( ( )\___ | '_ | '_| | '_ \/ _` | \ \ \ \
 \\/  ___)| |_)| | | | | || (_| |  ) ) ) )
  '  |____| .__|_| |_|_| |_\__, | / / / /
 =========|_|==============|___/=/_/_/_/
 :: Spring Boot ::   (v2.0.0.M5)
 ...
2017-10-20 22:29:34.319: Registering application images with eureka
 wi...
2017-10-20 22:29:34.320: Saw local status change event
 StatusChangeEve...
2017-10-20 22:29:34.321: DiscoveryClient_IMAGES/retina:images:
 registe...
2017-10-20 22:29:34.515: DiscoveryClient_IMAGES/retina:images -
 regist...
2017-10-20 22:29:34.522: Netty started on port(s): 8080 (http)
2017-10-20 22:29:34.523: Updating port to 8080
2017-10-20 22:29:34.906: Opened connection
[connectionId{localValue:2,...
2017-10-20 22:29:34.977: Started
LearningSpringBootImagesApplication i...
```

This preceding subsection of console output shows it registering itself with the Eureka service through DiscoveryClient under the name IMAGES.

At the same time, the following tidbit is logged on the Eureka Server:

```
Registered instance IMAGES/retina:images with status UP
(replication=false)
```

We can easily see that the `images` service has registered itself with the name `IMAGES`, and it's running on `retina` (my machine name).

Finally, let's launch the `comments` microservice:

```
  /\\ /  ___'_ _ _ _(_)_ _ _ _ \ \ \ \
 ( ( )\___ | '_ | '_| | '_ \/ _` | \ \ \ \
  \\/  ___)| |_)| | | | | || (_| |  ) ) ) )
   '  |____| .__|_| |_|_| |_\__, | / / / /
  =========|_|==============|___/=/_/_/_/
  :: Spring Boot ::    (v2.0.0.M5)
  ...
  2016-10-20 22:37:31.477: Registering application comments with
   eureka ...
  2016-10-20 22:37:31.478: Saw local status change event
   StatusChangeEve...
  2016-10-20 22:37:31.480:
   DiscoveryClient_COMMENTS/retina:comments:9000...
  2016-10-20 22:37:31.523:
   DiscoveryClient_COMMENTS/retina:comments:9000...
  2016-10-20 22:37:32.154: Netty started on port(s): 9000 (http)
  2016-10-20 22:37:32.155: Updating port to 9000
  2016-10-20 22:37:32.188: Opened connection
   [connectionId{localValue:2,...
  2016-10-20 22:37:32.209: Started
  LearningSpringBootCommentsApplication...
```

In this last output, our comment handling microservice has registered itself with Eureka under the logical name `COMMENTS`.

And again, in the Eureka Server logs, we can see a corresponding event:

```
Registered instance COMMENTS/retina:comments:9000 with status UP
(replication=false)
```

The `COMMENTS` service can be found at `retina:9000` (author alert--that's my laptop's hostname, yours will be different), which matches the port we configured that service to run on.

To see all this from a visual perspective, let's navigate to `http://localhost:8761`, and see Eureka's webpage:

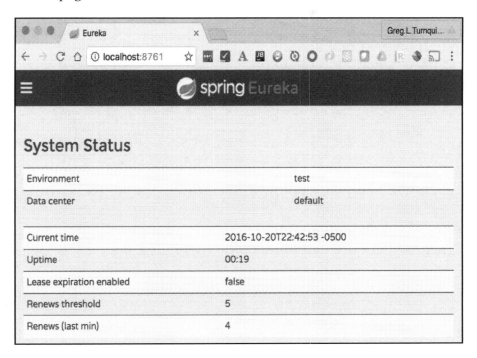

This preceding web page is not provided by Netflix Eureka, but is crafted by the Spring Cloud Netflix project (hence Spring Eureka at the top) instead. It has some basic details about the environment including uptime, refresh policies, and others.

Further down on the page is some more interesting information:

DS Replicas

Instances currently registered with Eureka

Application	AMIs	Availability Zones	Status
COMMENTS	n/a (1)	(1)	UP (1) - retina:comments:9000
IMAGES	n/a (1)	(1)	UP (1) - retina:images

DS (Discovery Service) Replica details are listed on the web page. Specifically, we can see the logical applications on the left (COMMENTS and IMAGES), their status on the right (both UP), and hyperlinks to every instance (retina:comments:9000 and retina:images).

If we actually click on the retina:comments:9000 hyperlink, it takes us to the Spring Boot info endpoint:

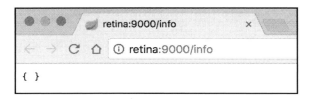

In this case, there is no custom info provided. But it also proves that the service is up and operational.

We may have verified everything is up, but let's prove that our new and improved microservice solution is in operation by visiting http://localhost:8080.

If we load up a couple of new images and submit some comments, things can now look like this:

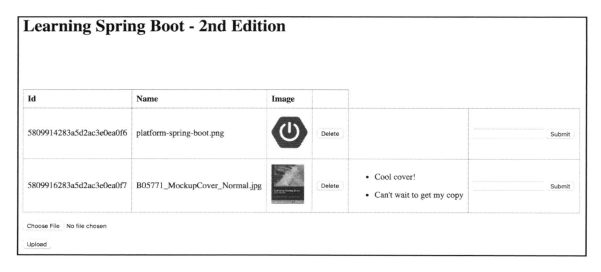

What's happening under the hood? If we look at the `images` microservice's console, we can see a little action:

```
2016-10-20 22:53:07.260  Flipping property:
COMMENTS.ribbon.ActiveConn...
2016-10-20 22:53:07.286  Shutdown hook installed for:
NFLoadBalancer-P...
2016-10-20 22:53:07.305  Client:COMMENTS instantiated a
LoadBalancer:D...
2016-10-20 22:53:07.308  Using serverListUpdater
PollingServerListUpda...
2016-10-20 22:53:07.325  Flipping property:
COMMENTS.ribbon.ActiveConn...
2016-10-20 22:53:07.326  DynamicServerListLoadBalancer for client
COMM...
    DynamicServerListLoadBalancer: {
        NFLoadBalancer:name=COMMENTS,
        current list of Servers=[retina:9000],
    }ServerList:org.springframework.cloud.netflix
    .ribbon.eureka.DomainExt...
2016-10-20 22:53:08.313  Flipping property:
COMMENTS.ribbon.ActiveConn...
2016-10-20 22:54:33.870  Resolving eureka endpoints via
configuration
```

There's a lot of detail in the preceding output, but we can see **Netflix Ribbon** at work handling software load balancing. We can also see `DynamicServerListLoadBalancer` with a current list of servers containing `[retina:9000]`.

So, what would happen if we launched a second copy of the `comments` service using `SERVER_PORT=9001` to ensure it didn't clash with the current one?

In the console output, we can spot the new instance registering itself with Eureka:

```
DiscoveryClient_COMMENTS/retina:comments:9001 - registration
status: 204
```

If we go back and visit the Spring Eureka web page again at `http://localhost:8761`, we can see this updated listing of replicas:

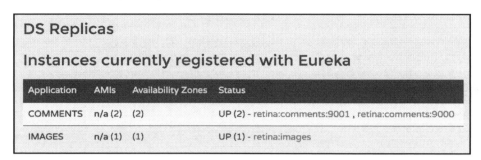

Application	AMIs	Availability Zones	Status
COMMENTS	n/a (2)	(2)	UP (2) - retina:comments:9001 , retina:comments:9000
IMAGES	n/a (1)	(1)	UP (1) - retina:images

If we start posting comments on the site, they will rotate, going between each `comments` microservice.

Normally, when using RabbitMQ, each instance of `comments` will register its own queue, and hence, receive its own copy of newly posted comments. This would result in double posting in this scenario. However, Spring Cloud Stream has a solution--**consumer groups**. By having `spring.cloud.stream.bindings.input.group=comments` in `comments` microservice's `application.yml`, we declare that only one such queue should receive each individual message. This ensures that only one of the microservices *actually* processes a given event. See `http://docs.spring.io/spring-cloud-stream/docs/Elmhurst.M1/refer ence/htmlsingle/index.html#consumer-groups` for more details.

With microservice-to-microservice remote calls tackled (and supported for scaling up), it's time to pursue another problem often seen in microservice-based solutions.

Implementing microservice circuit breakers

The ability to invoke a remote microservice comes with an implicit risk--there is always a chance that the remote service is down.

Remember using @SpringCloudApplication? As a reminder, that annotation contains:

```
@SpringBootApplication
@EnableDiscoveryClient
@EnableCircuitBreaker
public @interface SpringCloudApplication {
}
```

The last annotation, @EnableCircuitBreaker, enables **Netflix Hystrix**, the circuit breaker solution (http://martinfowler.com/bliki/CircuitBreaker.html).

In short, a circuit breaker is something that, when it detects a certain threshold of failure, will open the circuit and prevent any future remote calls for a certain amount of time. The purpose is to prevent cascade failures while giving the remote service an opportunity to heal itself and come back online. Slamming a service in the middle of startup might be detrimental.

For example, if the images microservice's HomeController makes a call to comments, and the system is down, it's possible for the calling thread to get hung up waiting for the request to timeout properly. In the meantime, incoming requests are served by a slightly reduced threadpool. If the problem is bad enough, it can hamper calls coming into the frontend controller, effectively spreading the remote service outage to users.

A side effect when operating multiple instances of such a service is that it can also speed up the failover to an alternate instance of the service.

In exchange for opening the circuit on a service (and failing a call), we can provide a fallback command. For example, if Netflix's recommendation engine happens to be down when a user finishes a show, it will fallback to showing a list of newly released shows. This is definitely better than a blank screen, or, worse, a cryptic stack trace on the website or someone's TV.

In the previous section, we had this fragment of code inside HomeController.index():

```
restTemplate.exchange(
  "http://COMMENTS/comments/{imageId}",
  HttpMethod.GET,
  null,
  new ParameterizedTypeReference<List<Comment>>() {},
  image.getId()).getBody());
```

We want to wrap this remote call to the comments system with a circuit breaker/fallback command.

First, we need to move the code into a separate method as follows:

```
@HystrixCommand(fallbackMethod = "defaultComments")
public List<Comment> getComments(Image image) {
  return restTemplate.exchange(
    "http://COMMENTS/comments/{imageId}",
    HttpMethod.GET,
    null,
    new ParameterizedTypeReference<List<Comment>>() {},
    image.getId()).getBody();

}
```

This tiny Hystrix command can be described as follows:

- This shows the exact same `restTemplate` call we wrote using Ribbon and Eureka earlier in this chapter
- `@HystrixCommand(fallback="defaultComments")` wraps the method with an aspect that hooks into a Hystrix proxy
- In the event the remote call fails, Hystrix will call `defaultComments`

What would make a good fallback command? Since we're talking about user comments, there is nothing better than an empty list, so a separate method with the same signature would be perfect:

```
public List<Comment> defaultComments(Image image) {
  return Collections.emptyList();
}
```

In this scenario, we return an empty list. But what makes a suitable fallback situation will invariably depend on the business context.

Hystrix commands operate using Spring **AOP (Aspect Oriented Programming)**. The standard approach is through Java proxies (as opposed to AspectJ weaving, which requires extra setup). A well-known issue with proxies is that in-class invocations don't trigger the enclosing advice. Hence, the Hystrix command method must be put inside another Spring bean, and injected into our controller.

There is some classic advice to offer when talking about Hystrix's AOP **advice**--be careful about using thread locals. However, the recommendation against thread locals is even stronger when we are talking about Reactor-powered applications, the basis for this entire book. That's because Project Reactor uses **work stealing**, a well-documented concept that involves different threads pulling work down when idle. Reactor's scheduler is thread agnostic, which means that we don't know where the work is actually being carried out. So don't use thread locals when writing Reactor applications. This impacts other areas too such as Spring Security, which uses thread locals to maintain contextual security status with SecurityContextHolder. We'll visit this subject in Chapter 9, *Securing Your App with Spring Boot*.

The following shows our method pulled into a separate class:

```
@Component
public class CommentHelper {
  private final RestTemplate restTemplate;

  CommentHelper(RestTemplate restTemplate) {
    this.restTemplate = restTemplate;
  }

  // @HystrixCommand code shown earlier

  // fallback method
}
```

We've already seen the @HystrixCommand code as well as the fallback. The other parts we wrote include:

- The CommentHelper class is flagged with an @Component annotation, so, it's picked up and registered as a separate Spring bean
- This component is injected with the restTemplate we defined earlier via constructor injection

To update our HomeController to use this instead, we need to adjust its injection point:

```
private final CommentHelper commentHelper;

public HomeController(ImageService imageService,
 CommentHelper commentHelper) {
   this.imageService = imageService;
   this.commentHelper = commentHelper;
}
```

The code in `HomeController` is almost the same, except that instead of injecting a `RestTemplate`, **it injects** `commentHelper`.

Finally, the call to populate comments in the `index()` method can be updated to use the new `commentHelper`:

```
put("comments", commentHelper.getComments(image));
```

At this point, instead of calling `restTemplate` to make a remote call, we are invoking `commentHelper`, which is wrapped with Hystrix advice to handle failures, and, potentially, open a circuit.

Notice earlier that I said, *"In the event the remote call fails, Hystrix will call defaultComments."*, but didn't mention anything about opening the circuit? Perhaps that's confusing, since this whole section has been about the circuit breaker pattern. Hystrix tabulates every failure, and *only* opens the circuit when a certain threshold has been breached. One missed remote call isn't enough to switch to an offline state.

Monitoring circuits

Okay, we've coded up a command with a circuit breaker, and given it a fallback command in the event the remote service is down. But how can we monitor it? Simply put--how can we detect if the circuit is open or closed?

Introducing the **Hystrix Dashboard**. With just a smidgeon of code, we can have another Spring Boot application provide us with a graphical view of things. And from there, we can test out what happens if we put the system under load, and then break the system.

To build the app, we first need to visit `http://start.spring.io`, and select **Hystrix Dashboard** and `Turbine`. If we also select `Gradle` and `Spring Boot 2.0.0`, and enter in our similar artifact details, we can produce another app. (Notice how handy it is to simply let *everything* be a Spring Boot app?)

The build file is the same except for these dependency settings:

```
buildscript {
  ext {
    springBootVersion = '2.0.0.M5'
    springCloudVersion = 'Finchley.M3'
  }
  ...
}
```

```
...
dependencies {
  compile('org.springframework.cloud:spring-cloud-starter-
    hystrix-dashboard')
}

dependencyManagement {
  imports {
    mavenBom "org.springframework.cloud:spring-cloud-
      dependencies:${springCloudVersion}"
  }
}
```

We can explain this preceding build file as follows:

- We pick up `spring-cloud-starter-hystrix-dashboard` to build a UI for monitoring circuits
- Again, we select Spring Cloud's **Finchley** BOM release with the `dependencyManagement` settings

To display the Hystrix dashboard, this is all we need:

```
@SpringBootApplication
@EnableHystrixDashboard
public class LearningSpringBootHystrixDashboard {

  public static void main(String[] args) {
    SpringApplication.run(
      LearningSpringBootHystrixDashboard.class);
  }
}
```

This previous tiny application can be described as such:

- `@SpringBootApplication` declares this to be a Spring Boot application. We don't need `@SpringCloudApplication`, because we don't intend to hook into Eureka, nor institute any circuit breakers.
- `@EnableHystrixDashboard` will start up a UI that we'll explore further in this section.
- The class `public static void main` is used to launch this class.

To configure this service, we need the following settings:

```
server:
  port: 7979
```

Hystrix Dashboard is usually run on port 7979.

With this in place, let's launch the application and take a peek. To see the dashboard, we must navigate to `http://localhost:7979/hystrix`:

Here we have a pretty simple interface, as seen in the preceding screenshot. It tells us we have options regarding what we want to view. The simplest variant is to have the dashboard look at one microservice's collection of circuits. This preceding screenshot shows the URL for the `images` service, the one we wrote a `@HystrixCommand` for.

Since each microservice that has `@EnableCircuitBreaker` (pulled in via `@SpringCloudApplication`) has a `/hystrix.stream` endpoint outputting circuit metrics, we can enter that service's URL.

After clicking `Monitor Stream`, we can see this nice visual display of our single circuit:

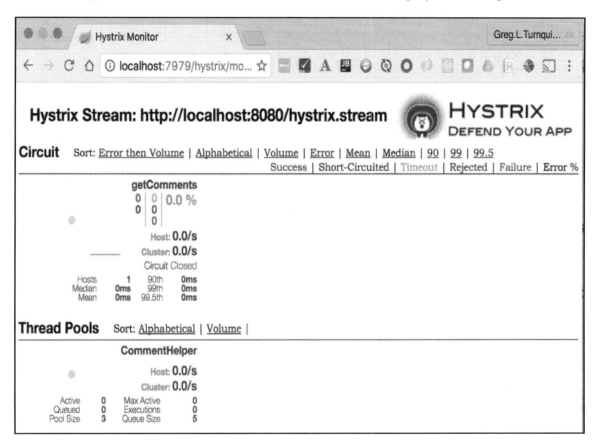

There's a lot on the preceding screen, so let's break it down:

- Across the top is the ability to sort various circuits based on different criteria. We only have one circuit, so it's not that important.
- `getComments` is shown underneath `Circuit`. The color coding of the numbers runs across the top, from `Success` to `Failure`, with everything currently showing 0.

- There is an overall failure percentage (also at 0%).
- There is a rate of activity for the host and for the cluster (also at 0/second).
- It may be hard to spot, but there's a flat horizontal line just left of Cluster. This will actually update based on traffic, showing spikes.
- Finally, it tracks the cost of making remote calls, and includes some statistics such as **Mean**, **Median**, **90** percentile, **95** percentile, and **99.5** percentile.
- The `Thread Pools` section can show how taxed the system is from a threading perspective. This can help us tune `@HystrixCommand` if we need to adjust thread-pool settings.

With circuit monitoring set up, why don't we institute a failure, and watch the whole thing go down and then recover?

To do that, we need to update our simulator that we created earlier in this book:

```
@Profile("simulator")
@Component
public class CommentSimulator {

    private final HomeController homeController;
    private final CommentController commentController;
    private final ImageRepository repository;

    private final AtomicInteger counter;

    public CommentSimulator(HomeController homeController,
      CommentController commentController,
      ImageRepository repository) {
        this.homeController = homeController;
        this.commentController = commentController;
        this.repository = repository;
        this.counter = new AtomicInteger(1);
    }

    @EventListener
    public void simulateComments(ApplicationReadyEvent event) {
      Flux
        .interval(Duration.ofMillis(1000))
        .flatMap(tick -> repository.findAll())
        .map(image -> {
          Comment comment = new Comment();
          comment.setImageId(image.getId());
          comment.setComment(
            "Comment #" + counter.getAndIncrement());
            return Mono.just(comment);
```

```
        })
        .flatMap(newComment ->
         Mono.defer(() ->
          commentController.addComment(newComment)))
          .subscribe();
    }

    @EventListener
    public void simulateUsersClicking(ApplicationReadyEvent event) {
      Flux
         .interval(Duration.ofMillis(500))
         .flatMap(tick ->
         Mono.defer(() ->
          homeController.index(new BindingAwareModelMap())))
          .subscribe();
    }
  }
```

The following are some key points to note about this preceding code:

- The @Profile annotation indicates that this component is only active when spring.profiles.active=simulator is set in the environment variables.
- By constructor injection, it gets copies of both, CommentController and HomeController.
- simulateActivity() is triggered when Spring Boot generates an ApplicationReadyEvent.
- The Flux generates a tick every 1000 ms. This tick is transformed into a request for all images, and then a new comment is created against each one, simulating user activity.
- simulateUsersClicking() is also triggered by the same ApplicationReadyEvent. It has a different Flux that simulates a user loading the home page every 500 ms.

In both of these simulation flows, the downstream activity needs to be wrapped in a Mono.defer in order to provide a target Mono for the downstream provider to subscribe to.

Finally, both of these Reactor flows must be subscribed to, or they will never run.

If we relaunch the `images` service, and watch the Hystrix Dashboard, we get a nice, rosy picture:

The bubble on the left of the preceding screenshot is green, and the green **60** at the top indicates that the volume of traffic for its window of monitoring shows **60** successful hits. Looking at the rate (**6.0/s**), we can deduce this is a 10-second window.

> I realize that in print, the bubble along with all the numbers are gray, but you can tell success/failure by noting that the circuit is **Closed**, meaning, traffic is flowing through it.

Let's switch over to our IDE, and kill the `comments` microservice:

> This preceding screenshot shows IntelliJ IDEA. Your IDE's kill switch may appear different.

If we jump back to the dashboard, things look very different:

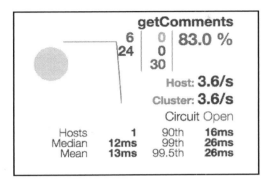

The 10 second window shows **6** successful calls, **30** failed calls, and **24** short circuited calls. The horizontal status line takes a precipitous drop, and the green bubble has now turned red. Additionally, the circuit is now **Open**.

 Again, you may not be able to discern the bubble is red in print, but the circuit is now **Open**, indicating the failures are being replaced with short-circuited calls.

If we follow this outage a little longer, things migrate all the way to 100% failure:

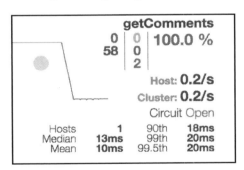

Now there are only two failures with **58** short-circuited calls. In essence, with the circuit **Open**, there is no point in trying to make remote calls and wasting resources. Instead, we use the fallback method without question. We can also see the graph has flatlined at the bottom.

We can simulate our ops team rushing in and fixing things by restarting the `comments` service:

With a little bit of time, this service will come back up and re-register with Eureka, making it available. After that, the circuit breaker must wait a minimum amount of time before a remote call will even be attempted.

Hystrix's default setting is 50% failure or higher to open the circuit. Another subtle property is that a minimum number of requests must be made to possibly open the circuit. The default is 20, meaning that 19 failures in a row would not open it. When the circuit is opened, Hystrix keeps the circuit open a minimum amount of time before looking at the rolling window (default: 5000 ms). Hystrix maintains a rolling window, by default, 10 seconds split up into 10 buckets. As a new bucket of metrics is gathered, the oldest is dropped. This collection of buckets is what is examined when deciding whether or not to open the circuit.

 As you can see, there is a lot of sophistication to Hystrix's metrics. We'll just use the defaults here. But if you're interested in adjusting Hystrix's various settings, visit `https://github.com/Netflix/Hystrix/wiki/configuration` where all its parameters are documented.

When we make a remote call, the circuit is immediately closed:

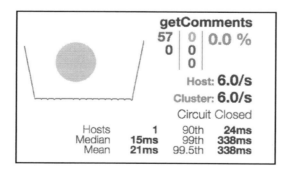

Successful calls climbs to **57**, and the number of short-circuited and failed calls clears out in a few seconds time. The graph turns around and climbs back up, showing a nice recovery.

> The circuit breaker we have in place watches REST calls from `images` to `comments`. The means the mechanism by which new `comments` are sent over the wire via RabbitMQ is, inherently, fault tolerant. While `comments` was down, the new comments pile up in RabbitMQ's exchange until the queue restored itself, and the system caught up.

This nice little scenario shows how we can keep a visual eye on microservice-to-microservice operations.

Offloading microservice settings to a configuration server

One thing that quickly adds up when building a microservice-based solution are all the properties that must be managed. It's one thing to manage a single application's `application.yml` file, and make tweaks and adjustments. But working with all these services, and having to jump to the correct file underneath each application's `src/main/resources` folder quickly becomes daunting. On top of that, when trying to make changes or adjustments, it is easy to overlook the settings of one microservice.

A key piece of the twelve-factor app (`https://12factor.net/`) is externalizing configuration. We already took a big step using Spring Boot's powerful property support. But Spring Cloud brings another key technology to the table that takes property support to the next level--**Spring Cloud Config Server**.

The **Config Server** let's us put all the properties into a centralized location, and feed them via an application to our existing microservices.

To see how, let's dive into creating one. First, go to `http://start.spring.io` and select `Config Server` (along with our other favorite settings).

When we do that, we get a familiar Gradle build file containing the following dependencies:

```
buildscript {
  ext {
    springBootVersion = '2.0.0.M5'
    springCloudVersion = 'Finchley.M3'
  }
  ...
}
...
dependencies {
  compile('org.springframework.cloud:spring-cloud-config-server')
}

dependencyManagement {
  imports {
    mavenBom "org.springframework.cloud:spring-cloud-
      dependencies:${springCloudVersion}"
  }
}
```

We can explain this preceding build file as follows:

- `spring-cloud-starter-config-server` is only needed to run a config server, not a config server client
- The `dependencyManagement` shows us the release train of Spring Cloud we are using

In a way very analogous to the Hystrix Dashboard, we will create a Config Server:

```
@SpringBootApplication
@EnableConfigServer
public class LearningSpringBootConfigServer {

  public static void main(String[] args) {
    SpringApplication.run(
      LearningSpringBootConfigServer.class, args);
  }
}
```

This preceding app isn't hard to unravel:

- `@SpringBootApplication` marks this as a Spring Boot application. Since this is the cornerstone of the rest of our microservices (including Eureka), it doesn't use Eureka.
- `@EnableConfigServer` launches an embedded Spring Cloud Config Server, full of options. We'll use the defaults as much as possible.
- It has a `public static void main` to launch itself.

With that, we just need a couple of property settings in `application.yml`:

```
server:
  port: 8888
spring:
  cloud:
    config:
      server:
        git:
          uri: https://github.com/gregturn/learning-spring-boot-
            config-repo
```

- Let's set its port to `8888`, since that is the default port for Spring Cloud Config clients
- By setting `spring.cloud.config.server.git.uri` to `https://github.com/gregturn/learning-spring-boot-config-repo`, we tell the Config Server where to get its property settings for all the other services

That's it! That's all we need to build a Config Server. We can launch it right now, but there is one thing missing--all the other properties of the application!

To configure properties for our Eureka Server, we need to add a `eureka.yml` that looks like this:

```
server:
  port: 8761

eureka:
  instance:
    hostname: localhost
  client:
    registerWithEureka: false
    fetchRegistry: false
    serviceUrl:
      defaultZone:
        http://${eureka.instance.hostname}:${server.port}/eureka/
```

If you'll notice, this is the *exact* same setting we put into the Eureka Server's `application.yml` earlier in this chapter. We are simply moving it into our config repo.

To make our Eureka Server talk to a Config Server, we need to add this to its build file:

```
compile('org.springframework.cloud:spring-cloud-starter-config')
```

What does this single dependency do?

- `spring-cloud-starter-config` empowers the Eureka Server to talk to the Config Server for property settings

 It's important to note that `spring-cloud-starter-config` is for *clients* to the Config Server. The dependency that was added to the Config Server itself was `spring-cloud-starter-config-server`, which is only needed to create a Config Server.

There is a certain order by which Spring Boot launches things. Suffice it to say, property sources must be read early in the Spring lifecycle in order to work properly. For this reason, Spring Cloud Config clients *must* have a `bootstrap.yml` file. The one for the Eureka Server must look like this:

```
spring:
  application:
    name: eureka
```

Not a whole lot needs to be in here, but at a minimum, `spring.application.name` needs to be set so that the Config Server knows which property file to fetch from its config repo. By default, Spring Cloud Config clients will seek `{spring.application.name}.yml`, so in this case, `eureka.yml`.

Assuming we have committed `eureka.yml` to our GitHub-based config repo and launched the config server, we can actually see what is served up:

```
1    // 20170813194344
2    // http://localhost:8888/eureka/default
3
4  ▾ {
5      "name": "eureka",
6  ▾   "profiles": [
7        "default"
8      ],
9      "label": null,
10     "version": "a69475c00e47bc91949e76c79d2df39720967a21",
11     "state": null,
12 ▾   "propertySources": [
13 ▾     {
14         "name": "https://github.com/gregturn/learning-spring-boot-config-repo/eureka.yml",
15 ▾       "source": {
16           "server.port": 8761,
17           "eureka.instance.hostname": "localhost",
18           "eureka.client.registerWithEureka": false,
19           "eureka.client.fetchRegistry": false,
20           "eureka.client.serviceUrl.defaultZone": "http://${eureka.instance.hostname}:${server.port}/eureka/"
21         }
22       }
23     ]
24   }
```

Let's tear apart the details of this preceding screenshot:

- `http://localhost:8888/eureka/default` looks up `spring.application.name=eureka`, and finds the default state of things
- The name `eureka` is at the top along with information like its label and SHA version
- The config server entry lists the available Spring property sources (`eureka.yml`) along with each property found in that property source

It's possible to retrieve different versions of configuration settings. All we have to do is set `spring.cloud.config.label=foo` in `bootstrap.yml` to fetch an alternative label. When we use Git as the repository, a label can refer to either a branch or a tag.

In essence, the Spring Cloud Config Server is Yet Another Way™ to craft a property source that the Spring Framework can intrinsically consume.

Next, let's move all the properties for `images` from its `application.yml` file into the config repo's `images.yml` like this:

```
eureka:
  client:
    serviceUrl:
      defaultZone: http://localhost:8761/eureka/

spring:
  cloud:
    stream:
      bindings:
        output:
          destination: learning-spring-boot-comments
          group: comments-service
          content-type: application/json
```

With all these settings moved to the Config Server's `images.yml` file, we can replace the `application.yml` with the following `src/main/resources/bootstrap.yml` file:

```
spring:
  application:
    name: images
```

Earlier in this chapter, `spring.application.name=images`, along with all the other settings, were combined in `application.yml`. To work with Spring Cloud Config Server, we split out `spring.application.name`, and put it inside `bootstrap.yml`.

We can do the same for `comments` by moving all of its property settings into `comments.yml`. You can see it at https://github.com/gregturn/learning-spring-boot-config-repo/blob/master/comments.yml, if you wish, along with `hystrix-dashboard.yml`.

Instead, we'll give `comments` the following `src/main/resources/bootstrap.yml` file:

```
spring:
  application:
    name: comments
```

And do the same for our Hystrix Dashboard app:

```
spring:
  application:
    name: hystrix-dashboard
```

You know what's truly amazing about all this? We don't have to touch the services. At all.

Is running *lots* of microservices inside your IDE driving you nuts? Constantly starting and stopping can get old, real fast. IntelliJ IDEA has the Multirun (https://plugins.jetbrains.com/plugin/7248) plugin that lets you group together several launch configurations into a single command. If you use Eclipse, the CDT (C/C++ Development Tooling) module provides a component called **Launch Groups** that lets you do the same. The following screenshot shows the IntelliJ IDEA Multirun plugin configured for our microservices.

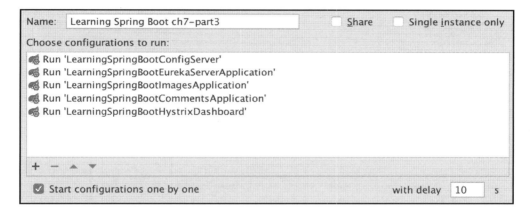

Notice the little 10 second delay in the bottom-right corner of the preceding screenshot? The Config Server needs to be up and operational before any other services start, or they'll fall on default settings.

Using the Multirun plugin, if we launch everything, we should have a nice little system up:

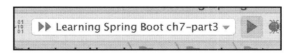

Each service, when it launches, should show something like this:

```
or : Fetching config from server at: http://localhost:8888
or : Located environment: name=comments, profiles=[default], label=master, v
on : Located property source: CompositePropertySource [name='configService',
on : No active profile set, falling back to default profiles: default
```

Without touching a line of code, and simply moving most of what we've already written into another location (or into `bootstrap.yml`), we have extracted the entire configuration of our social media site to a remote location, making configuration a snap to maintain.

So, is our little snap-a-picture social media platform ready for IPO? Heh, maybe not *yet*. But we've made a major enhancement that will make us more stable and ready for growth by breaking things up into microservices without breaking the bank.

There are *lots* of options in the Spring Cloud Config Server. You can register it with Eureka, direct clients to fail fast if it's not up, have clients retry if its down at startup, and more. Security options include the ability to secure the Config Server so that not just anyone can access it (something we'll visit in `Chapter 9`, *Securing Your App with Spring Boot*). For more details, see `http://cloud.spring.io/spring-cloud-config`.

Spring Cloud Config Server currently supports GitHub, GitLab, and Bitbucket out of the box. This means that you can quickly put your configuration on a publicly hosted GitHub repository, but you can also install GitLab inside your data center, and point there, instead, to reduce the risk of public repository outages.

Summary

In this chapter, we took a quick tour of building a microservice-based solution using several Spring Cloud projects combined with their Netflix OSS counterparts. This lets us make each component smaller, easier to maintain, and more scalable in the long run.

With little effort, we made it possible to run multiple copies of services, and not have other microservices be impacted by such changes. Services could call other services, we were able to introduce some resiliency, and we could offload the configuration of this system to an externalized, centralized repository.

In the next chapter, we will shift our focus back to user experience, and introduce Spring's WebSocket support to help make the UX more dynamic.

8
WebSockets with Spring Boot

Hell yeah @springboot rocks! (after winning JAX Innovation Award 2016)

– Andrew Rubalcaba @Han_Cholo

In the previous chapter, we learned how to split our application into microservices driven by bounded contexts. Yet, we still linked things together in an efficient manner using Spring Cloud.

When it comes to building a social media platform, the standard has been set very high. We all expect dynamic updates to whatever content we view. If someone comments on a topic that we are also viewing, we expect to be alerted to the update immediately. Such fluid changes are made possible through the power of WebSockets.

In this chapter, we will cover the following topics:

- Publishing saved comments to a chat service
- Broadcasting saved comments to web subscribers
- Configuring a WebSocket broker
- Consuming messages from the web asynchronously
- Introducing user chatting with channel-wide and user-specific messages

We will use Spring's reactive WebSocket API found in WebFlux while also using a little JavaScript in our template.

Publishing saved comments to a chat service

In the previous chapter, we connected our images service to the comments service via Spring Cloud Stream. This let us transmit new comments over the wire to a service dedicated to storing them in a MongoDB data store.

The following screenshot shows us entering a new comment:

To carry on this use case to its natural conclusion, it's expected that after storing a message, we'd want to share it with everyone, right? To do so, let's pick up with the comment microservice's CommentService.

In the previous chapter, the comments service transformed an incoming stream of Flux<Comment> into a Flux<Void>, a stream of voids. This had the effect of, essentially, dropping the stream at this point. In this chapter, we want to take that incoming stream of comments and forward them.

This is accomplished by altering the Comment.save() operation as follows:

```
@StreamListener
@Output(Processor.OUTPUT)
public Flux<Comment> save(@Input(Processor.INPUT) Flux<Comment>
  newComment) {
    return repository
     .saveAll(newComment)
     .map(comment -> {
       log.info("Saving new comment " + comment);
       meterRegistry
         .counter("comments.consumed", "imageId", comment.getImageId())
         .increment();
       return comment;
```

```
    });
  }
```

This previous code is almost identical to what we had before except for the following changes:

- The last step of the map operation now returns `comment` instead of `Mono.empty()`
- The method now has a return type of `Flux<Comment>`

With this tweak, the return results from `save()` are transmitted over the `Source.OUTPUT` channel.

 `Processor.INPUT` and `Processor.OUTPUT` are just channel names. They don't say *where* anything goes. That's why we need to configure `bindings`.

Our `comments.yml` properties file stored on the Config Server needs to be upgraded as follows:

```
server:
  port: 9000

spring:
  cloud:
    stream:
      bindings:
        input:
          destination: learning-spring-boot-comments
          group: comments-service
          content-type: application/json
        output:
          destination: learning-spring-boot-chat
          group: comments-chat
          content-type: application/json
```

The preceding code is mostly the same as the previous chapter, but with the following:

- `spring.cloud.stream.bindings.input` and its properties are the same as before
- `spring.cloud.stream.bindings.output.destination` points to a different exchange to avoid colliding with the one feeding messages *into* this service

- `spring.cloud.stream.bindings.output.group` provides a logical grouping to ensure proper handling if we ever scale up to more than one instance of `comments` service
- `spring.cloud.stream.bindings.output.content-type` is marked `application/json`, indicating we don't expect the consumer to use the same domain class, but will probably deserialize into their own POJO instead

With these changes, we can expect an output as follows:

```
2017-07-05 00:00:36.769  INFO 92207 --- [ments-service-1]
c.g.l.comments.CommentService : Saving new comment Comment(id=null,
imageId=581d6669596aec65dc9e6c05, comment=Nice cover!)
```

With all these changes, our `comments` microservice is geared up to transmit saved comments to someone else able to broadcast to users. It may be tempting to send them *back* to the `images` service. But let's continue with the concept of keeping a narrow scope, and send this traffic to a different, chat-focused microservice instead. We can even call it the `chat` service!

Creating a chat service to handle WebSocket traffic

If we visit `http://start.spring.io`, select **Gradle**, **Spring Boot 2.0**, **Eureka Discovery**, **Config Client**, **Stream Rabbit**, **Lombok**, and **Reactive Web**, we'll have a nice little service ready to chat:

```
compile('org.springframework.boot:spring-boot-starter-webflux')
compile('org.projectlombok:lombok')
compile('org.springframework.cloud:spring-cloud-starter-stream-
  rabbit')
compile('org.springframework.cloud:spring-cloud-stream-reactive')
compile('org.springframework.cloud:spring-cloud-starter-eureka')
compile('org.springframework.cloud:spring-cloud-starter-config')
```

These aforementioned dependencies in our new chat service can be described as follows:

- `spring-boot-starter-webflux`: This comes with a Reactive Streams capable WebSocket API
- `lombok`: This is the library that gets us out of the business of coding getters, setters, and other boilerplate Java code

- `spring-cloud-starter-stream-rabbit`: This is the Spring Cloud Stream library that uses RabbitMQ as the underlying technology
- `spring-cloud-stream-reactive`: This layers on Reactive Streams support
- `spring-cloud-starter-eureka`: This makes the microservice capable of registering itself with our Eureka Server and of consuming other Eureka-based services
- `spring-cloud-starter-config`: This lets the microservice get its configuration details from the Config Server

There is little value in looking at the rest of the build file, since it's the same as our other microservices.

With these dependencies, the only thing needed to make this Yet Another Microservice™ is to fashion our Spring Boot `public static void main` like this:

```
@SpringCloudApplication
@EnableEurekaClient
public class LearningSpringBootChatApplication {

  public static void main(String[] args) {
    SpringApplication.run(
      LearningSpringBootChatApplication.class, args);
  }
}
```

The last code can be described quite simply:

- `@SpringCloudAppplication` is a `@SpringBootApplication` combined with a Eureka Discovery, and with circuit breaker enabled

We're close. Early in this book, we would put the needed settings in `application.yml` (or `application.properties`), but since we have adopted Spring Cloud Config Server, we, instead, need to create the following `bootstrap.yml` file:

```
spring:
  application:
    name: chat
```

This `bootstrap.yml` file now identifies our application as the `chat` microservice to Eureka, and will cause it to ask the Config Server for `chat.yml` on startup.

To support that, we need to add the following to our Config Server's Git repository:

```
server:
  port: 8200

spring:
  cloud:
    stream:
      bindings:
        input:
          destination: learning-spring-boot-chat
          group: comments-chat
          content-type: application/json
        newComments:
          destination: learning-spring-boot-chat
          group: comments-chat
          content-type: application/json
        clientToBroker:
          destination: learning-spring-boot-chat-user-messages
          group: app-chatMessages
        brokerToClient:
          destination: learning-spring-boot-chat-user-messages
          group: topic-chatMessages
```

Wow! That's a lot of settings. Let's take them apart:

- `server.port` shows this service will listen on port `8200`. (Why not?)
- `spring.cloud.stream.bindings.input` contains the *exact* same settings we saw earlier in the comments `spring.cloud.stream.bindings.output` settings. This ensures that the two are talking to each other.
- We also have `spring.cloud.stream.bindings.newComments`, `.clientToBroker`, and `.brokerToClient`. This part is a little complex, so let's discuss what happens.

> Before we dig into moving WebSocket messages around, don't forget to commit this change, and *push* to origin!

Brokering WebSocket messages

Something that's important to understand is the flow of messages. So far, we have seen messages sent from the website into the `comments` service, stored into a MongoDB database, and then forwarded to our `chat` service.

At this point, we are trying to onramp these messages to WebSockets. But what does that mean? A WebSocket is a very lightweight, two-way channel between a web page and the server. WebSockets, on their own, don't dictate much about what travels over this thin pipe, but one thing is for certain--each web page, when connected to a server, has a separate **session**.

Spring WebFlux provides an API that lets us hook into this WebSocket-oriented session, whether to transmit or receive. But no WebSocket session is immediately linked to another WebSocket session. If we were using Spring Framework 4's WebSocket API, we would be leveraging its most sophisticated Messaging API. This API was born in Spring Integration, and is the same concept found in Spring Cloud Streams. Spring MVC comes with a built-in broker to help bridge messages between different sessions. In essence, a message that originates in one WebSocket session must be transmitted to the broker where it can then be forwarded to any *other* WebSocket session that might be interested.

With Spring WebFlux, we have no such Messaging API, no such broker, and no higher level constructs such as user-based messaging. But it's no big deal! We can fashion it ourselves--using the Spring Cloud Stream tools we are already familiar with.

Through the rest of this chapter, we will chain together these streams of messages, and it will be most elegant.

Broadcasting saved comments

To consume messages sent via Spring Cloud Stream, the `chat` application needs its own `CommentService`:

```
@Service
@EnableBinding(Sink.class)
public class CommentService implements WebSocketHandler {

  private final static Logger log =
    LoggerFactory.getLogger(CommentService.class);
    ...
}
```

The preceding code can be described as follows:

- @Service marks this as a Spring bean, picked up automatically when the **chat** microservice starts
- @EnableBinding(Sink.class) shows this to be a receiver for Spring Cloud Stream messages
- Our service implements WebSocketHandler, a WebFlux interface that comes with a handle(WebSocketSession) method (which we'll use shortly)
- An Slf4j Logger is used to print out traffic passing through

This service needs to consume the messages sent from Spring Cloud Stream. However, the destination for these messages is *not* another Spring Cloud Stream destination. Instead, we want to pipe them into a WebSocket session.

To do that, we need to pull messages down from a RabbitMQ-based Flux, and forward them to a Flux connected to a WebSocket session. This is where we need another one of those FluxSink objects:

```
private ObjectMapper mapper;
private Flux<Comment> flux;
private FluxSink<Comment> webSocketCommentSink;

CommentService(ObjectMapper mapper) {
  this.mapper = mapper;
  this.flux = Flux.<Comment>create(
    emitter -> this.webSocketCommentSink = emitter,
    FluxSink.OverflowStrategy.IGNORE)
    .publish()
    .autoConnect();
}
```

This last bit of code can easily be described as follows:

- We need a Jackson ObjectMapper, and will get it from Spring's container through constructor injection.
- To create a FluxSink that lets us put comments one by one onto a Flux, we use Flux.create(), and let it initialize our sink, webSocketCommentSink.
- When it comes to backpressure policy, it's wired to ignore backpressure signals for simplicity's sake. There may be other scenarios where we would select differently.
- publish() and autoConnect() kick our Flux into action so that it's ready to start transmitting once hooked into the WebSocket session.

The idea we are shooting for is to put events directly onto `webSocketCommentSink`, and then hitch the corresponding `flux` into the WebSocket API. Think of it like `webSocketCommentSink` as the object we can append comments to, and `flux` being the consumer pulling them off on the other end (after the consumer subscribes).

With our `webSocketCommentSink` configured, we can now hook it into our Spring Cloud Stream `Sink`, as follows:

```
@StreamListener(Sink.INPUT)
public void broadcast(Comment comment) {
  if (webSocketCommentSink != null) {
    log.info("Publishing " + comment.toString() +
    " to websocket...");
    webSocketCommentSink.next(comment);
  }
}
```

The preceding code can be described as follows:

- The `broadcast()` method is marked as a `@StreamListener` for `Sink.INPUT`. Messages get deserialized as `Comment` objects thanks to the `application/json` setting.
- The code checks if our `webSocketCommentSink` is null, indicating whether or not it's been created.
- A log message is printed.
- The `Comment` is dropped into our `webSocketSink`, which means that it will become available to our corresponding `flux` automatically.

With this service in place, we can expect to see the following in the **chat** service's logs when a new comment arrives:

```
2017-08-05 : Publishing Comment(id=581d6774596aec682ffd07be,
imageId=581d6669596aec65dc9e6c05, comment=Nice cover!) to websocket...
```

The last step is to push this `Flux` of comments out over a WebSocket session. Remember the `WebSocketHandler` interface at the top of our class? Let's implement it:

```
@Override
public Mono<Void> handle(WebSocketSession session) {
  return session.send(this.flux
    .map(comment -> {
      try {
        return mapper.writeValueAsString(comment);
      } catch (JsonProcessingException e) {
        throw new RuntimeException(e);
```

```
        }
    })
    .log("encode-as-json")
    .map(session::textMessage)
    .log("wrap-as-websocket-message"))
  .log("publish-to-websocket");
}
```

This `WebSocketHandler` can be described as follows:

- We are handed a `WebSocketSession` which has a very simple API
- The `Comment`-based `Flux` is piped into the WebSocket via its `send()` method
- This `Flux` itself is transformed from a series of `Comment` objects into a series of JSON objects courtesy of Jackson, and then, finally, into a series of `WebSocketMessage` objects

It's important to point out that in Spring Framework 4, much of this was handled by the inner working of Spring's WebSocket API as well as its Messaging API. There was no need to serialize and deserialize Java POJOs into JSON representations. That was provided out of the box by Spring's converter services.

In Spring Framework 5, in the WebFlux module, the WebSocket API is very simple. Think of it as streams of messages coming and going. So, the duty of transforming a chain of `Comment` objects into one of JSON-encoded text messages is paramount. As we've just seen, with the functional paradigm of Reactor, this is no bother.

 Getting bogged down in POJO overload? Seeing `Comment` domain objects in every microservice? Don't panic! While we *could* write some common module that was used by every microservice to hold this domain object, that may not be the best idea. By letting each microservice manage their own domain objects, we reduce coupling. For example, only the `comments` service actually marks the `id` field with Spring Data Commons's `@Id` annotation, since it's the only one talking to MongoDB. What may appear identical in code actually carries slightly semantic differences that can arise down the road.

Configuring WebSocket handlers

We've coded our `CommentService` to implement Spring's `WebSocketHandler` interface, meaning, it's *ready* to transmit traffic over a WebSocket. The next step is to hook this service into the machinery.

We can start by creating a Spring configuration class:

```
@Configuration
public class WebSocketConfig {
  ...
}
```

This Spring configuration class is devoted to configuring WebSocket support, and is marked up with the `@Configuration` annotation, indicating it's a source of Spring bean definitions.

With that in place, we now come to the core piece of registering WebSocket functionality:

```
@Bean
HandlerMapping webSocketMapping(CommentService commentService) {
  Map<String, WebSocketHandler> urlMap = new HashMap<>();
  urlMap.put("/topic/comments.new", commentService);

  Map<String, CorsConfiguration> corsConfigurationMap =
    new HashMap<>();
  CorsConfiguration corsConfiguration = new CorsConfiguration();
  corsConfiguration.addAllowedOrigin("http://localhost:8080");
  corsConfigurationMap.put(
    "/topic/comments.new", corsConfiguration);

  SimpleUrlHandlerMapping mapping = new SimpleUrlHandlerMapping();
  mapping.setOrder(10);
  mapping.setUrlMap(urlMap);
  mapping.setCorsConfigurations(corsConfigurationMap);

  return mapping;
}
```

This preceding little chunk of code can be taken apart as follows:

- `@Bean` indicates this entire method is used to construct a Spring bean.
- It's a `HandlerMapping` bean, Spring's interface for linking routes with handler methods.
- The name of the method, `webSocketMapping`, indicates this method is about wiring routes for WebSocket message handling.

- It asks for a copy of the `CommentService` bean we defined earlier. Since Spring Boot activates component scanning, an instance of that service will be created automatically, thanks to the `@Service` annotation we put on it earlier.
- We create a Java `Map`, designed for mapping string-based routes onto `WebSocketHandler` objects, and dub it a `urlMap`.
- We load the map with `/topic/comments.new`, and link it with our `CommentService`, a class that implements the `WebSocketHandler` interface.
- There's the sticky issue of microservices, whereby, our `chat` service runs on a different port from the frontend `image` service. Any modern web browser will deny a web page calling a different port from the original port it was served. To satisfy security restrictions (for now), we must implement a custom **Cross-origin Resource Sharing** or **CORS** policy. In this case, we add an **Allowed Origin** of `http://localhost:8080`, the address where the frontend `image` service resides.
- With both the `urlMap` and the `corsConfiguration` policy, we construct `SimpleUrlHandlerMapping`. It also needs an order level of `10` to get viewed ahead of certain other route handlers provided automatically by Spring Boot.

Essentially, this bean is responsible for mapping WebSocket routes to handlers, whether that is to target client-to-server, or server-to-client messaging. The message route we've designed so far is a WebSocket message that originates on the server when a new comment is created, and is pushed out to all clients so they can be alerted to the new comment.

In Spring Framework 4, there is an annotation-based mechanism that lets us configure these routes directly on the handlers themselves. But for Spring Framework 5 (WebFlux), we must configure things by hand. CORS is also critical to handle given the way we split things up across multiple microservices.

Another critical component in the same configuration class is listed next:

```
@Bean
WebSocketHandlerAdapter handlerAdapter() {
    return new WebSocketHandlerAdapter();
}
```

This preceding, somewhat boring looking, Spring bean is critical to the infrastructure of WebSocket messaging. It connects Spring's `DispatcherHandler` to a `WebSocketHandler`, allowing URIs to be mapped onto handler methods.

Don't confuse `DispatcherHandler`, a Reactive Spring component responsible for handling Reactor-based web requests with the venerable `DispatcherServlet`, a servlet-based component that performs an analogous function. This WebSocket handling is purely Reactive Streams-oriented.

Consuming WebSocket messages from the web page

With everything configured on the server, it's time to wire things up in the client. Because JavaScript has a WebSocket API, and we aren't using subprotocols such as **Simple** (or **Streaming) Text Oriented Message Protocol (STOMP)**, we don't need any extra libraries.

So we can augment our Thymeleaf template, `index.html`. It's important to point out that our template is in the `images` microservice, not the `chat` microservice we just created. Add the following chunk of code toward the bottom of the HTML:

```
<script th:inline="javascript">
    /*<![CDATA[*/
    (function() {
        ... custom JavaScript code here...
    })();
    /*]]>*/
</script>
```

This preceding chunk of code can be explained as follows:

- The HTML `<script>` tag combined with `th:inline="javascript"` allows Thymeleaf to process it.
- To avoid HTML parsing in various browsers as well as our IDE, the entire code is wrapped with `CDATA` tags.
- To ensure our JavaScript code doesn't litter the global namespace, we have enclosed it in an **immediately-invoked function expression (IIFE)** `(function() { /* code */ })();`. The code inside this block *cannot* be reached from anywhere outside, and this is a Good Thing™. There is no chance we'll run into anyone else's variables without deliberate action.

To repeat this point--we write any JavaScript used to send and receive messages over the WebSocket in the `images` microservice. That's because it's where our Thymeleaf template is served from. To actually send and receive WebSocket messages, it will connect to the **chat** microservice.

To subscribe to WebSocket messages, we need to subscribe as follows:

```
var socket = new WebSocket(
  'ws://localhost:8200/topic/comments.new');
socket.onopen = function(event) {
  console.log('Connected to chat service!');
  console.log(event);
}
socket.onmessage = function(event) {
  console.log('Received ' + event.data + '!');
  var parsedMessage = JSON.parse(event.data);
  var ul = document.getElementById(
    'comments-' + parsedMessage.imageId);
  var li = document.createElement('li');
  li.appendChild(
    document.createTextNode(parsedMessage.comment));
  ul.appendChild(li);
}
```

The last code can be described as follows:

- We start by creating a WebSocket connection at `ws://localhost:8200/topic/comments.new`.
- With a JavaScript `WebSocket` object assigned to our `socket` variable, we then assign event handlers to `onopen` and `onmessage`.
- The `onopen` handler is processed when a connection is first opened on the server. In this case, it merely logs that we have connected.
- The `onmessage` handler is processed everytime a message is issued from the server. In this case, we log the event's `data`, parse it (assuming it's JSON), construct an HTML LI, and append it to the page's already existing UL based on the comment's `imageId`.

 This code uses native JavaScript, but if you're using React.js, jQuery, or some other JavaScript toolkit, feel free to use its APIs to generate new DOM elements.

Moving to a fully asynchronous web client

Now we are geared up to receive asynchronous messages from the server as comments are created, and display them dynamically on the site. However, there is something else that warrants attention.

Remember how, in the previous chapter, we had an HTML form for the user to fill out comments? The previous chapter's controller responded to such POSTs like this:

```
@PostMapping("/comments")
public Mono<String> addComment(Mono<Comment> newComment) {

  /* stream comments to COMMENTS service */

  return Mono.just("redirect:/");
}
```

`redirect:/` is a Spring Web signal to re-render the page at / via an HTTP redirect. Since we are shifting into dynamically updating the page based on asynchronous WebSocket messages, this is no longer the best way.

What are the issues? A few can be listed as follows:

- If the comment hasn't been saved (yet), the redirect would re-render the page with no change at all.
- The redirect may cause an update in the midst of handling the new comment's WebSocket message. Based on the race conditions, the comment may not yet be saved, causing it to not appear, and the refresh may miss the asynchronous message, causing the entire comment to not be displayed unless the page is manually refreshed.
- Setting up a WebSocket handler with every new comment isn't efficient.

Either way, this isn't a good use of resources, and could introduce timing issues. Instead, it's best if we convert this into an AJAX call.

To do so, we need to alter the HTML like this:

```
<td>
  <input th:id="'comment-' + ${image.id}" type="text" value="" />
  <button th:id="${image.id}" class="comment">Submit</button>
</td>
```

Instead of a form with a text input and a `Submit` input, we remove the HTML form and replace it with a button:

- The `<input>` contains an `id` attribute unique to its corresponding image
- The `<button>` has a similar `id` attribute

The `<button>` also has `class="comment"`, which we'll use to find, and decorate it with an event handler to process clicks as follows:

```
// Register a handler for each button to make an AJAX call
document.querySelectorAll('button.comment')
 .forEach(function(button) {
    button.addEventListener('click', function() {
      var comment = document.getElementById(
        'comment-' + button.id);

      var xhr = new XMLHttpRequest();
      xhr.open('POST', /*[[@{'/comments'}]]*/'', true);

      var formData = new FormData();
      formData.append('comment', comment.value);
      formData.append('imageId', button.id);

      xhr.send(formData);

      comment.value = '';
    });
});
```

This last block of JavaScript, contained inside our tidy little `(function(){})()`, has the following:

- `document.querySelectorAll('button.comment')` uses a native JavaScript query selector to find all the HTML buttons that have the class `comment`.
- Iterating over each button, an event listener is added, responding to the `click` events.
- When a click is received, it fetches the corresponding comment input.
- Then it fashions an `XMLHttpRequest` object, opening a `POST` operation set for asynchronous communications.
- With Thymeleaf's JavaScript support, it will plug in the URL for `@{'/comments'}` upon rendering.
- Then it constructs a `FormData`, and loads the same fields as the previous chapter as if we had filled out an HTML form on the page.

- It transmits the form data over the wire. Since we don't depend on the results, they are ignored.
- Finally, it clears out the comment input's entry box.

 In this example, we're using JavaScript's native APIs. But if you're using Rest.js, jQuery, Restangular, lodash, or any other toolkit, feel free to assemble your AJAX call using that instead. The point is to asynchronously transmit the data instead of navigating to another page.

Handling AJAX calls on the server

To support the fact that we are now making an AJAX call, and not expecting a redirect, we need to make alterations on the server side.

For one thing, we need to change the `image` microservice's `CommentController` from being view-based to being a REST controller. Earlier in this book, it looked like this:

```
@Controller
@EnableBinding(Source.class)
public class CommentController {
    ...
}
```

`@Controller` marked it as a Spring WebFlux controller that was expected to return the HTTP redirect.

To tweak things for AJAX calls, update it to look like this:

```
@RestController
@EnableBinding(Source.class)
public class CommentController {
    ...
}
```

By replacing `@Controller` with `@RestController`, we have marked this class as a Spring WebFlux controller with results written directly into the HTTP response body.

With that in place, we can now rewrite `addComment` as shown here:

```
@PostMapping("/comments")
public Mono<ResponseEntity<?>> addComment(Mono<Comment> newComment)
{
  if (commentSink != null) {
    return newComment
      .map(comment -> {
        commentSink.next(MessageBuilder
          .withPayload(comment)
          .setHeader(MessageHeaders.CONTENT_TYPE,
          MediaType.APPLICATION_JSON_VALUE)
          .build());
        return comment;
      })
      .flatMap(comment -> {
        meterRegistry
          .counter("comments.produced", "imageId", comment.getImageId())
          .increment();
        return Mono.just(ResponseEntity.noContent().build());
      });
  } else {
      return Mono.just(ResponseEntity.noContent().build());
  }
}
```

What did we change? The following:

- The return type has switched from `Mono<String>` to `Mono<ResponseEntity<?>>`. `ResponseEntity<?>` is a Spring Web container that holds HTTP response headers, body, and status code.
- The logic for forwarding messages to the `comments` service over a `FluxSink` to Spring Cloud Stream is the same as the previous chapter.
- The last line of both the `if` and the `else` clauses uses the static builder methods of `ResponseEntity` to generate an `HTTP 204 (No Content)` response. It indicates success, but no response body is included. Considering the client isn't interested in any content, that's good enough!

Let's check our handiwork. If we start up everything (remember to launch the Config Server before the others), and open two separate browser tabs, we can see the effects.

In the following screenshot, one user enters a new comment (`Nice cover!`):

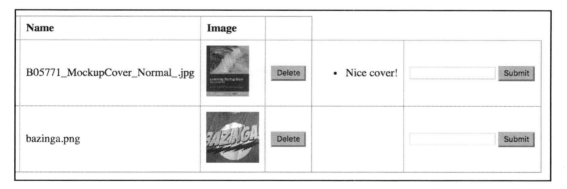

Another user with their own browser is looking at the same images. When the first user clicks on **Submit**, the message automatically appears on the second user's window, as follows:

Name	Image			
B05771_MockupCover_Normal_.jpg		Delete	• Nice cover!	Submit
bazinga.png		Delete		Submit

No page reloads, and no need to refresh the data and pull it from the `comments` service.

We can also see the message activity in the second user's browser console:

```
Received {"id":"599b90cec4d95697c2bea08b","imageId":"0a84bee9-f441-48bf-9c6a-558dab29c9d2","comment":"Nice cover!"}!
```

Introducing user chatting

What social media platform doesn't provide a means for users to communicate with each other? In this section, we'll enhance our application to allow chatting between users. This is another way to use asynchronous WebSocket messaging between clients and servers.

To start, let's add a new HTML element at the bottom of our template like this:

```
<div id="chatBox">
    Greetings!
    <br/>
    <textarea id="chatDisplay" rows="10" cols="80"
        disabled="true"></textarea>
    <br/>
    <input id="chatInput" type="text" style="width: 500px"
        value="" />
    <br/>
    <button id="chatButton">Send</button>
    <br/>
</div>
```

This preceding HTML code is placed right underneath the Upload widget for sending new pictures. It contains:

- A simple greeting.
- An HTML `textarea` for displaying messages, 80 columns wide and 10 rows tall. It is disabled to make it a read-only message output.
- A text input for entering new messages.
- A button to submit new messages.

 It's true that any and all styling should be done through CSS, but we are trying to keep things simple, and not turn this into a UX-based book.

To post new messages from the text input box, we need to add another bit of code inside our piece of JavaScript:

```
var outboundChatMessages = new
 WebSocket('ws://localhost:8200/app/chatMessage.new');
// Post new chat messages
outboundChatMessages.onopen = function(event) {
  document.getElementById('chatButton')
    .addEventListener('click', function () {
      var chatInput = document.getElementById('chatInput');
```

```
    console.log('Publishing "' + chatInput.value + '"');
    outboundChatMessages.send(chatInput.value);
    chatInput.value = '';
    chatInput.focus();
  });
}
```

This last bit of code does the following:

- It creates another WebSocket connection, this time to `ws://localhost:8200/app/chatMessage.new` (which we'll code further down).
- Registers a handler function to be invoked when the `onopen` event of the WebSocket is triggered.
- Finds the `chatButton`, and registers an event handler for the `click` events.
- When clicked, fetches the `chatInput` text input.
- Using the WebSocket variable, it sends the value of the `chatInput` text input. NOTE: This is pure text. No JSON encoding needed.
- Clears out `chatInput`, and switches focus back to it.

This will transport raw strings to the server. How these messages are received will be defined shortly, but while we're here, why not go ahead and code up the other side, that is, when these messages are transmitted from server to client?

 Are you getting nervous about seeing `http://localhost:8200`? It's appeared in a couple places so far (and will again as we write more code). It's a bit arbitrary, and also doesn't lend itself to scaling in production, right? We could stuff this value into the Config Server Git repo, and then write some JavaScript to scarf it out, but that sounds a little complicated. And it still wouldn't solve the scaling issue. The truth is that there is a much simpler solution in Chapter 9, *Securing Your App with Spring Boot*. So we'll stick with hard-coded URLs for now.

To display chat messages as they arrive, add the following:

```
var inboundChatMessages =
  new WebSocket('ws://localhost:8200/topic/chatMessage.new');
// Listen for new chat messages
inboundChatMessages.onmessage = function (event) {
  console.log('Received ' + event.data);
  var chatDisplay = document.getElementById('chatDisplay');
  chatDisplay.value = chatDisplay.value + event.data + '\n';
};
```

The preceding code does the following:

- Creates a third WebSocket connection to
  `ws://localhost:8200/topic/chatMessage.new`
- On the WebSocket's `onmessage` handler, registers a function handler to be invoked with every new message
- When an event arrives, grabs hold of the `chatDisplay`
- Appends the message's `data` to the `chatDisplay`, and adds a newline character

Confused by the paths `/app/chatMessage.new` and `/topic/chatMessage.new`? The first is for sending messages from the client to our server-side application, while the latter is for sending messages from server to client. There is no requirement that they be prefixed by `/app` or `/topic`. It's just a convention to help denote where the messages are traveling.

We just defined a route to *send* user messages to the server as well as a route to *receive* messages from the server. The next step is to register these routes in our server-side code. We do so by updating our `WebSocketConfig` class's `webSocketMapping` like this:

```
@Bean
HandlerMapping webSocketMapping(CommentService commentService,
  InboundChatService inboundChatService,
  OutboundChatService outboundChatService) {
    Map<String, WebSocketHandler> urlMap = new HashMap<>();
    urlMap.put("/topic/comments.new", commentService);
    urlMap.put("/app/chatMessage.new", inboundChatService);
    urlMap.put("/topic/chatMessage.new", outboundChatService);

    Map<String, CorsConfiguration> corsConfigurationMap =
     new HashMap<>();
    CorsConfiguration corsConfiguration = new CorsConfiguration();
    corsConfiguration.addAllowedOrigin("http://localhost:8080");
    corsConfigurationMap.put(
      "/topic/comments.new", corsConfiguration);
    corsConfigurationMap.put(
      "/app/chatMessage.new", corsConfiguration);
    corsConfigurationMap.put(
      "/topic/chatMessage.new", corsConfiguration);

    SimpleUrlHandlerMapping mapping = new
     SimpleUrlHandlerMapping();
    mapping.setOrder(10);
    mapping.setUrlMap(urlMap);
    mapping.setCorsConfigurations(corsConfigurationMap);
```

```
        return mapping;
    }
```

This last code contains many changes, so let's take them apart one by one:

- Previously, this method only injected `CommentService`. Now we *also* inject `InboundChatService` as well as `OutboundChatService`. These are two services we must define based on the need to **broker** WebSocket messages between sessions. (Don't panic! We'll get to that real soon).
- We have two new routes added to the `urlMap`--`/app/chatMessage.new` and `/topic/chatMessage.new`--which we just saw used in the web layer.
- These same routes must also be added to our CORS policy.

 Are you a little nervous about the CORS policy? Worried about managing hard-coded ports in your code when we just showed how that's not necessary in the previous chapter? Concerned about what this means when it comes time to secure everything? Don't worry, we'll show how this can be handled in `Chapter 9`, *Securing Your App with Spring Boot*.

With this adjustment to our `chat` microservice's `WebSocketConfig`, we must now configure how incoming WebSocket messages are handled. It's important to realize that if we receive the `Flux` of messages, and turn around and broadcast them on the same `WebSocketSession`, the only person receiving the messages will be the person that sent them--an echo server if you will.

This is why we need a broker if we want to broadcast such messages. Incoming messages must be received, relayed to a broker, and then picked up on the other side by *all* clients.

Now, where can we find a broker? We already have one! We've been using Spring Cloud Stream to transport messages over RabbitMQ on our behalf. We can do the same for these messages as well.

It's important to remember that Spring Cloud Stream operates on the channel paradigm. Everything is sent and received over channels. Up until now, we've gotten by using `Source`, `Sink`, and `Processor`, three interfaces that work with `output` and `input`. To handle new comment-based messages, client-to-server user messages, and server-to-client user messages, those two channels aren't enough.

So, we need to define a new set of streams. We can do that by creating our own interface, ChatServiceStreams in the chat microservice, as shown here:

```
public interface ChatServiceStreams {

    String NEW_COMMENTS = "newComments";
    String CLIENT_TO_BROKER = "clientToBroker";
    String BROKER_TO_CLIENT = "brokerToClient";

    @Input(NEW_COMMENTS)
    SubscribableChannel newComments();

    @Output(CLIENT_TO_BROKER)
    MessageChannel clientToBroker();

    @Input(BROKER_TO_CLIENT)
    SubscribableChannel brokerToClient();
}
```

This preceding declarative cornerstone of our **chat** service can be described as follows:

- Three channel names are defined at the top--NEW_COMMENTS, CLIENT_TO_BROKER, and BROKER_TO_CLIENT. They each map onto a channel name of newComments, clientToBroker, and brokerToClient.
- newComments() is defined as an input linked to the NEW_COMMENTS channel via the @Input annotation, and has a return type of SubscribableChannel, meaning, it can be used to consume messages.
- clientToBroker() is defined as an output linked to the CLIENT_TO_BROKER channel via the @Output annotation, and has a return type of MessageChannel, which means that it can be used to transmit messages.
- brokerToClient() is defined as an input linked to the BROKER_TO_CLIENT channel via the @Input annotation, and also has a return type of SubscribableChannel, which means it, too, can be used to consume messages.

We need this interface in place so we can then dive into creating that InboundChatService we promised to build earlier:

```
@Service
@EnableBinding(ChatServiceStreams.class)
public class InboundChatService implements WebSocketHandler {

    private final ChatServiceStreams chatServiceStreams;

    public InboundChatService(ChatServiceStreams chatServiceStreams)
```

```
  {
    this.chatServiceStreams = chatServiceStreams;
  }

  @Override
  public Mono<Void> handle(WebSocketSession session) {
    return session
      .receive()
      .log("inbound-incoming-chat-message")
      .map(WebSocketMessage::getPayloadAsText)
      .log("inbound-convert-to-text")
      .map(s -> session.getId() + ": " + s)
      .log("inbound-mark-with-session-id")
      .flatMap(this::broadcast)
      .log("inbound-broadcast-to-broker")
      .then();
  }

  public Mono<?> broadcast(String message) {
    return Mono.fromRunnable(() -> {
      chatServiceStreams.clientToBroker().send(
        MessageBuilder
          .withPayload(message)
          .build());
    });
  }
}
```

This preceding service code, registered to handle messages coming in on
`/app/chatMessage.new` can be described as follows:

- `@Service` marks it as a Spring service that should launch automatically thanks to Spring Boot's component scanning.
- `@EnableBinding(ChatServiceStreams.class)` signals Spring Cloud Stream to connect this component to its broker-handling machinery.
- It implements the `WebSocketHandler` interface--when a client connects, the `handle(WebSocketSession)` method will be invoked.
- Instead of using the `@StreamListener` annotation as in the previous code, this class injects a `ChatServiceStreams` bean (same as the binding annotation) via constructor injection.
- To handle a new `WebSocketSession`, we grab it and invoke its `receive()` method. This hands us a `Flux` of potentially endless `WebSocketMessage` objects. These would be the incoming messages sent in by the client that just connected. NOTE: Every client that connects will invoke this method independently.

- We map the `Flux<WebSocketMessage>` object's stream of payload data into a `Flux<String>` via `getPayloadAsText()`.
- From there, we transform each raw message into a formatted message with the WebSocket's session ID prefixing each message.
- Satisfied with our formatting of the message, we `flatMap` it onto our `broadcast()` message in order to broadcast it to RabbitMQ.
- To hand control to the framework, we put a `then()` on the tail of this Reactor flow so Spring can subscribe to this `Flux`.
- The `broadcast` method, invoked as every message is pulled down, marshals and transmits the message by first building a Spring Cloud Streams `Message<String>` object. It is pushed out over the `ChatServiceStreams.clientToBroker()` object's `MessageChannel` via the `send()` API. To **reactorize** it, we wrap it with `Mono.fromRunnable`.

Whew! That's a lot of code! Such is the effect of **functional reactive programming (FRP)**. Not a lot of effort is spent on imperative constructs and intermediate results. Instead, each step is chained to the next step, forming a transforming flow, pulling data from one input (the `WebSocketSession` in this case), and steering it into a channel for the broker (`ChatServiceStreams.clientToBroker()`).

Remember earlier when we created a `chat.yml` file in our Config Server's Git repo? Here's the key fragment:

```
spring:
  cloud:
    stream:
      bindings:
        clientToBroker:
          destination: learning-spring-boot-chat-user-messages
          group: app-chatMessages
```

It contains an entry for `spring.cloud.stream.bindings.clientToBroker`, where `clientToBroker` matches the *channel name* we set in `ChatServiceStreams`. It indicates that messages transmitted over the `clientToBroker` channel will be put on RabbitMQ's `learning-spring-boot-chat-user-messages` exchange, and grouped with other messages marked `app-chatMessages`.

This sets things up to broadcast any user-based chat message to everyone. We just need to have every user listen for them!

To do so, we need to create that *other* service we promised to build earlier, OutboundChatService:

```
@Service
@EnableBinding(ChatServiceStreams.class)
public class OutboundChatService implements WebSocketHandler {

  private final static Logger log =
    LoggerFactory.getLogger(CommentService.class);

  private Flux<String> flux;
  private FluxSink<String> chatMessageSink;

  public OutboundChatService() {
    this.flux = Flux.<String>create(
      emitter -> this.chatMessageSink = emitter,
      FluxSink.OverflowStrategy.IGNORE)
      .publish()
      .autoConnect();
  }

  @StreamListener(ChatServiceStreams.BROKER_TO_CLIENT)
  public void listen(String message) {
    if (chatMessageSink != null) {
      log.info("Publishing " + message +
        " to websocket...");
      chatMessageSink.next(message);
    }
  }

  @Override
  public Mono<Void> handle(WebSocketSession session) {
    return session
      .send(this.flux
      .map(session::textMessage)
      .log("outbound-wrap-as-websocket-message"))
      .log("outbound-publish-to-websocket");

  }
}
```

The code can be described as follows:

- Again, the `@Service` annotation marks this as an automatically wired Spring service.
- It has the same `EnableBinding(ChatServicesStreams.class)` as the inbound service, indicating that this, too, will participate with Spring Cloud Streams.
- The constructor call wires up another one of those `FluxSink` objects, this time for a `Flux` or strings.
- `@StreamListener(ChatServiceStreams.BROKER_TO_CLIENT)` indicates that this service will be listening for incoming messages on the `brokerToClient` channel. When it receives one, it will forward it to `chatMessageSink`.
- This class also implements `WebSocketHandler`, and each client attaches via the `handle(WebSocketSession)` method. It is there that we connect the `flux` of incoming messages to the `WebSocketSession` via its `send()` method.
- Because `WebSocketSession.send()` requires `Flux<WebSocketMessage>`, we map the `Flux<String>` into it using `session::textMessage`. Nothing to serialize.
- There is a custom log flag when the `Flux` finished, and another for when the entire `Flux` is handled.

That's it!

With `InboundChatService` routing individual messages from client to server to broker, we are able to take individual messages and broadcast them to ALL users. Then, with `OutboundChatService` pulling down copies of the message *for each WebSocket session*, each user is able to receive a copy.

Don't forget, we also added a binding to `chat.yml` on the Config Server to `OutboundChatService` as well:

```
spring:
  cloud:
    stream:
      bindings:
        brokerToClient:
          destination: learning-spring-boot-chat-user-messages
          group: topic-chatMessages
```

And remember that little bit of JavaScript we wrote to subscribe to
`ws://localhost:8200/topic/chatMessage.new`? It will receive the broadcast
messages.

 `Flux` and `FluxSink`--if you haven't caught on, linking async operations
with pre-established `Flux` objects is easily handled by this pattern. We've
seen it several times now. If both sides of an async service use a `Flux`, it's
not necessary. But if something bars hooking them directly, this
mechanism easily bridges the gap.

The names `InboundChatService` and `OutboundChatService` are somewhat arbitrary.
The important point to note is that one is responsible for transporting WebSocket messages
from the client to the broker through the server. Those are *incoming*. After crossing the
broker, we describe them at this stage as being *outgoing*. The naming convention is meant to
help remember what does what. Neither Spring Boot nor Spring Cloud Stream care about
what these classes are named.

With this enhancement, we can fire things up and see what it looks like.

In the following screenshot of our new chat box there is a conversation involving two users:

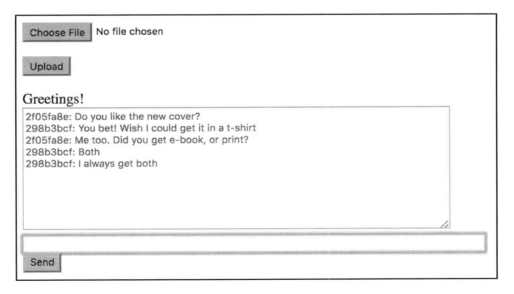

The prefix values (`2f05fa8e` and `298b3bcf`) are pure WebSocket session IDs. Kind of tricky to connect with a human user, ehh? Nevertheless, this interchange is what is seen by all parties. (Since both sides see the same exchange, no need to show *both* browser tabs.)

However, if we peek inside the browser's JavaScript console, we get a new insight. The following is a screenshot from the user with `2f05fa8e` as their session ID:

```
Publishing "Do you like the new cover?"
Received 2f05fa8e: Do you like the new cover?
Received 298b3bcf: You bet! Wish I could get it in a t-shirt
Publishing "Me too. Did you get e-book, or print?"
Received 2f05fa8e: Me too. Did you get e-book, or print?
Received 298b3bcf: Both
Received 298b3bcf: I always get both
>  |
```

We can immediately see the first message (`Do you like the new cover?`) being published, and received right back. Following that, the other user sends a separate message (`You bet! Wish I could get a t-shirt`).

If we inspect the other user's JavaScript console, we can see the other side of the conversation:

```
Received 2f05fa8e: Do you like the new cover?
Publishing "You bet! Wish I could get it in a t-shirt"
Received 298b3bcf: You bet! Wish I could get it in a t-shirt
Received 2f05fa8e: Me too. Did you get e-book, or print?
Publishing "Both"
Received 298b3bcf: Both
Publishing "I always get both"
Received 298b3bcf: I always get both
>
```

The first message was from the first user (`Do you like the new cover?`) followed by the second user's response (`You bet!...`), and so forth.

Simple. Elegant. Asynchronous. That's what WebSockets are for. And here we have a simple usage.

Sending user-specific messages

So far, we have crafted a relatively rich application using different types of broadcast messages.

For example, when a new comment is written, it's sent to every client. Only the clients actually displaying the relevant image will update anything. But the message was sent nonetheless. Also, when a user enters a new chat message, it's sent to everybody. For these use cases, this solution is fine. WebSockets make the process quite efficient.

But there are definitely scenarios when we want to send a message to just one subscriber. A perfect example we'll pursue in this section is adding the ability to "@" a user with a chat message. We only want such a message sent to that specific user. What would be even better? If we could do this without ripping up everything we've done so far.

We can start with the `ChatController` inside the `chat` microservice. We should be able to look at the incoming message, and sniff out anything starting with @. If we find it, then we should be able to extract the username, and send the message to that user and that user alone. If a message does NOT start with @, simply broadcast the message to everyone as before.

Registering users without authentication

In this chapter, we haven't yet picked up security. That will be covered in `Chapter 9`, *Securing Your App with Spring Boot*. For now, we need something to take its place.

As a workaround, we can introduce the concept of the user entering his or her own username and sending it with the HTTP-based request used to create the WebSocket.

To offer the user a place to enter their username, we can put this at the top of the Thymeleaf template:

```
<input id="username" type="text" />
<button id="connect">Connect</button>
<button id="disconnect" style="display: none">Disconnect</button>
```

There is a both a `Connect` and a `Disconnect` button to analogously log in/log out of the WebSocket session.

Now we can wire it so that clicking the `Connect` button, actually creates the WebSocket connection:

```
document.getElementById('connect')
 .addEventListener('click', function () {
   document.getElementById('connect').style.display = 'none';
   document.getElementById('disconnect').style.display = 'inline';

   var usernameInput = document.getElementById('username');

   document.getElementById('chatBox').style.display = 'inline';
```

This is what happens when `Connect` is clicked:

- The `connect` button is hidden while the `disconnect` button is shown
- We get hold of the `username` input
- The `chatBox` is switched from hidden to displayed

From here, the rest of the flow of creating a WebSocket is followed, including the extra `user` parameter supplied by the `userInput` input as we subscribe for `/topic/chatMessage.new`:

```
inboundChatMessages =
  new WebSocket(
    'ws://localhost:8200/topic/chatMessage.new?user='
    + usernameInput.value);
inboundChatMessages.onmessage = function (event) {
  console.log('Received ' + event.data);
  var chatDisplay = document.getElementById('chatDisplay');
  chatDisplay.value = chatDisplay.value + event.data + '\n';
};
```

This preceding subscription code for incoming chat messages works as follows:

- We again create a JavaScript `WebSocket`, but it has an extra query argument, `user`, populated with the `usernameInput` value
- The route we subscribe to is `/topic/chatMessage.new`, the same one that `OutboundChatService` publishes to
- The `onmessage` handler is assigned a function that updates the `chatDisplay` textarea with the new event's `data`

To wrap things up, we add the following event listener in case `Disconnect` is clicked:

```
document.getElementById('disconnect')
  .addEventListener('click', function () {
    document.getElementById('connect').style.display = 'inline';
    document.getElementById('disconnect').style.display = 'none';
    document.getElementById('chatBox').style.display = 'none';

    if (newComments != null) {
      newComments.close();
    }
    if (outboundChatMessages != null) {
      outboundChatMessages.close();
    }
    if (inboundChatMessages != null) {
      inboundChatMessages.close();
    }
});
```

This last code nicely does the following things:

- It hides the `Disconnect` button and the chat box while showing the `Connect` button
- It closes all the WebSockets

Linking a user to a session

We are still missing a critical ingredient--linking the username entered to the user's WebSocket session.

Since every one of our `WebSocketHandler` services we built may need access to this user data, we should build a **shim** called `UserParsingHandshakeHandler` to slip in like this:

```
abstract class UserParsingHandshakeHandler
  implements WebSocketHandler {

    private final Map<String, String> userMap;

    UserParsingHandshakeHandler() {
      this.userMap = new HashMap<>();
    }

    @Override
    public final Mono<Void> handle(WebSocketSession session) {
```

```
        this.userMap.put(session.getId(),
          Stream.of(session.getHandshakeInfo().getUri()
            .getQuery().split("&"))
            .map(s -> s.split("="))
            .filter(strings -> strings[0].equals("user"))
            .findFirst()
            .map(strings -> strings[1])
            .orElse(""));

        return handleInternal(session);
    }

    abstract protected Mono<Void> handleInternal(
      WebSocketSession session);

    String getUser(String id) {
      return userMap.get(id);
    }
}
```

The previous code can be described as follows:

- This abstract class implements `WebSocketHandler`; it will be invoked when a new `WebSocketSession` is created
- It contains a mapping between session ID and username, called `userMap`, initialized in the constructor
- The implementation of `handle(WebSocketSession)` takes the `userMap` and puts a new entry keyed off the session's ID
- The value stored under that session ID is extracted from the session's handshake, granting access to the original URI
- With some Java 8 stream magic, we can extract the query string from this URI, and find the user argument
- `findFirst()` produces an `Optional`, so we can either map over the answer or fall back to an empty string (no user)
- Having loaded the `userMap`, we then invoke the concrete subclass through a custom abstract method, `handleInternal(WebSocketMessage)`
- To facilitate looking up the current username, `getUser(String)` is provided to look up user based on session ID

This chunk of code will handle user details, allowing each concrete `WebSocketHandler` to do its thing while also having access to the current session's username.

To use this new handshake handler, we need to update the `InboundChatService` like this:

```
@Service
@EnableBinding(ChatServiceStreams.class)
public class InboundChatService extends UserParsingHandshakeHandler
{

  private final ChatServiceStreams chatServiceStreams;

  public InboundChatService(ChatServiceStreams chatServiceStreams){
    this.chatServiceStreams = chatServiceStreams;
  }

  @Override
  protected Mono<Void> handleInternal(WebSocketSession session) {
    return session
      .receive()
      .log(getUser(session.getId())
          + "-inbound-incoming-chat-message")
      .map(WebSocketMessage::getPayloadAsText)
      .log(getUser(session.getId())
          + "-inbound-convert-to-text")
      .flatMap(message ->
          broadcast(message, getUser(session.getId())))
      .log(getUser(session.getId())
          + "-inbound-broadcast-to-broker")
      .then();
  }

  public Mono<?> broadcast(String message, String user) {
    return Mono.fromRunnable(() -> {
      chatServiceStreams.clientToBroker().send(
        MessageBuilder
          .withPayload(message)
          .setHeader(ChatServiceStreams.USER_HEADER, user)
          .build());
    });
  }

}
```

It's almost the same as what we coded earlier in this chapter, with a few key differences:

- It now extends `UserParsingHandshakeHandler` instead of `WebSocketHandler`.
- Instead of implementing `handle(WebSocketSession)`, we must now write `handleInternal(WebSocketSession)`. This is a classic pattern of using a parent abstract class to intercept and then delegate.
- `broadcast()` takes two arguments--`message` and `user`. The `user` field is populated using `getUser(session.getId())`.
- `broadcast()` builds a `Message` like it did earlier in this chapter, but also adds a custom header containing the user of the creator of the message.

 Part of the power of the Message API are headers. You can use standard headers as well as make up your own to suit your needs. In this case, we mark up every message with the originator. Other useful details could include the timestamp of creation and origin address. Really, anything.

Sending user-to-user messages

The last step in implementing user-to-user messages is to apply a filter to `OutboundChatService`. Since we coded up `UserParsingHandshakeHandler`, we have to adjust the service to handle this:

```
@Service
@EnableBinding(ChatServiceStreams.class)
public class OutboundChatService
  extends UserParsingHandshakeHandler {
    ...
}
```

For starters, we need to change this class to extend `UserParsingHandshakeHandler` instead of `WebSocketHandler`.

There's no need to alter the constructor call where our `FluxSink` is configured. However, the handler itself must be adjusted as follows:

```
@Override
protected Mono<Void> handleInternal(WebSocketSession session) {
  return session
    .send(this.flux
      .filter(s -> validate(s, getUser(session.getId())))
      .map(this::transform)
```

```
            .map(session::textMessage)
            .log(getUser(session.getId()) +
                "-outbound-wrap-as-websocket-message"))
        .log(getUser(session.getId()) +
            "-outbound-publish-to-websocket");
    }
```

The details can be explained as follows:

- Just like `InboundChatService`, we must now implement `handleInternal(WebSocketSession)`.
- It has the same `session.send(Flux)` call, but that `Flux` has a couple of extra steps added, including a filter and an extra map.
- The `filter` call validates each message, deciding whether or not *this* user should get it. (We'll write that `validate()` method in a moment).
- Assuming the message is valid for this user, it uses a local `transform` method to tweak it.
- The rest of the machinery used to convert this string message into a `WebSocketMessage<String>` and pipe it over the WebSocket is the same as before.

When dealing with streams of messages, layering in a filter is no biggie. See how in the following code:

```
private boolean validate(Message<String> message, String user) {
    if (message.getPayload().startsWith("@")) {
        String targetUser = message.getPayload()
            .substring(1, message.getPayload().indexOf(" "));

        String sender = message.getHeaders()
            .get(ChatServiceStreams.USER_HEADER, String.class);

        return user.equals(sender) || user.equals(targetUser);
    } else {
        return true;
    }
}
```

This last code can be described as follows:

- `validate` accepts a `Message<String>` and the name of the current user (not the user that sent the message).
- It first checks the payload, and if it starts with @, it looks deeper. If the message does NOT start with @, it just lets it on through.
- If the message starts with @, it proceeds to extract the target user by parsing the text between @ and the first space. It also extracts the original sender of the message using the `User` header.
- If the current user is either the sender or the receiver, the message is allowed through. Otherwise, it is dropped.

A filtering function like this makes it easy to layer various options. We used it to target user-specific messages. But imagine putting things like security checks, regional messages, time-based messages, and more!

To wrap this up, we need to also code a little transformation to make the user-to-user experience top notch:

```
private String transform(Message<String> message) {
  String user = message.getHeaders()
    .get(ChatServiceStreams.USER_HEADER, String.class);
  if (message.getPayload().startsWith("@")) {
    return "(" + user + "): " + message.getPayload();
  } else {
      return "(" + user + ")(all): " + message.getPayload();
  }
}
```

This preceding nice little transformation can be described as follows:

- `transform` accepts a `Message<String>`, and converts it into a plain old string message
- It extracts the `User` header to find who wrote the message
- If the message starts with @, then it assumes the message is targeted, and prefixes it with the author wrapped in parentheses
- If the message does NOT start with @, then it prefixes it with the author wrapped in parentheses plus `(all)`, to make it clear that this is a broadcast message

With this change in place, we have coded a sophisticated user-to-user chat service, running on top of RabbitMQ, using Reactive Streams.

Checking out the final product

By hooking up a username with a WebSocket ID, let's see how all this runs. Restart everything, and visit the site.

First, we login as shown in this screenshot:

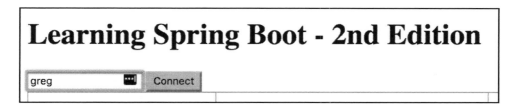

As seen in the last screenshot, the user logs in as greg. After that, the chat box will display itself at the bottom of the page. If we assume that oliver and phil have also logged in, we can see an exchange of messages as follows:

Greg asks how everyone likes the cover:

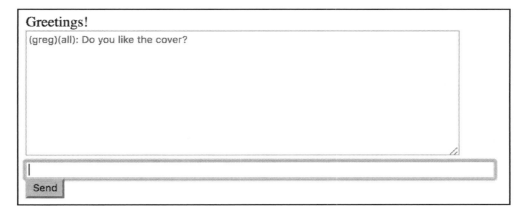

This preceding message is seen by everyone. Again, no reason to display all three users' views, since it is identical at this stage.

Oliver gives his $0.02:

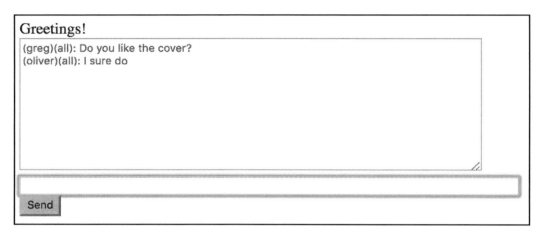

So far, the conversation is wide open, as depicted by the (all) tag on each message. By the way, isn't this user-based interaction easier to follow the conversation than the earlier version where we used session IDs?

Phil writes a direct question to Greg:

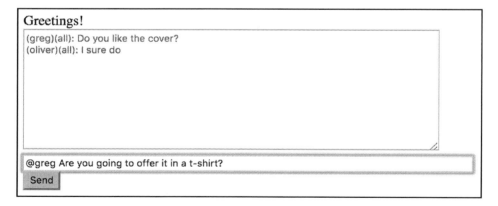

After Phil clicks on **Send**, the following appears in Greg's browser:

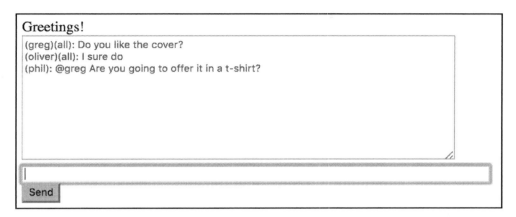

Notice how this message does NOT have (`all`)? We know this message is direct, which is further verified by looking at Oliver's browser:

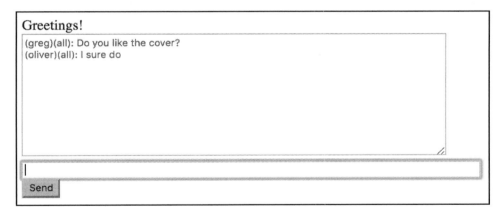

No sign of a followup question about t-shirt availability.

And if we look at Greg's JavaScript console, we can see all of this:

```
Publishing "Do you like the new cover?"
Received (greg)(all): Do you like the new cover?
Received (oliver)(all): I sure do.
Received (phil): @greg Are you going to offer it in a t-shirt?
>  |
```

This preceding interchange shows the following:

- One message is sent from Greg's session to the server
- Two broadcast messages are received via the broker from Greg and Oliver
- One direct message is received from Phil

In conclusion, it's nice to see that by chaining together streams of messages across the system with Spring Cloud Stream, we were able to pipe exactly the messages we wanted to whom we wanted to receive them. We were able to leverage a sturdy transport broker, RabbitMQ, without getting caught up in messy details.

We took advantage of things like headers to mark up our messages, and filtered things as needed to implement business requirements. And we didn't spend all our time configuring brokers, servlet containers, or anything else. Instead, we logically defined channels and what was posted/consumed from those channels.

JSR 356 versus Spring WebFlux messaging

Perhaps, you're wondering why this chapter doesn't delve into Java's standard WebSocket API? In truth, the standard API is a good piece of technology, but due to several limitations, it doesn't suit our needs.

A big limitation of JSR 356 is that it's based on the Servlet 3.1 spec. If we were running Apache Tomcat, we'd have access to that. But being a Reactive Streams application, we are using Netty, putting it off limits.

Even if we *did* switch to Apache Tomcat, there is no support for Reactor types. This is partly due to its blocking API, despite being hitched to an asynchronous programming model.

Summary

In this chapter, we made our social media platform asynchronous, front to back, through the usage of WebSocket messages. We published new comments to all users. We introduced a way for our users to chat amongst themselves, whether that was by broadcasting to everyone, or by sending individual messages directly to each other.

In the next chapter, we will apply one of the most critical components needed for production, security.

9
Securing Your App with Spring Boot

It's not real until it's secured.

– Greg L. Turnquist @gregturn

In the previous chapter, you learned how to turn our application into a fully asynchronous, message-based app using WebSockets.

Security is hard. Even among the experts. Rob Winch, the lead for **Spring Security**, has stated in multiple forums, *"Do not implement security on your own."* A classic example is when someone wrote a utility to crack password-protected Microsoft Word documents. It had an intentional delay so that it didn't operate in subsecond time. Get it? The author of the tool didn't want to show how *easy* it was to break a Word document.

Suffice it to say, there are lots of attack vectors. Especially on the web. The fact that our applications partially run in a remote location (the browser) on someone else's machine leaves little in guarantees. In fact, whole books have been written on Spring Security. We can't cover everything, but we will cover Just Enough™ to secure our microservice-based social media platform.

In this chapter, we will cover the following topics:

- Using Spring Session to share state between services
- Creating a Gateway API
- Securing the `chat` microservice
- Securing the `images` microservice

- Authorizing methods
- Securing WebSockets
- Securing the Config Server
- Securing the Eureka Server

Securing a Spring Boot application

In this chapter, we will secure our microservice-based social media platform. This will introduce some interesting use cases, ones that Spring Security can easily handle. However, it's important to know that almost every situation is slightly different. Spring Security can handle them, but it requires understanding how it operates so that you can adapt what you learn in this chapter to our unique situation.

To kick things off, we just need one dependency added to our project:

```
compile('org.springframework.boot:spring-boot-starter-security-
    reactive')
```

In addition to adding Spring Security, we will need to define a policy, and also include authorization rules. As we move through this chapter, you'll learn what all this means.

By the way, remember the microservice-based solution we've developed in the previous chapters? What is the side effect of splitting our app into multiple services? We have to secure each and every one. This means, we have to add these dependencies to each module. Yikes! Can you imagine logging in to the **user interface** (**UI**), clicking on a link, and logging in again?

Yech!

Using Spring Session

Before we can dig into those nice security policies and authorization rules we just talked about, we need a solution to secure multiple microservices.

What is the exact problem? When we log in to the first piece of our social media platform, we want that status to be carried through to the other components with ease.

The solution is Spring Session (`http://projects.spring.io/spring-session/`), which supports multiple third-party data stores to offload session state including Redis, MongoDB, GemFire, Hazelcast, and others. Instead of the session data being stored in memory, it is externalized to a separate data store.

This provides multiple benefits such as the following:

- Provides scalability when running multiple instances of various services
- Avoids the need for session affinity (sticky sessions) by not requiring load balancers to route clients to the same instance
- Leverages a data store's built-in expiration options (if desired)
- Multi-user profiles

There is one other, hidden benefit that we will take immediate advantage of in this chapter--sharing session state between different microservices. Log in to the user-facing microservice, create a session with that security state, and share the session with all microservices. Bam! Automatic access.

Since we are already using MongoDB, let's use that to also store our session.

The first thing we need to do in getting Spring Session off the ground is to update each microservice with the following dependencies:

```
compile('org.springframework.boot:spring-boot-starter-security-
  reactive')
compile('org.springframework.session:spring-session-data-mongodb')
```

These preceding dependencies can be described as follows:

- `spring-boot-starter-security-reactive` brings in all the configuration support we need to define a security policy, including some critical annotations, as well as Spring WebFlux-based security components to implement our policy, including various filters
- `spring-session-data-mongodb` will bring in Spring Session MongoDB and Spring Data MongoDB, making it possible to write session data to our MongoDB service reactively

 It's important to understand that sessions and security are orthogonal concepts that nicely leverage each other. We can use one or the other for different purposes. However, when used in concert, the effect is most elegant.

To configure Spring Session to use MongoDB, we need the following added to each microservice:

```
@EnableMongoWebSession
public class SessionConfig {

}
```

This new `SessionConfig` class does the following:

- `@EnableMongoWebSession` activates Spring Session MongoDB, signaling to use MongoDB as the place to read and write any session data

This is all it takes to enable using MongoDB for session data. However, there are some lingering issues we have to sort out due to the structure of our microservice-based application that bars us from moving forward.

We used this code in the previous chapter:

```
Map<String, CorsConfiguration> corsConfigurationMap =
  new HashMap<>();
CorsConfiguration corsConfiguration = new CorsConfiguration();
corsConfiguration.addAllowedOrigin("http://localhost:8080");
corsConfigurationMap.put(
  "/topic/comments.new", corsConfiguration);
corsConfigurationMap.put(
  "/app/chatMessage.new", corsConfiguration);
corsConfigurationMap.put(
  "/topic/chatMessage.new", corsConfiguration);
```

To make our WebSocket `chat` microservice integrate with the `images`-based web page, we needed `addAllowedOrigin("http://localhost:8080")`. That way, a web request from a service on port `8080` was permitted to cross over to a service on port `8200`.

When it comes to security and sessions, stitching together two different services on two different ports in the browser isn't the best way to approach things. Not only is it technically daunting, it is really a code smell--a hint that our application is leaking too much of its structure to the outside world.

The solution is to create a **Gateway API**.

Creating a Gateway API

What is a Gateway API? It's a one-stop facade where we can make all our various web requests. The facade then dispatches the requests to the proper backend service based on the configuration settings.

In our case, we don't want the browser talking to two different ports. Instead, we'd rather serve up a single, unified service with different URL paths.

In Chapter 7, *Microservices with Spring Boot*, we used Spring Cloud for several microservice tasks, including service discovery, circuit breaker, and load balancing. Another microservice-based tool we will make use of is **Spring Cloud Gateway**, a tool for building just such a proxy service.

Let's start by adding this to our chat microservice:

```
compile('org.springframework.cloud:spring-cloud-starter-gateway')
```

With Spring Cloud Gateway on the classpath, we don't have to do a single thing to activate it in our chat microservice. Out of the box, Spring Cloud Gateway makes the chat microservice our *front door* for all client calls. What does that mean?

Spring Cloud Gateway forwards various web calls based on patterns to its respective backend service. This allows us to split up the backend into various services with some simple settings, yet offer a seamless API to any client.

 Spring Cloud Gateway also allows us to pull together legacy services into one unified service. Older clients can continue talking to the old system, while newer clients adopt the new gateway. This is known as API *strangling* (http://www.kennybastani.com/2016/08/strangling-legacy-microserv ices-spring-cloud.html).

To configure which URL patterns are forwarded where, we need to add this to our chat.yml stored in the Config Server:

```
spring:
  cloud:
    gateway:
      routes:
      # =========================================================
      - id: imagesService
        uri: lb://IMAGES
        predicates:
        - Path=/imagesService/**
```

```
            filters:
            - RewritePath=/imagesService/(?<segment>.*), /$\{segment}
            - RewritePath=/imagesService, /
            - SaveSession
        - id: images
          uri: lb://IMAGES
          predicates:
          - Path=/images/**
          filters:
          - SaveSession
        - id: mainCss
          uri: lb://IMAGES
          predicates:
          - Path=/main.css
          filters:
          - SaveSession
        - id: commentsService
          uri: lb://IMAGES
          predicates:
          - Path=/comments/**
          filters:
          - SaveSession
```

Looking at the preceding code, we can discern the following:

- Each entry has an `id`, a `uri`, an optional collection of `predicates`, and an optional list of `filters`.
- Looking at the first entry, we can see that requests to `/imagesService` are routed to the load-balanced (`lb:` prefix), Eureka-registered `IMAGES` service. There are filters to strip the `imagesService` prefix.
- All requests to `/images` will also be sent to the `images` microservice. However, compared to `/imagesServices`, the full path of the request will be sent. For example, a request to `/images/abc123` will be forwarded to the `images` service as `/images/abc123`, and not as `/abc123`. We'll soon see why this is important.
- Asking for `/main.css` will get routed to `images` as well.
- All requests to `/comments` will get sent to `images`, full path intact. (Remember that `images` uses Ribbon to remotely invoke `comments`, and we don't want to change that right now).
- All of these rules include the `SaveSession` filter, a custom Spring Cloud Gateway filter we'll write shortly to ensure our session data is saved before making any remote call.

Don't forget to restart the Config Server after committing changes!

What's going on?

First and foremost, we create a Gateway API, because we want to keep image management and chatting as separate, nicely defined services. At one point in time, there was only HTTP support. WebSocket support is newly added to Spring Cloud Gateway, so we don't use it yet, but keep all of our WebSocket handling code in the gateway instead. In essence, the chat microservice moves to the front, and the images microservice moves to the back.

Additionally, with WebSocket handling kept in the gateway, we can eliminate the latency of forwarding WebSocket messages to another service. It's left as an exercise for you to move WebSocket messaging into another service, configure Spring Cloud Gateway to forward them and measure the effects.

This suggests that we should have chat serve up the main Thymeleaf template, but have it fetch image-specific bits of HTML from the images service.

To go along with this adjustment to our social media platform, let's create a Thymeleaf template at src/main/resources/templates/index.html in chat like this:

```
<!DOCTYPE html>
<html xmlns:th="http://www.thymeleaf.org">
    <head>
        <meta charset="UTF-8" />
        <title>Learning Spring Boot: Spring-a-Gram</title>
        <link rel="stylesheet" href="/main.css" />
    </head>
    <body>
        <div>
            <span th:text="${authentication.name}" />
            <span th:text="${authentication.authorities}" />
        </div>
        <hr />

        <h1>Learning Spring Boot - 2nd Edition</h1>

        <div id="images"></div>

        <div id="chatBox">
            Greetings!
            <br/>
```

```
            <textarea id="chatDisplay"
                    rows="10" cols="80"
                    disabled="true" ></textarea>
            <br/>
            <input id="chatInput" type="text"
                    style="width: 500px" value="" />
            <br/>
            <button id="chatButton">Send</button>
            <br/>
        </div>

    </body>
</html>
```

This preceding template can be described as follows:

- It's the same header as we saw in the previous chapter, including the main.css stylesheet.
- The <h1> header has been pulled in from the image service.
- For images, we have a tiny <div> identified as images. We need to write a little code to populate that from our images microservice.
- Finally, we have the same chat box shown in the earlier chapter.
- By the way, we remove the connect/disconnect buttons, since we will soon leverage Spring Security's user information for WebSocket messaging!

To populate the images <div>, we need to write a tiny piece of JavaScript and stick it at the bottom of the page:

```
<script th:inline="javascript">
    /*<![CDATA[*/
    (function() {
        var xhr = new XMLHttpRequest();
        xhr.open('GET', /*[[@{'/imagesService'}]]*/'', true);
        xhr.onload = function(e) {
            if (xhr.readyState === 4) {
                if (xhr.status === 200) {
                    document.getElementById('images').innerHTML =
                        xhr.responseText;

                    // Register a handler for each button
                    document.querySelectorAll('button.comment')
                        .forEach(function(button) {
                            button.addEventListener('click',
                                function() {
                                    e.preventDefault();
                                    var comment =
```

```
                            document.getElementById(
                            'comment-' + button.id);

                var xhr = new XMLHttpRequest();
                xhr.open('POST',
                    /*[[@{'/comments'}]]*/'',
                    true);

                var formData = new FormData();
                formData.append('comment',
                            comment.value);
                formData.append('imageId',
                                button.id);

                xhr.send(formData);

                comment.value = '';
            });
        });

    document.querySelectorAll('button.delete')
        .forEach(function(button) {
            button.addEventListener('click',
                function() {
                e.preventDefault();
                var xhr = new XMLHttpRequest();
                xhr.open('DELETE', button.id, true);
                xhr.withCredentials = true;
                xhr.send(null);
            });
        });

    document.getElementById('upload')
        .addEventListener('click', function() {
            e.preventDefault();
            var xhr = new XMLHttpRequest();
            xhr.open('POST',
                    /*[[@{'/images'}]]*/'',
                    true);

            var files = document
                .getElementById('file').files;

            var formData  = new FormData();
            formData.append('file', files[0],
                files[0].name);

            xhr.send(formData);
```

```
                               })
                         }
                     }
                 }
             xhr.send(null);
         })();
         /*]]>*/
     </script>
```

This code can be explained as follows:

- The whole thing is an **immediately invoked function expression** (**IIFE**), meaning no risk of global variable collisions.
- It creates an `XMLHttpRequest` named `xhr` to do the legwork, opening an asynchronous `GET` request to `/imagesService`.
- A callback is defined with the `onload` function. When it completes with a successful response status, the images `<div>` will have its `innerHTML` replaced by the response, ensuring that the DOM content is updated using `document.getElementById('images').innerHTML = xhr.responseText`.
- After that, it will register handlers for each of the image's comment buttons (something we've already seen). The delete buttons and one upload button will also be wired up.
- With the callback defined, the request is sent.

 Don't get confused by the fact that there are four `xhr` objects. One is used to fetch the image-based HTML content, the other three are used to handle new comments, delete images, and upload new images, when the corresponding button is clicked. They are in separate scopes and have no chance of bumping into each other.

Since we only need the image-specific bits of HTML from the `images` microservice, we should tweak that template to serve up a subset of what it did in the previous chapter, like this:

```html
<!DOCTYPE html>
<div xmlns:th="http://www.thymeleaf.org">

    <table>

    <!-- ...the rest of the image stuff we've already seen... -->
```

This last fragment of HTML can be explained as follows:

- This is no longer a complete page of HTML, hence, no `<html>`, `<head>`, and `<body>` tags. Instead, it's just a `<div>`.
- Despite being just a `<div>`, we need the Thymeleaf namespace `th` to give the IDE the right information to help us with code completion.
- From there, it goes into the table structure used to display images. The rest is commented out, since it hasn't changed.

With these changes to `chat` and `images`, along with the Spring Cloud Gateway settings, we have been able to merge what appeared as two different services into one. Now that these requests will be forwarded by Spring Cloud Gateway, there is no longer any need for CORS settings. Yeah!

This means we can slim down our WebSocket configuration as follows:

```
@Bean
HandlerMapping webSocketMapping(CommentService commentService,
  InboundChatService inboundChatService,
  OutboundChatService outboundChatService) {
    Map<String, WebSocketHandler> urlMap = new HashMap<>();
    urlMap.put("/topic/comments.new", commentService);
    urlMap.put("/app/chatMessage.new", inboundChatService);
    urlMap.put("/topic/chatMessage.new", outboundChatService);

    SimpleUrlHandlerMapping mapping = new SimpleUrlHandlerMapping();
    mapping.setOrder(10);
    mapping.setUrlMap(urlMap);

    return mapping;
}
```

The preceding code is the same as shown earlier in this chapter, but with the CORS settings, which we briefly saw earlier, removed.

As a reminder, we are focusing on writing Java code. However, in this day and age, writing JavaScript is unavoidable when we talk about dynamic updates over WebSockets. For a full-blown social media platform with a frontend team, something like webpack (https://webpack.github.io/) and babel.js (https://babeljs.io/) would be more suitable than embedding all this JavaScript at the bottom of the page. Nevertheless, this book isn't about writing JavaScript-based apps. Let's leave it as an exercise to pull out all this JavaScript from the Thymeleaf template and move it into a suitable module-loading solution.

Securing the chat microservice

Okay, this chapter is titled *Securing Your App with Spring Boot*, yet we have spent a fair amount of time... NOT securing our app! That is about to change. Thanks to this little bit of restructuring, we can move forward with locking things down as desired.

Let's take a crack at writing some security policies, starting with the `chat` microservice:

```
@EnableWebFluxSecurity
public class SecurityConfiguration {

  @Bean
  SecurityWebFilterChain springWebFilterChain(HttpSecurity http) {
    return http
        .authorizeExchange()
            .pathMatchers("/**").authenticated()
            .and()
        .build();
  }
}
```

The preceding security policy can be defined as follows:

- `@EnableWebFluxSecurity` activates the Spring WebFlux security filters needed to secure our application
- `@Bean` marks the one method as a bean definition
- `HttpSecurity.http()` lets us define a simple set of authentication and authorization rules
- In this case, every Spring WebFlux exchange (denoted by /**) must be `authenticated`

 The `.pathMatchers("/**").authenticated()` rule is the first rule based upon URLs. It's also possible to put additional requirements at the method level, which we'll explore later in this chapter.

This is a nice beginning to define a security policy, but we need some way to track user data to *authenticate* against. To do so, we need a `User` domain object and a way to store such data. To minimize our effort at storing user information in a database, let's leverage Spring Data again.

First, we'll create a `User` domain object like this:

```
@Data
@AllArgsConstructor
@NoArgsConstructor
public class User {

  @Id private String id;
  private String username;
  private String password;
  private String[] roles;
}
```

This preceding `User` class can easily be described as follows:

- `@Data` uses the Lombok annotation to mark this for getters, setters, `equals`, `toString`, and `hashCode` functions
- `@AllArgsConstructor` creates a constructor call for all of the attributes
- `@NoArgsConstructor` creates an empty constructor call
- `@Id` marks this `id` field as the key in MongoDB
- `username`, `password`, and `roles` are critical fields required to properly integrate with Spring Security, as shown further in the chapter

> The names of these fields don't matter when it comes to integrating with Spring Security, as we'll soon see.

To interact with MongoDB, we need to create a Spring Data repository as follows:

```
public interface UserRepository
 extends Repository<User, String> {

  Mono<User> findByUsername(String username);
}
```

This is similar to the other repositories we have built so far in the following ways:

- It extends Spring Data Commons' `Repository`, indicating that the domain type is `User` and the ID type is `String`
- It has one finder needed for security lookups, `findByUsername`, which is returned as a reactive `Mono<User>`, signaling Spring Data MongoDB to use reactive MongoDB operations

With this handy repository defined, let's preload some user data into our system by creating an `InitUsers` class, as shown here:

```
@Configuration
public class InitUsers {

  @Bean
  CommandLineRunner initializeUsers(MongoOperations operations) {
    return args -> {
      operations.dropCollection(User.class);

      operations.insert(
        new User(
          null,
          "greg", "turnquist",
          new String[]{"ROLE_USER", "ROLE_ADMIN"}));
      operations.insert(
        new User(
          null,
          "phil", "webb",
          new String[]{"ROLE_USER"}));

      operations.findAll(User.class).forEach(user -> {
        System.out.println("Loaded " + user);
      });
    };
  }
}
```

This preceding user-loading class can be described as follows:

- `@Configuration` indicates this class contains bean definitions
- `@Bean` marks the `initializeUsers` method as a Spring bean
- `initializeUsers` requires a copy of the blocking `MongoOperations` bean defined by Spring Boot's MongoDB autoconfiguration code
- The return type is `CommandLineRunner`, which we'll supply with a lambda function
- Inside our lambda function, we drop the `User` based collection, insert two new users, and then print out the collection

Now, let's see how to put that to good use! To hook into Reactive Spring Security, we must implement its `UserDetailsRepository` interface. This interface is designed to look up a user record through any means necessary and bridge it to Spring Security as a `Mono<UserDetails>` return type. The solution can be found here:

```
@Component
public class SpringDataUserDetailsRepository implements
 UserDetailsRepository {

  private final UserRepository repository;

  public SpringDataUserDetailsRepository(UserRepository
   repository)
  {
    this.repository = repository;
  }

  @Override
  public Mono<UserDetails> findByUsername(String username) {
    return repository.findByUsername(username)
     .map(user -> new User(
       user.getUsername(),
       user.getPassword(),
       AuthorityUtils.createAuthorityList(user.getRoles())
     ));
  }
}
```

The previous code can be described as follows:

- It injects a `UserRepository` we just defined through constructor injection
- It implements the interface's one method, `findByUsername`, by invoking our repository's `findByUsername` method and then mapping it onto a Spring Security `User` object (which implements the `UserDetails` interface)
- `AuthorityUtils.createAuthorityList` is a convenient utility to translate a `String[]` of roles into a `List<GrantedAuthority>`
- If no such user exists in MongoDB, it will return a `Mono.empty()`, which is the Reactor equivalent of `null`

We map our MongoDB User domain object onto Spring Security's org.springframework.security.core.userdetails.User object to satisfy the UserDetails requirement. However, that doesn't mean we can't implement a custom version of this interface. Imagine we were building a medical tracking system and needed each patient record to contain a detailed profile. A custom implementation would allow us to fill in the critical fields while also adding all the other data needed to track a person.

By hooking MongoDB-stored users into Spring Security, we can now attempt to access the system.

When we try to access localhost:8080, we can expect a login prompt, as shown in this screenshot:

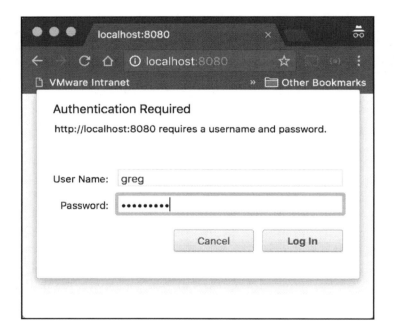

This popup (run from an incognito window to ensure there are no cookies or lingering session data) lets us nicely log in to the gateway.

Authentication versus authorization

Spring Security operates on two fundamental concepts--**authentication** and **authorization**.

These two concepts can be described as follows:

- **Authentication**: This defines who you are
- **Authorization**: This defines what you are allowed to do

The first step in any security system is to confirm the user's identify. This often involves a username and a password, but these credentialed bits can be stored in many different systems, including relational databases, directory servers, certificates, and other things. However, these are implementation details that surround verifying someone's identity. Until we know **who you are**, we can't make any determination.

HTTP Basic, HTTP FORM, and other forms of authentication are supported by Spring Security. Right now, we are using HTTP Basic on the frontend as well as the cross-service calls, given that it's the only version currently supported with Reactive Spring Security.

The second step in any security system is to decide **what the user is authorized to do**. Both a teller and a vice president at a bank can be authenticated, but they will certainly have differing permissions on what they are each allowed to do. The teller may be granted permission to open his assigned cash drawer, while the vice president may be authorized to open her customer's account.

With the `SecurityConfig` code given earlier, our `chat` microservice has instituted authentication, which is linked to the session. However, it also chose a very simple authorization strategy: anyone that is authenticated can do anything. Since the `chat` microservice does little more than communicate via a WebSocket, that is fine. In the next section, we'll see a different policy, where certain operations are restricted to a subset of users.

Sharing session details with other microservices

Something that's critical to our microservice-based social media platform is sharing the session details when putting things together. When we load the main page, it may have to pull together bits of data from multiple places. This means that after logging in to the system, the session ID that is generated has to be passed along seamlessly.

Spring Cloud Gateway can forward various requests, but Spring Session has a lazy approach to things. This means, we need to step up and save the session immediately; otherwise, the first few remote calls might fail.

To do so, we need to create a custom Spring Cloud Gateway filter as follows:

```
@Configuration
public class GatewayConfig {

  private static final Logger log =
    LoggerFactory.getLogger(GatewayConfig.class);

  /**
  * Force the current WebSession to get saved
  */
  static class SaveSessionGatewayFilterFactory
   implements GatewayFilterFactory {
     @Override
     public GatewayFilter apply(Tuple args) {
       return (exchange, chain) -> exchange.getSession()
        .map(webSession -> {
          log.debug("Session id: " + webSession.getId());
          webSession.getAttributes().entrySet()
           .forEach(entry ->
           log.debug(entry.getKey() + " => " +
            entry.getValue())));
           return webSession;
        })
        .map(WebSession::save)
        .then(chain.filter(exchange));
     }
  }

  @Bean
  SaveSessionGatewayFilterFactory saveSessionGatewayFilterFactory() {
    return new SaveSessionGatewayFilterFactory();
  }
}
```

This preceding filter can be described as follows:

- The @Configuration annotation indicates that this class contains beans to be picked up by Boot's component scanning
- There is an Slf4j Logger to print out debug statements

- `static class SaveSessionGatewayFilterFactory` implements the Spring Cloud Gateway's `GatewayFilterFactory` interface, allowing us to write a custom filter, which is, essentially, a function call where the inputs are transformed into a `GatewayFilter`
- To implement this functional interface, we write a lambda, accepting a WebFlux `WebServerExchange` and `GatewayFilterChain`, which gives us access to the request as well as the chain of filters to hand it off to
- We grab the exchange's `WebSession` and map over it in order to print out all its details
- Next, we map over the same `WebSession` and invoke its `save` function through a method reference
- We wrap things up with a `then()` call to invoke the filter chain on the exchange
- With `@Bean`, we define a bean in the application context that implements `SaveSessionGatewayFilterFactory`

Spring Cloud Gateway's default policy is to use the classname of the filter with `GatewayFilterFactory` removed as the name of the filter itself. Hence, `SaveSessionGatewayFilterFactory` becomes simply `SaveSession` for purposes of inserting into our configuration file, as we saw earlier.

```
spring:
  cloud:
    gateway:
      routes:
      - id: imagesService
        uri: lb://IMAGES
        predicates:
        - Path=/imagesService/**
        filters:
        - RewritePath=/imagesService/(?<segment>.*), /${segment}
        - RewritePath=/imagesService, /
        - SaveSession
        ...
```

With the preceding little filter in place, we can guarantee that all the forwarded calls made by Spring Cloud Gateway will first ensure that the current `WebSession` has been saved.

The default Spring WebFlux behavior for a web call with a `WebSession` is to issue a `Set-Cookie` directive (with the `SESSION` entry configured with the ID) back to the client in its response. Subsequent calls into WebFlux will automatically parse this cookie entry and load `WebSession` details. Spring Cloud Gateway itself forwards cookies unless explicitly configured not to. Hence, the session entry gets propagated. All that we do is ensure the security details automatically linked to the session are properly stored *before* a forwarded call is made.

Securing the images microservice

Having secured the frontend and also embedded a session ID in every gateway call to the backend, we can shift our focus to securing those backend services.

Let's start with the `images` service. First of all, we need to configure session management by creating `SessionConfig` as follows:

```
@EnableMongoWebSession
public class SessionConfig {

}
```

This preceding code can be described as follows:

- `@EnableMongoWebSession` activates the Reactor-based Spring Session MongoDB

Next, we can lock things down by creating a `SecurityConfiguration` class like this:

```
@EnableWebFluxSecurity
@EnableReactiveMethodSecurity
public class SecurityConfiguration {

  @Bean
  SecurityWebFilterChain springWebFilterChain() {
    return HttpSecurity.http()
        .securityContextRepository(
            new WebSessionSecurityContextRepository())
        .authorizeExchange()
          .anyExchange().authenticated()
          .and()
        .build();
  }
}
```

The preceding class definition can be described as follows:

- `@EnableWebFluxSecurity` activates a collection of filters and components needed to secure Spring WebFlux endpoints.
- `@EnableReactiveMethodSecurity` adds additional support for putting annotations on methods and classes where we can plug in sophisticated security expressions (as we'll soon see).
- Next, we create a `SecurityWebFilterChain`. This is, actually, a collection of filters defined in a very specific order using Spring Security's fluent API. This API nicely lets us define what we need while leaving Spring Security to put it together in the right order.
- In this case, we want HTTP support, but with a `WebSession`-based `SecurityContextRepository`. This activates a filter that will load the exchange with a `Principal` object from our session store.
- As a minimum for authorization, all exchanges must be authenticated.

Some of this is the same as earlier, and some of it is different.

What's different? The `images` service has **method security**, meaning, it can annotate individual methods with *additional* authorization rules, which we'll see shortly. We are no longer confined to securing things based on URLs and HTTP verbs. There are also no account definitions. That's because the `images` service is not creating new sessions, but riding on the one created in the gateway by the `chat` microservice instead; (do we really want to create a separate `User` domain object in every microservice?).

Both services respond to `Authorization` headers as well as `SESSION` headers, which means that once logged in, the two can easily share information. Both, essentially, route all URLs into the same authorization rule, `.anyExchange().authenticated()`. (That's the same net effect as that of `.pathMatchers("/**").authenticated()`).

Wiring in image ownership

Spring WebFlux's `ServerWebExchange` comes prepared for security by providing a `getPrincipal()` API that returns `Mono<Principal>`. While the default version, straight out of Spring Framework, supplies `Mono.empty()`, Spring Security automatically hooks in a filter to supply a real value via `WebSessionSecurityContextRepository`.

With Spring Security and Spring Session hooked into all our web calls, we can leverage this information every time a new image is uploaded.

First of all, we can adjust our `Image` domain object as follows:

```
@Data
@AllArgsConstructor
public class Image {

  @Id private String id;
  private String name;
  private String owner;
}
```

This last code is the same POJO that we've used throughout this book with one change:

- It now has a `String owner` property. This lets us associate an image with whoever uploaded it (which we'll see shortly).

Spring Security makes it possible to inject any Spring WebFlux controller with an authentication object as follows:

```
@PostMapping(value = BASE_PATH)
public Mono<String> createFile(
  @RequestPart("file") Flux<FilePart> files,
  @AuthenticationPrincipal Principal principal) {
    return imageService.createImage(files, principal)
      .then(Mono.just("redirect:/"));
}
```

This change to our `image` service's `UploadController.createFile`, as shown in the preceding code, can be described as follows:

- Using Spring Security's `@AuthenticationPrincipal` annotation, the second parameter allows us to find out the security context of the caller.
- The actual type can be flexible, whether we want a Java `Principal`, a Spring Security subinterface `Authentication`, or a concrete instance (`UsernamePasswordAuthenticationToken` by default). This parameter can also be wrapped as a `Mono<T>` of this type.
- For simplicity, we grab it unwrapped and pass it along to `ImageService` as a new argument.

So, let's go update `ImageService.createImage()`, where `Image` objects are actually created:

```
public Mono<Void> createImage(Flux<FilePart> files,
  Principal auth) {
    return files
```

```
      .log("createImage-files")
      .flatMap(file -> {
        Mono<Image> saveDatabaseImage = imageRepository.save(
          new Image(
            UUID.randomUUID().toString(),
            file.filename(),
            auth.getName()))
            .log("createImage-save");

        ...the rest that hasn't changed...
      }
  }
```

The parts that have changed in the preceding code can be described as follows:

- This method now accepts a second argument, `Principal`. This is a Java standard token.
- The code where we actually create a new `Image` is populated in the same as done earlier for the first two fields, with a random ID and the name of the file.
- The `owner` field is now populated with `auth.getName()`, supplied to us by Spring Security's context-enabling advice.

The last link in the chain of ownership is to display it on the page. To do this, we can update the model fed to that HTML fragment in `HomeController`, as follows:

```
model.addAttribute("images",
  imageService
   .findAllImages()
   .map(image -> new HashMap<String, Object>() {{
     put("id", image.getId());
     put("name", image.getName());
     put("owner", image.getOwner());
     put("comments",
       commentHelper.getComments(image,
         webSession.getId())));
   }})
);
```

This preceding fragment from `public String index()` has been updated to include the new `owner` attribute.

With that added to the template's model, we can display it by adding the following bit of HTML to our Thymeleaf template, like this:

```
<td th:text="${image.owner}" />
```

This attribute can now be seen when we log in and check things out, as seen in this screenshot:

Name	Image		Owner	C
bazinga.png		Delete	greg	
B05771_MockupCover_Normal.png		Delete	phil	

In the preceding screenshot, we see one image loaded by **greg** and one image loaded by **phil**.

Authorizing methods

For a security framework to be of value, it needs flexibility. Security rules are never confined to simple use cases. We have all dealt with customers needing very complex settings for certain operations. Spring Security makes this possible through its special dialect of **SpEL** or **Spring Expression Language**.

To get a taste of it, let's augment the images microservice's ImageService.delete() method with an authorization rule:

```
@PreAuthorize("hasRole('ADMIN') or " +
  "@imageRepository.findByName(#filename).owner " +
    "== authentication.name")
public Mono<Void> deleteImage(String filename) {

    ... rest of the method unchanged ...
}
```

This preceding code for deleting images is only different in the new annotation in the following manner:

- The method is flagged with a `@PreAuthorize` annotation, indicating that the SpEL expression must evaluate to `true` in order for the method to get called
- `hasRole('ADMIN')` indicates that a user with ROLE_ADMIN is allowed access
- `or @imageRepository.findByName(#filename).owner == authentication.name")` indicates that access is *also* granted if the user's `name` matches the image's `owner` property

> Why do we need this authorization rule again? Because without it, *any* authenticated user can delete *any* image. Probably not a good idea.

This authorization rule is just one example of the types of rules we can write. The following table lists the prebuilt rules provided by Spring Security:

SpEL function	Description
`hasAuthority('ROLE_USER')`	Access is granted if user has ROLE_USER
`hasAnyAuthority('ROLE_USER', 'ROLE_ADMIN')`	Access is granted if user has any of the listed authorities
`hasRole('USER')`	Shorthand for `hasAuthority('ROLE_USER')`
`hasAnyRole('USER', 'ADMIN')`	Shorthand for `hasAnyAuthority('ROLE_USER', 'ROLE_ADMIN')`
`principal`	Direct access to the `Principal` object representing the user
`authentication`	Direct access to the `Authentication` object obtained from the security context
`permitAll`	Evaluates to `true`
`denyAll`	Evaluates to `false`
`isAnonymous()`	Returns `true` if user is an anonymous user
`isRememberMe()`	Returns `true` if user is a remember-me user
`isAuthenticated()`	Returns `true` if user is not anonymous

`isFullyAuthenticated()`	Returns `true` if user is neither anonymous nor a remember-me user

It's possible to combine these SpEL functions with `and` and `or`.

As we saw demonstrated earlier, we can also write security checks like this:

```
@PreAuthorize("#contact.name == authentication.name")
public void doSomething(Contact contact);
```

This preceding security check will grab the method's `contact` argument and compare its `name` field against the current `authentication` object's name field, looking for a match.

By the way, these types of parameter-specific rules are great when we want to restrict operations to the owner of the record, a common use case. In essence, if you are logged in and operating on *your* data, then you can do something.

In addition to all these functions and comparators, we can also invoke beans (another thing shown earlier). Look at the following code, for example:

```
@PreAuthorize("@imageRepository.findByName(#filename).owner ==
    authentication.name")
```

This last security check will invoke the bean named `imageRepository` and use its `findByName` function to look up an image's owner and then compare it against the current `authentication` object.

> `@PreAuthorize` rules can be applied to any Spring bean, but it's recommended you apply them to your **service layer methods**. In essence, any code that invokes the service layer, whether it was from a web call or somewhere else, should be secured. Wrapping higher up at the web handler can leave your service layer susceptible to unauthorized access. To guard against improper web calls, it's recommended that you use route-based rules (as shown earlier in the `chat` microservice's `SecurityConfiguration` policy).

Tailoring the UI with authorization checks

With the REST endpoints locked down, it's nice to know things are secure. However, it doesn't make sense to display options in the UI that will get cut off. Instead, it's better to simply not show them. For that, we can leverage a custom Thymeleaf security rule.

Normally, we would make use of Thymeleaf's Spring Security extension. Unfortunately, the Thymeleaf team has yet to write such support for Spring Framework 5's WebFlux module. No problem! We can craft our own and register it inside the Thymeleaf engine.

For starters, we want to define an **authorization** scoped operation that could be embedded inside a Thymeleaf th:if="${}" expression, conditionally displaying HTML elements. We can start by adding SecurityExpressionObjectFactory to the images microservice, since that fragment of HTML is where we wish to apply it:

```
public class SecurityExpressionObjectFactory
  implements IExpressionObjectFactory {

  private final
    SecurityExpressionHandler<MethodInvocation> handler;

  public SecurityExpressionObjectFactory(
    SecurityExpressionHandler<MethodInvocation> handler) {
      this.handler = handler;
  }

  @Override
  public Set<String> getAllExpressionObjectNames() {
    return Collections.unmodifiableSet(
      new HashSet<>(Arrays.asList(
        "authorization"
    )));
  }

  @Override
  public boolean isCacheable(String expressionObjectName) {
    return true;
  }

  @Override
  public Object buildObject(IExpressionContext context,
    String expressionObjectName) {
      if (expressionObjectName.equals("authorization")) {
        if (context instanceof ISpringWebFluxContext) {
          return new Authorization(
            (ISpringWebFluxContext) context, handler);
        }
      }
      return null;
  }
}
```

The preceding Thymeleaf expression object factory can be described as follows:

- This class implements Thymeleaf's `IExpressionObjectFactory`, the key toward writing custom expressions.
- To do its thing, this factory requires a copy of Spring Security's `SecurityExpressionHandler`, aimed at method invocations. It's injected into this factory through constructor injection.
- To advertize the expression objects provided in this class, we implement `getAllExpressionObjectNames`, which returns an unmodifiable `Set` containing `authorization`, the token of our custom expression.
- We implement the interface's `isCacheable` and point blank say that all expressions may be cached by the Thymeleaf engine.
- `buildObject` is where we create objects based on the token name. When we see **authorization**, we narrow the template's context down to a WebFlux-based context and then create an `Authorization` object with the context, Spring Security's expression handler, and a copy of the current `ServerWebExchange`, giving us all the details we need.
- Anything else, and we return `null`, indicating this factory doesn't apply.

Our expression object, `Authorization`, is defined as follows:

```
public class Authorization {

    private static final Logger log =
        LoggerFactory.getLogger(Authorization.class);

    private ISpringWebFluxContext context;
    private SecurityExpressionHandler<MethodInvocation> handler;

    public Authorization(ISpringWebFluxContext context,
        SecurityExpressionHandler<MethodInvocation> handler) {
        this.context = context;
        this.handler = handler;
    }
    ...
}
```

The code can be described as follows:

- It has an Slf4j `log` so that we can print access checks to the console, giving developers the ability to debug their authorization expressions

- Through constructor injection, we load a copy of the Thymeleaf
  `ISpringWebFluxContext` and the Spring Security
  `SecurityExpressionHandler`

With this setup, we can now code the actual function we wish to use,
`authorization.expr()`, as follows:

```
public boolean expr(String accessExpression) {
  Authentication authentication =
    (Authentication) this.context.getExchange()
    .getPrincipal().block();

  log.debug("Checking if user \"{}\" meets expr \"{}\".",
   new Object[] {
      (authentication == null ?
       null : authentication.getName()),
       accessExpression});

  /*
   * In case this expression is specified as a standard
   * variable expression (${...}), clean it.
   */
  String expr =
    ((accessExpression != null
        &&
        accessExpression.startsWith("${")
        &&
        accessExpression.endsWith("}")) ?

        accessExpression.substring(2,
            accessExpression.length()-1) :
        accessExpression);

  try {
    if (ExpressionUtils.evaluateAsBoolean(
      handler.getExpressionParser().parseExpression(expr),
      handler.createEvaluationContext(authentication,
      new SimpleMethodInvocation())))) {

        log.debug("Checked \"{}\" for user \"{}\". " +
            "Access GRANTED",
          new Object[] {
            accessExpression,
            (authentication == null ?
              null : authentication.getName())});

        return true;
```

```
            } else {
                log.debug("Checked \"{}\" for user \"{}\". " +
                "Access DENIED",
                new Object[] {
                    accessExpression,
                    (authentication == null ?
                    null : authentication.getName())});

                return false;
            }
        } catch (ParseException e) {
            throw new TemplateProcessingException(
            "An error happened parsing \"" + expr + "\"", e);
        }
    }
```

This last Thymeleaf custom function can be described as follows:

- Our custom `expr()` function is named in the first line, is publicly visible, and returns a Boolean, making it suitable for `th:if={}` expressions.
- The first thing we need is to grab the `Authentication` object from the context's `ServerWebExchange`. Because we are inside an inherently blocking API, we must use `block()` and cast it to a Spring Security `Authentication`.
- To help developers, we log the current user's authentication details along with the authorization expression.
- In the event the whole expression is wrapped with `${}`, we need to strip that off.
- We tap into Spring Security's SpEL support by invoking `ExpressionUtils.evaluateAsBoolean()`.
- That method requires that we parse the expression via `handler.getExpressionParser().parseExpression(expr)`.
- We must also supply the SpEL evaluator with a context, including the current **authentication** as well as `SimpleMethodInvocation`, since we are focused on method-level security expressions.
- If the results are `true`, it means access has been granted. We log it and return `true`.
- If the results are `false`, it means access has been denied. We log that and return `false`.
- In the event of a badly written SpEL expression, we catch it with an exception handler and throw a Thymeleaf `TemplateProcessingException`.

The preceding code defines the `expr()` function, while the enclosing `SecurityExpressionObjectFactory` scopes the function inside `authorization`, setting us up to embed `#authorization.expr(/* my Spring Security SpEL expression*/)` inside Thymeleaf templates.

The next step in extending Thymeleaf is to define a **Dialect** with our expression object factory, as follows:

```
public class SecurityDialect extends AbstractDialect
  implements IExpressionObjectDialect {

    private final
      SecurityExpressionHandler<MethodInvocation> handler;

    public SecurityDialect(
       SecurityExpressionHandler<MethodInvocation> handler) {
         super("Security Dialect");
         this.handler = handler;
    }

    @Override
    public IExpressionObjectFactory getExpressionObjectFactory()
    {
        return new SecurityExpressionObjectFactory(handler);
    }
}
```

This previous code can be described as follows:

- `SecurityDialect` extends `AbstractDialect` and implements `IExpressionObjectDialect`
- We need a copy of Spring Security's `SecurityExpressionHandler` in order to parse Spring Security SpEL expression, and it's provided by constructor injection
- To support `IExpressionObjectDialect`, we supply a copy of our custom `SecurityExpressionObjectFactory` factory inside the `getExpressionObjectFactory()` method

With our tiny extension dialect defined, we must register it with Thymeleaf's template engine. To do so, the easiest thing is to write a custom Spring post processor, like this:

```
@Component
public class SecurityDialectPostProcessor
  implements BeanPostProcessor, ApplicationContextAware {

    private ApplicationContext applicationContext;
```

```
    @Override
    public void setApplicationContext(
      ApplicationContext applicationContext)
      throws BeansException {
        this.applicationContext = applicationContext;
    }

    @Override
    public Object postProcessBeforeInitialization(
      Object bean, String beanName) throws BeansException {
        if (bean instanceof SpringTemplateEngine) {
          SpringTemplateEngine engine =
            (SpringTemplateEngine) bean;
          SecurityExpressionHandler<MethodInvocation> handler =
            applicationContext.getBean(
              SecurityExpressionHandler.class);
          SecurityDialect dialect =
            new SecurityDialect(handler);
          engine.addDialect(dialect);
        }
        return bean;
    }

    @Override
    public Object postProcessAfterInitialization(
      Object bean, String beanName) throws BeansException {
        return bean;
    }
}
```

The preceding code can be defined as follows:

- @Component signals Spring Boot to register this class.
- By implementing the BeanPostProcessor interface, Spring will run every bean in the application context through it, giving our SecurityDialectPostProcessor the opportunity to find Thymeleaf's engine and register our custom dialect.
- Since our custom dialect needs a handle on the SecurityExpressionHandler bean, we also implement the ApplicationContextAware interface, giving it a handle on the application context.

- It all comes together in `postProcessBeforeInitialization`, which is invoked against every bean in the application context. When we spot one that implements Thymeleaf's `SpringTemplateEngine`, we grab that bean, fetch `SecurityExpressionHandler` from the app context, create a new `SecurityDialect`, and add that dialect to the engine. Every bean, modified or not, is returned back to the app context.
- Because we don't need any processing *before* initialization, `postProcessAfterInitialization` just passes through every bean.

With all this in place, we are ready to make some security-specific tweaks to our templates.

In the main page (`chat` microservice's `index.html` template), it would be handy to put some user-specific information. To display the username and their roles, we can update the `HomeController` like this:

```
@GetMapping("/")
public String index(@AuthenticationPrincipal Authentication auth,
  Model model) {
    model.addAttribute("authentication", auth);
    return "index";
}
```

This preceding adjustment to the home controller can be described as follows:

- `@AuthenticationPrincipal Authentication auth` grants us a copy of the current user's `Authentication` object
- `Model model` gives us a model object to add data to the template
- By simply sticking the `Authentication` object into the model, we can use it to display security details on the web page

Now, we can display the username and their roles, as follows:

```
<div>
  <span th:text="${authentication.name}" />
  <span th:text="${authentication.authorities}" />
</div>
<hr />
```

This little DIV element that we just defined includes the following:

- Displays the authentication's `name` property, which is the username
- Displays the authentication's `authorities` properties, which are the user's roles
- Draws a horizontal line, setting this bit of user specifics apart from the rest of the page

 Since we are using HTTP Basic security, there is no value in putting a logout button on the screen. You have to shut down the browser (or close the incognito tab) to clear out security credentials and start afresh.

We can now expect to see the following when we log in as **greg**:

We mentioned limiting things that the user can't do. The big one in our social media platform is restricted access to deleting images. To enforce this in the UI, we need to parallel the authorization rule we wrote earlier in the `images` microservice's `index.html`, as shown here:

```
<td>
  <button th:if="${#authorization.expr('hasRole(''ROLE_ADMIN'')')
  or #authorization.expr('''__${image.owner}__'' ==
  authentication.name')}"
        th:id="'/images/' + ${image.name}"
         class="delete">Delete</button>
</td>
```

This last code looks a bit more complex than the `@PreAuthorize` rule wrapping `ImageService.deleteImage()`, so let's take it apart:

- We use Thymeleaf's `th:if="..."` expression along with `${}` to construct a complex expression consisting of two `#authorization.expr()` functions chained by `or`.
- `#authorization.expr('hasRole(''ROLE_ADMIN'')')` grants access if the user has `ROLE_ADMIN`.
- `#authorization.expr('''__${image.owner}__'' == authentication.name')` grants access if the `image.owner` attribute matches the current `authentication.name`.
- By the way, the double underscore before and after `${image.owner}` is Thymeleaf's **preprocessor**. It indicates that this is done before any other part of the expression is evaluated. In essence, we need the image's owner attribute parsed first, stuffed into the authorization expression, and finally run through our custom tie-in to Spring Security's SpEL parser.

> The expressions inside `#authorization.expr()` are supposed to be wrapped in single quotes. Literal values themselves have to be wrapped in single quotes. To escape a single quote in this context requires a double single quote. Confused yet? Thymeleaf's rules for concatenation, preprocessing, and nesting expressions can, at times, be daunting. To help debug an expression, pull up the `Authorization` class coded earlier inside your IDE and set breakpoints inside the proper security expression. This will pause code execution, allowing you to see the final expression before it gets passed, hopefully making it easier to craft a suitable authorization rule.

With our nice tweaks to the UI, let's see what things look like if we have two different images uploaded, one from an admin and one from a regular user.

If **greg** is logged in, we can see the following screenshot:

In the preceding screenshot, both images have a **Delete** button, since **greg** has ROLE_ADMIN.

If **phil** is logged in, we can see the following screenshot:

In the earlier screenshot, only the second image has the **Delete** button, since **phil** owns it.

With these nice details in place, we can easily check out the headers relayed to the backend using the browser's debug tools, as seen in this screenshot:

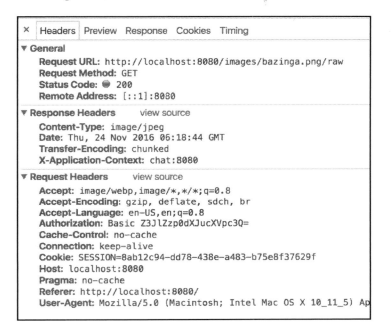

This collection of request and response headers shown in the last image lets us see the following things:

- The session ID, 8ab12c94-dd78-438e-a483-b75e8f37629f, is captured in SESSION in the cookie and sent over the wire.
- There is an Authorization header that is transmitted once we have been authenticated.
- More security-based headers are used to further protect us from other attack vectors. See http://docs.spring.io/spring-security/site/docs/current/reference/html/headers.html for more details.

When we started building this social media platform early in this book, we had several operations tied into our Thymeleaf template. This type of tight interaction between controllers and views is of classic design. However, the more things shift to piecing together bits of HTML and leveraging JavaScript, the more it becomes useful to have REST-based services. Writing AJAX calls decouples the HTML from the server-side controls, which can be further leveraged if we use tools such as React.js (`https://facebook.github.io/react/`). This gets us out of the business of assembling DOM elements and lets us focus on the state of the frontend instead.

Securing WebSockets

So far, we have secured the `chat` service and the `images` service.

Or have we?

Well, we configured chat as the Gateway API for our microservices using Spring Cloud Gateway. To do that, we made it the sole source of HTTP session creation. Given that the session details were also included in forwarded web requests, our Gateway API is nicely buttoned up.

However, the `chat` microservice's critical function is brokering WebSocket messages. And we haven't lifted a finger to secure that component. Time to roll up our sleeves and get to work.

Since our WebSocket handlers are stream oriented, we merely need to slip in a parent class that authorizes things when the WebSocket session is configured, as follows:

```
abstract class AuthorizedWebSocketHandler
  implements WebSocketHandler {

  @Override
  public final Mono<Void> handle(WebSocketSession session) {
    return session.getHandshakeInfo().getPrincipal()
      .filter(this::isAuthorized)
      .then(doHandle(session));
  }

  private boolean isAuthorized(Principal principal) {
    Authentication authentication = (Authentication) principal;
    return authentication.isAuthenticated() &&
      authentication.getAuthorities().contains("ROLE_USER");
```

```
    }

    abstract protected Mono<Void> doHandle(
      WebSocketSession session);
  }
```

The preceding code can be described as follows:

- This abstract class implements the `WebSocketHandler` interface with a Reactor-based `handle()` function
- The `handle` method looks up `handshakeInfo`, finding the `Principal` that will be populated by Spring Security, and filters against a custom `isAuthorized` function
- If the session is indeed authorized, an abstract `doHandle` is invoked, handing over `WebSocketSession` to the actual handlers
- The `isAuthorized` function takes the session's `Principal`, casts it to a Spring Security `Authentication`, and verifies that the user is both authenticated and also contains ROLE_USER

With this in place, we can update our `InboundChatService` like this:

```
@Service
@EnableBinding(ChatServiceStreams.class)
public class InboundChatService extends AuthorizedWebSocketHandler
{

  private final ChatServiceStreams chatServiceStreams;

  public InboundChatService(ChatServiceStreams chatServiceStreams) {
    this.chatServiceStreams = chatServiceStreams;
  }

  @Override
  protected Mono<Void> doHandle(WebSocketSession session) {

    ...
  }
```

The changes in the previous code can be described as follows:

- `InboundChatService` now extends `AuthorizedWebSocketHandler`, forcing it to accept those upstream checks
- We have replaced `handle(WebSocketSession)` with `doHandle(WebSocketSession)`
- The rest of the code is the same, so there's no reason to show it

If we apply the same changes to `OutboundChatService` and `CommentService`, we can ensure that all of our WebSocket services are locked down.

Admittedly, our policy is quite simple. However, we can easily scale based on requirements. For example, if the Admins wanted their own channel, it wouldn't be hard to add `/topic/admin/**` and require `ROLE_ADMIN`.

It's also important to recognize that this level of security is aimed at the whole channel. Adding per-message security checks could *also* be layered in by going to each concrete service, and, essentially, embedding `.filter()`, based on the details of the message.

And that's all it takes! Our WebSocket channels are now secured such that only proper incoming messages are allowed through, and only HTML served from our site will have the means to connect and send such messages.

Tracing calls

Earlier, we saw a screenshot from Chrome's debug tools, showing request and response headers. There is another tool we can use as well--Spring Boot Actuator's `trace` endpoint.

By visiting `http://localhost:8080/application/trace`, we can see all the web calls, going back in time. For example, look at this request to negotiate the WebSocket:

```
{
  "timestamp": 1480805242289,
  "info": {
    "method": "GET",
    "path": "/learning-spring-boot/160/ge00bkmu/websocket",
    "headers": {
      "request": {
        "host": "localhost:8080",
        "connection": "Upgrade",
        "pragma": "no-cache",
        "cache-control": "no-cache",
        "authorization": "Basic Z3JlZzp0dXJucXVpc3Q=",
```

```
        "upgrade": "websocket",
        "origin": "http://localhost:8080",
        "sec-websocket-version": "13",
        "user-agent": "Mozilla/5.0 (Macintosh; Intel Mac OS X
          10_11_5) AppleWebKit/537.36 (KHTML, like Gecko)
          Chrome/54.0.2840.98 Safari/537.36",
        "accept-encoding": "gzip, deflate, sdch, br",
        "accept-language": "en-US,en;q=0.8",
        "cookie": "SESSION=3f0668ec-d528-43d8-a6e8-87a369571745",
        "sec-websocket-key": "L8fkEK8VtxXfxx4jBzOC9Q==",
        "sec-websocket-extensions": "permessage-deflate;
          client_max_window_bits"
      },
      "response": {
        "X-Application-Context": "chat:8080",
        "Upgrade": "websocket",
        "Connection": "upgrade",
        "Sec-WebSocket-Accept": "m8xyQSUtHR/qMEUp1xog4wwUS0E=",
        "Sec-WebSocket-Extensions": "permessage-
          deflate;client_max_window_bits=15",
        "status": "101"
      }
    }
  }
}
```

The following are some key bits that can be pointed out in the preceding code:

- The `authorization` header has a `Basic` token value, us having logged in
- The `cookie` is loaded with our SESSION ID
- The upgrade protocol to go from HTTP to WebSocket is evident in the response headers and the `101` status code

Let's look at one more, the request to view our `bazinga.png` image:

```
{
  "timestamp": 1480805242286,
  "info": {
    "method": "GET",
    "path": "/images/bazinga.png/raw",
    "headers": {
      "request": {
        "host": "localhost:8080",
        "connection": "keep-alive",
        "authorization": "Basic Z3J1Zzp0dXJucXVpc3Q=",
        "user-agent": "Mozilla/5.0 (Macintosh; Intel Mac OS X
          10_11_5) AppleWebKit/537.36 (KHTML, like Gecko)
```

```
            Chrome/54.0.2840.98 Safari/537.36",
          "accept": "image/webp,image/*,*/*;q=0.8",
          "referer": "http://localhost:8080/",
          "accept-encoding": "gzip, deflate, sdch, br",
          "accept-language": "en-US,en;q=0.8",
          "cookie": "SESSION=3f0668ec-d528-43d8-a6e8-87a369571745"
        },
        "response": {
          "X-Application-Context": "chat:8080",
          "Date": "Sat, 03 Dec 2016 22:47:21 GMT",
          "Content-Type": "image/jpeg",
          "Transfer-Encoding": "chunked",
          "status": "200"
        }
      }
    }
  }
```

Some interesting fields in the last code include the following:

- The `cookie` header contains our `SESSION` ID.
- The `authorization` header includes the same token.
- The `referer` header shows the origin of the request as `http://localhost:8080/`.
- The `accept-encoding` header indicates the formats that the browser will accept, including zipped images and deflated ones.
- The `content-type` response header has JPEG, a value we hard-coded into our controller. Since all images get handled by the same part of the browser, it doesn't matter if it's not PNG.

Spring Boot Actuator's `trace` endpoint will track the last one hundred requests. It's a handy way to peek at past web calls in case you don't have the browser's development tools open at the time.

 You can inject `TraceRepository` into your code and use `add(Map)` on any structure you want, with it getting serialized into JSON.

Securing the Config Server

So, we've locked down `chat`, `images`, and `comments`. But what about the Config Server itself? Seeing how critical it is with each microservice's configuration details, we need to insulate ourselves from a malevolent Config Server being stood up in its place.

The simplest thing to do is to add Spring Security to our Config Server. So, let's do it!

```
compile('org.springframework.boot:spring-boot-starter-security')
```

By default, Spring Security will set username to `user` and password to something random. Since we can't be updating the other services every time we restart, let's override that with a fixed password, as follows:

```
@Bean
UserDetailsService userDetailsService() {
  return new InMemoryUserDetailsManager(
    User
      .withUsername("user")
      .password("password")
      .roles("USER").build());
}
```

In Spring Boot 1.x, there was a `security.password` property to override. In the spirit of simplification, this property has been removed in Spring Boot 2.x. The new approach is to inject a `UserDetailsService` bean, as shown in the previous code fragment (which can be added to `LearningSpringBootConfigServer`). This code shows a single user, `user/password`, defined.

That's all it takes to secure our Config Server!

To signal the other services, we need to adjust their `bootstrap.yml` files. Let's start with the Eureka Server, like this:

```
spring:
  application:
    name: eureka
  cloud:
    config:
      label: session
      password: password
```

This change shown in the last code adds `spring.cloud.config.password` set to the same password we just chose.

Let's continue with `chat`:

```
spring:
  application:
    name: chat
  cloud:
    config:
      label: session
      password: password
```

In the preceding code, we have `spring.cloud.config.password` and `spring.cloud.config.label` properly set.

We can make the same changes to `images`, as follows:

```
spring:
  application:
    name: images
  cloud:
    config:
      label: session
      password: password
```

This will secure things with the exact same settings.

And finally, let's make the following changes to `comments`:

```
spring:
  application:
    name: comments
  cloud:
    config:
      label: session
      password: password
```

This will lock things down, preventing others from getting access to our settings. If someone attempted to stand up a bogus Config Server, they would have to somehow secure it with the same password on the same network address. (Not likely!).

Securing the Eureka Server

The last bastion to secure is our Eureka Server. To do so, we need to adopt similar steps to what we did with the Config Server.

First, add Spring Security to the Eureka Server, as follows:

```
compile('org.springframework.boot:spring-boot-starter-security')
```

This preceding dependency will enable Spring Security automatically. However, just like Config Server, it will generate a random password every time it launches. To pin the password, we need to add the same `UserDetailsService` bean as follows:

```
@Bean
UserDetailsService userDetailsService() {
  return new InMemoryUserDetailsManager(
    User
      .withUsername("user")
      .password("password")
      .roles("USER").build());
}
```

The recommended way to plug in the username/password settings for a Eureka client is by using the URL notation. For the `chat` service, we need to update the Config Server with this:

```
eureka:
  client:
    serviceUrl:
      defaultZone: http://user:password@localhost:8761/eureka
```

This preceding adjustment will have the `chat` microservice signing into the Eureka Server with a username, password, hostname, port, and path--all standard options with URLs.

These options can be applied to the Config Server's `images.yml` file, like this:

```
eureka:
  client:
    serviceUrl:
      defaultZone: http://user:password@localhost:8761/eureka/
```

This can also be applied to the Config Server's `comments.yml` file, as follows:

```
eureka:
  client:
    serviceUrl:
      defaultZone: http://user:password@localhost:8761/eureka/
```

Are you unsure that this is working? Enable security in the Eureka Server as described, but do not make these changes to the Eureka clients. When they are launched, they'll report inability to connect to Eureka. Make the changes to the Config Server, restart it, then make the changes to the clients. They will then connect. Ta dah!

We now have every component secured. We also have session state shared between the services, making it easy to expand and add new services or to refine the existing roles. Pretty much anything we can think of.

So... does it smell like too many hard-coded values? Getting nervous about this system being able to roll with the punches of the network changing underneath it? Your concern is justified. We'll soon see in `Chapter 10`, *Taking Your App to Production with Spring Boot*, how we can take our social media platform to the cloud, scale its components, and with minimal adjustments, overcome what *may* appear as brittle settings.

Summary

In this chapter, we applied Spring Security to each of our microservices. We then configured our `chat` service as a Gateway API using Spring Cloud Gateway. Finally, we brought on board Spring Session MongoDB and had it share session details with the other *backend* microservices.

After ensuring that SESSION IDs were propagated by Spring Cloud Gateway to all the backend services, we wrote authorization rules, both for REST endpoints as well as for WebSocket messages.

To wrap things up, we also secured our Config Server and our Eureka Server so that only our system can talk to them.

In the next chapter, we will take our social media platform to production. We'll deploy our microservices-based application to the cloud, and see how to scale and adjust various things. We'll also discover how Spring Boot makes adjusting things a breeze.

10

Taking Your App to Production with Spring Boot

Here is my source code

Run it on the cloud for me

I do not care how

– Cloud Foundry haiku (Onsi Fakhouri @onsijoe)

In the previous chapter, we learned how to secure our microservice-based social media platform.

In this chapter, we will cover the following topics:

- Configuring profile-specific beans
- Creating configuration property beans
- Overriding property settings in production
- Deploying our social media platform to the cloud

So, today is the day. We worked for weeks to build this system. And now we want to take it to production. What could happen? What could go wrong?

Answer: A lot. And...a lot.

Spring Boot comes with powerful features to make it easy to tune and adjust things in production, allowing us to minimize the code. Some of the concepts presented here are rooted in *The Twelve-Factor App* (https://12factor.net/) and the ability to externalize configuration settings. We've already seen parts of that through the Config Server. However, now we'll dig in and apply more as we go to production.

Profile-based sets of beans

Many cloud-based platforms use proxies wrapped around applications. This enables the platform to support many features, including caching, **content delivery networks** (CDN), load balancing, and SSL termination. After all, why put such common infrastructure requirements on developers?

However, the side effect can break security protocols designed to protect us in the web. For example, our application may be running on a private IP address, while original requests come in on a public-facing URL. When our application sees a forwarded web request, how are we to distinguish it between a proper request versus some nefarious cross site scripting attack leveraging our service?

The first place this can affect our application is the `chat` service's WebSocket handling. It requires explicit configuration to handle such a hop. However, we only want such an adjustment in our code to apply when we are in production, not when running things in development on our workstation.

The solution is **profile-based beans**. Spring lets us configure beans to only be created if certain profiles are enabled.

In the previous chapter, we had our entire WebSocket configuration in a top-level class. We need to change that configuration class and turn it into a container class with different options based on whether or not we are in production.

The first step is to move the existing bean definitions into a new, static inner class as shown here:

```
@Configuration
public class WebSocketConfig {

  ...
  @Profile("!cloud")
```

```
@Configuration
static class LocalWebSocketConfig {
  ...
  }
}
```

So far, we haven't changed a lot. What we have, can be described as follows:

- The outer class, `WebSocketConfig`, looks the same
- This new inner class, `LocalWebSocketConfig`, is annotated `@Profile("!cloud")`, meaning it only runs if there is *no* `cloud` profile
- The new class is called `LocalWebSocketConfig` to clarify that it only operates when we run things locally

 What is a **cloud** profile? Spring allows settings various profiles through the `spring.profiles.active` application property. We can create all the profiles we want, even overlapping ones. However, any application deployed to **Cloud Foundry** automatically has an extra profile, that is, **cloud**, applied.

Since we plan to have both a local as well as a cloud-based configuration, it's important to distinguish what is the same and what is different. Something that will be the same are the WebSocket route mappings.

To support this, we need a single `configureUrlMappings()` method to configure this `SimpleUrlHandlerMapping`:

```
private static SimpleUrlHandlerMapping configureUrlMappings(
   CommentService commentService,
   InboundChatService inboundChatService,
   OutboundChatService outboundChatService) {
   Map<String, WebSocketHandler> urlMap = new HashMap<>();
   urlMap.put("/topic/comments.new", commentService);
   urlMap.put("/app/chatMessage.new", inboundChatService);
   urlMap.put("/topic/chatMessage.new", outboundChatService);

   SimpleUrlHandlerMapping mapping = new
    SimpleUrlHandlerMapping();
   mapping.setOrder(10);
   mapping.setUrlMap(urlMap);

   return mapping;
}
```

This is the same code we saw in the last chapter, just moved around a little:

- The three endpoints are tied to their respective services in `Map` of routes-to-`WebSocketHandlers`
- A `SimpleUrlHandlerMapping` is defined with this map of handlers
- The order is set to `10`
- The method is static since it will be placed *outside* our new `LocalWebSocketConfig` (but *inside* `WebSocketConfig`)

To tap this, we simply need to write a bean definition inside `LocalWebSocketConfig` like this:

```
@Bean HandlerMapping webSocketMapping(CommentService
 commentService, InboundChatService inboundChatService,
 OutboundChatService outboundChatService) {
    return configureUrlMappings(commentService,
        InboundChatService, outboundChatService);
}
```

This method does nothing more than invoke our WebSocket configuring method.

With the local configuration set up, we can now turn our attention towards configuring the WebSocket broker to work in the cloud. To do so, we need another inner static class inside `WebSocketConfig`, as follows:

```
@Profile("cloud")
@Configuration
@EnableConfigurationProperties(ChatConfigProperties.class)
static class CloudBasedWebSocketConfig {
```

It can be explained as follows:

- It's marked as `@Profile("cloud")`, meaning this only applies if the `cloud` profile is in force, the opposite of `LocalWebSocketConfig`
- It contains `@EnableConfigurationProperties(ChatConfigProperties.class)`, used to provide an extra set of properties
- It's named `CloudBasedWebSocketConfig` to point out its role

If you're wondering what `@EnableConfigurationProperties` means, it leads us into the next section.

Creating configuration property beans

`@EnableConfigurationProperties`, applied anywhere in our application, will cause a bean of the named type, `ChatConfigProperties`, to get added to the application context. A **configuration property bean** is meant to hold various settings that can be configured with optional defaults and can be overridden through various means.

Remember properties like `server.port` where we adjusted the default port our Netty web container listened for web requests? All the properties we've seen through this book are all configuration property beans. This annotation simply gives us the means to define our own property settings specific to our application.

In this case, `ChatConfigProperties` is aimed at configuring the WebSocket broker.

 It's not critical that the annotation be applied to this specific class. It's just convenient since it's the place where we intend to use it.

Despite enabling such property settings, we still have to inject the bean into our `CloudBasedWebSocketConfig` configuration class, as shown here:

```
private final ChatConfigProperties chatConfigProperties;

CloudBasedWebSocketConfig(ChatConfigProperties
  chatConfigProperties) {
    this.chatConfigProperties = chatConfigProperties;
}
```

Using constructor injection, we now have access to whatever property settings are provided by this configuration property bean.

 Configuration property beans are simply Spring beans with the added ability to override. It means they can be injected just like any other Spring bean.

Digging into the WebSocket broker configuration, what we need is the remote host we are willing to accept WebSocket connection requests from. Essentially, the public-facing URL of our `chat` microservice. To do that, we'll define a property called `origin` and use it as shown here:

```
@Bean HandlerMapping webSocketMapping(CommentService
  commentService, InboundChatService inboundChatService,
  OutboundChatService outboundChatService) {
```

```
SimpleUrlHandlerMapping mapping =
  configureUrlMappings(commentService,
  InboundChatService, outboundChatService);

Map<String, CorsConfiguration> corsConfigurationMap =
  new HashMap<>();
CorsConfiguration corsConfiguration = new CorsConfiguration();
corsConfiguration
  .addAllowedOrigin(chatConfigProperties.getOrigin());

mapping.getUrlMap().keySet().forEach(route ->
  corsConfigurationMap.put(route, corsConfiguration)
);

mapping.setCorsConfigurations(corsConfigurationMap);

return mapping;
}
```

This code has the same endpoints as `LocalWebSocketConfig`, thanks to the `configureUrlMappings` method. It additionally creates a CORS map, like we did in Chapter 8, *WebSockets with Spring Boot*. Only, this time, it uses the injected `getOrigin()` to plug in the public-facing URL of the `chat` service (hold tight--we'll see how shortly).

What's missing is the definition of this configuration property bean. It's shown here:

```
@Data
@ConfigurationProperties(prefix = "lsb")
public class ChatConfigProperties {

  @Value("https://${vcap.application.uris[0]}")
  private String origin;

}
```

The code can be explained as follows:

- Once again, we use Project Lombok's `@Data` annotation to avoid writing getters and setters. This is ideal for configuration property beans.
- `@ConfigurationProperty(prefix="lsb")` flags this bean as a candidate for Spring Boot's property reading rules, starting with the `lsb` prefix.
- There is a single property named `origin` that is initialized using Spring's `@Value()` annotation.

- On Cloud Foundry, `vcap.application.uris` is a property applied to every application that lists publicly visible URLs. Assuming that the first is the one we wish to use, we are applying it to our `origin` property.
- By combining the prefix (`lsb`) and the name of the property (`origin`), the full path of this property is `lsb.origin`, and it can be overridden at any time.

Overriding property settings in production

Everytime we take our application to a new environment, there are always settings that have to be adjusted. We don't want to edit code. Instead, it's easier if we could just override various properties. And we can!

This was touched on briefly in `Chapter 1`, *Quick Start with Java*, under the guise of overriding Spring Boot's property settings. However, the fact that we can write our own custom configuration property beans makes this a powerful feature for application customization.

To recap the rules listed in `Chapter 1`, *Quick Start with Java*, property settings can be overridden in the following order, highest to lowest:

1. `@TestPropertySource` annotations on test classes.
2. Command-line arguments.
3. Properties found inside `SPRING_APPLICATION_JSON` (inline JSON embedded in an env variable or system property).
4. `ServletConfig` init parameters.
5. `ServletContext` init parameters.
6. JNDI attributes from `java:comp/env`.
7. Java System properties (`System.getProperties()`).
8. OS environment variables.
9. `RandomValuePropertySource` that only has properties in `random.*`.
10. Profile-specific properties outside the packaged JAR file (`application-{profile}.properties` and YAML variants).
11. Profile-specific properties inside the packaged JAR file (`application-{profile}.properties` and YAML variants).
12. Application properties outside the package JAR file (`application.properties` and YAML variants).

13. Application properties inside the packaged JAR file (`application.properties` and YAML variants).

14. `@PropertySource` annotations on any `@Configuration` classes.

15. Default properties (specified using `SpringApplication.setDefaultProperties`).

 By default, we can run with `vcap.application.uris[0]`. However, if we take it to another cloud solution, we can simply plug in an override to `lsb.origin` and leverage whatever environment variables the new cloud provides. This lets us escape having to alter the code again and instead focus on getting things running.

One of the most common tactics is to create an `application-{profile}.yml` file that will be automatically applied when <profile> is in effect. Since Cloud Foundry apps get the **cloud** profile, it would be natural to create an `application-cloud.yml` file.

However, since we adopted the Spring Cloud Config Server and specified that the chat service is governed by `chat.yml`, we instead merely need to add a `chat-cloud.yml` file. Then we know the following cloud-specific settings will be applied when deployed to Cloud Foundry:

```
server:
  port: 8080

eureka:
  client:
    serviceUrl:
      defaultZone: http://user:password@learning-spring-boot-
      eureka-server.cfapps.io/eureka/
    instance:
      hostname: ${vcap.application.uris[0]}
      nonSecurePort: 80
```

These settings can be explained as follows:

- The `server.port` is the same as before
- The `eureka.client.serviceUrl.defaultZone` is changed to the public-facing URL for our Eureka service, so the `chat` service can find it

- Since the public-facing URL for our `chat` service is terminated by a proxy, we have to override `eureka.instance.hostname` with `${vcap.application.uris[0]}` to avoid registering an unreachable IP address with Eureka
- We must also register that we are visible (non-secure) on port `80`

The following settings are identical for `comments-cloud.yml`:

```
server:
  port: 8080

eureka:
  client:
    serviceUrl:
      defaultZone: http://user:password@learning-spring-boot-
        eureka-server.cfapps.io/eureka/
    instance:
      hostname: ${vcap.application.uris[0]}
      nonSecurePort: 80
```

And the same for `images-cloud.yml`:

```
server:
  port: 8080

eureka:
  client:
    serviceUrl:
      defaultZone: http://user:password@learning-spring-boot-
        eureka-server.cfapps.io/eureka/
    instance:
      hostname: ${vcap.application.uris[0]}
      nonSecurePort: 80
```

Finally, we need to set the same instance details for the Eureka service itself via `eureka-cloud.yml`, as shown here:

```
server:
  port: 8080

eureka:
  instance:
    hostname: ${vcap.application.uris[0]}
    nonSecurePort: 80
```

If you'll notice, there is no `eureka.client.serviceUrl.defaultZone` given that this IS the Eureka service!

These additional settings added to `https://github.com/greglturn/learning-spring-boot-config-repo/tree/production` will ensure that our apps function smoothly in the cloud.

If we want to see our newly minted property settings, we can visit `http://learning-spring-boot.cfapps.io/configprops` and look for `ChatConfigProperties`.

The configuration properties can be described as follows:

- The name is captured as the prefix + the canonical path of the class
- The prefix, `lsb`, is displayed
- The `properties` lists the named properties we can tap (nesting displayed if that were the case)

From this, we can easily glean that `lsb.origin` is the property to override should we have some reason to adjust this.

@ConfigurationProperties versus @Value

In our code, we have used both strongly-type `@ConfigurationProperties` based classes as well as `@Value` labeled attributes. It's important to understand the differences before using them in your application.

@Value is old, preceding Spring Boot by years. It is a powerful annotation, able to inject values as well as accept default values. However, it misses several features many of us have come to rely upon when writing Boot apps, as shown in the following table:

Feature	@ConfigurationProperties	@Value
Relaxed binding	Yes	No
Meta-data support	Yes	No
SpEL evaluation	No	Yes

This matrix documents three critical features:

- **Relaxed binding**: The ability to match `server.port`, `SERVER_PORT`, and `sErVeR.pOrT` to the same attribute is quite valuable.
- **Meta-data support**: The ability to include code completion for property settings is also of incredible value, along with hover-over tips. Anything that speeds up developer effort cannot be understated in value.
- **SpEL evaluation**: The ability to write SpEL expressions to populate properties.

There is a strong suggestion to start with `@ConfigurationProperties`. When you bundle together a set of properties inside a POJO, it really is a shortcut for a fist full of `@Value` attributes. And the property binding is supercharged.

However, when you *need* SpEL expression support, as we do to get a hold of the application's URI (`${vcap.application.uris[0]}`), then it's okay to break from `@ConfigurationProperties` and switch to `@Value`.

However, if you'll notice, we continue to leverage it inside `@ConfigurationProperties`. The real hint of doing it wrong is if we try to construct a collection of properties using `@Value`. Configuration properties is a nice way to build a hierarchy of properties with little effort.

Pushing app to Cloud Foundry and adjusting the settings

Keep calm and cf push.

- Denizens of the Internet

If there's one thing critical to any smooth-running Ops center, it's the need for automation. If we do things by hand, we introduce the risk of drift among our various components in production.

The following section shows some BASH scripts for deploying our microservices-based social media platform, a first step on the path towards automated deployment.

Assuming we've built everything with Gradle, let's kick things off by deploying our Spring Boot uber JARs to Cloud Foundry:

```bash
#!/usr/bin/env bash

cf push learning-spring-boot-config-server -p config-
server/build/libs/learning-spring-boot-config-server-0.0.1-SNAPSHOT.jar &
cf push learning-spring-boot-eureka-server -p eureka-
server/build/libs/learning-spring-boot-eureka-server-0.0.1-SNAPSHOT.jar &
cf push learning-spring-boot -p chat/build/libs/learning-spring-boot-
chat-0.0.1-SNAPSHOT.jar &
cf push learning-spring-boot-comments -p comments/build/libs/learning-
spring-boot-comments-0.0.1-SNAPSHOT.jar &
cf push learning-spring-boot-images -p images/build/libs/learning-spring-
boot-images-0.0.1-SNAPSHOT.jar &
cf push learning-spring-boot-hystrix-dashboard -p hystrix-
dashboard/build/libs/learning-spring-boot-hystrix-dashboard-0.0.1-
SNAPSHOT.jar &
```

It can be described as follows:

- Each module is deployed using the CF CLI (https://github.com/cloudfoundry/cli), deploying with both a name and the JAR file
- Each command is backgrounded to speed up release

A real microservice-based solution presumes different teams responsible for different modules. Hence, each team may have a different deployment script as well as different release schedules.

Let's get things underway and deploy! The console output shows us running our deployment script:

```
gturnquist$ ./deploy.sh

Creating app learning-spring-boot-comments in org cosmos-refarch / space
development as gturnquist@pivotal.io...
Creating app learning-spring-boot in org cosmos-refarch / space development
as gturnquist@pivotal.io...
Creating app learning-spring-boot-config-server in org cosmos-refarch /
space development as gturnquist@pivotal.io...
Creating app learning-spring-boot-images in org cosmos-refarch / space
development as gturnquist@pivotal.io...
Creating app learning-spring-boot-hystrix-dashboard in org cosmos-refarch /
space development as gturnquist@pivotal.io...
Creating app learning-spring-boot-eureka-server in org cosmos-refarch /
space development as gturnquist@pivotal.io...
...
Using route learning-spring-boot-config-server.cfapps.io
Binding learning-spring-boot-config-server.cfapps.io to learning-spring-
boot-config-server...
Using route learning-spring-boot-comments.cfapps.io
Binding learning-spring-boot-comments.cfapps.io to learning-spring-boot-
comments...
Using route learning-spring-boot-eureka-server.cfapps.io
Binding learning-spring-boot-eureka-server.cfapps.io to learning-spring-
boot-eureka-server...
Using route learning-spring-boot-images.cfapps.io
Binding learning-spring-boot-images.cfapps.io to learning-spring-boot-
images...
Using route learning-spring-boot.cfapps.io
Binding learning-spring-boot.cfapps.io to learning-spring-boot...
Using route learning-spring-boot-hystrix-dashboard.cfapps.io
Binding learning-spring-boot-hystrix-dashboard.cfapps.io to learning-
spring-boot-hystrix-dashboard...
...
Uploading learning-spring-boot-config-server...
Uploading learning-spring-boot-hystrix-dashboard...
Uploading learning-spring-boot-comments...
Uploading learning-spring-boot-eureka-server...
Uploading learning-spring-boot-images...
Uploading learning-spring-boot...
```

```
...
Starting app learning-spring-boot-hystrix-dashboard in org cosmos-refarch /
space development as gturnquist@pivotal.io...
Starting app learning-spring-boot-comments in org cosmos-refarch / space
development as gturnquist@pivotal.io...
Starting app learning-spring-boot-images in org cosmos-refarch / space
development as gturnquist@pivotal.io...
Starting app learning-spring-boot-eureka-server in org cosmos-refarch /
space development as gturnquist@pivotal.io...
Starting app learning-spring-boot in org cosmos-refarch / space development
as gturnquist@pivotal.io...
Starting app learning-spring-boot-config-server in org cosmos-refarch /
space development as gturnquist@pivotal.io...
...
App started

(the rest ommitted for brevity)
```

All components of our social media platform are now deployed to the cloud.

Be warned! This isn't enough. There are custom settings that must be applied after the bits are uploaded.

Let's start with the section that configures our Eureka server, as shown here:

```
#!/usr/bin/env bash

cf set-env learning-spring-boot-eureka-server spring.cloud.config.uri
https://learning-spring-boot-config-server.cfapps.io
cf set-env learning-spring-boot-eureka-server spring.cloud.config.label
production
```

Eureka needs to be configured with a Config Server URI and which label to fetch from GitHub, as done using `cf set-env`.

Next, we can look at the settings for the `chat` microservice:

```
cf set-env learning-spring-boot spring.cloud.config.uri
https://learning-spring-boot-config-server.cfapps.io
cf set-env learning-spring-boot spring.cloud.config.label production

cf bind-service learning-spring-boot learning-spring-boot-mongodb
cf set-env learning-spring-boot spring.data.mongodb.uri
\${vcap.services.learning-spring-boot-mongodb.credentials.uri}

cf bind-service learning-spring-boot learning-spring-boot-rabbitmq
```

The `chat` service needs a Config Server URI (with the GitHub label), a MongoDB service binding and URI setting, and a RabbitMQ service binding.

Next, we can look at the settings for the `comments` microservice, as shown here:

```
cf set-env learning-spring-boot-comments spring.cloud.config.uri
https://learning-spring-boot-config-server.cfapps.io
cf set-env learning-spring-boot-comments spring.cloud.config.label
production

cf bind-service learning-spring-boot-comments learning-spring-boot-mongodb
cf set-env learning-spring-boot-comments spring.data.mongodb.uri
\${vcap.services.learning-spring-boot-mongodb.credentials.uri}

cf bind-service learning-spring-boot-comments learning-spring-boot-rabbitmq
```

The `comments` service needs a Config Server URI (with the GitHub label), a MongoDB service binding and URI setting, and a RabbitMQ service binding.

Next, we can look at the settings for the `images` microservice, as shown here:

```
cf set-env learning-spring-boot-images spring.cloud.config.uri
https://learning-spring-boot-config-server.cfapps.io
cf set-env learning-spring-boot-images spring.cloud.config.label production

cf bind-service learning-spring-boot-images learning-spring-boot-mongodb
cf set-env learning-spring-boot-images spring.data.mongodb.uri
\${vcap.services.learning-spring-boot-mongodb.credentials.uri}

cf bind-service learning-spring-boot-images learning-spring-boot-rabbitmq
```

The `images` service needs a Config Server URI (with the GitHub label), a MongoDB service binding and URI setting, and a RabbitMQ service binding.

> While all three services are binding to the same MongoDB service, they could actually use separate MongoDB services. The code was carefully written to avoid integrating inside the database. Each service has separate collections. However, for the sake of brevity, just one service is used in this code.

With this in place, let's run the following configuration script:

```
gturnquist$ ./config.sh

Setting env variable 'spring.cloud.config.uri' to
'https://learning-spring-boot-config-server.cfapps.io' for app learning-
spring-boot-eureka-server in org cosmos-refarch / space development as
```

```
gturnquist@pivotal.io...
Setting env variable 'spring.cloud.config.label' to 'production' for app
learning-spring-boot-eureka-server in org cosmos-refarch / space
development as gturnquist@pivotal.io...
Setting env variable 'spring.cloud.config.uri' to
'https://learning-spring-boot-config-server.cfapps.io' for app learning-
spring-boot in org cosmos-refarch / space development as
gturnquist@pivotal.io...
Setting env variable 'spring.cloud.config.label' to 'production' for app
learning-spring-boot in org cosmos-refarch / space development as
gturnquist@pivotal.io...
Binding service learning-spring-boot-mongodb to app learning-spring-boot in
org cosmos-refarch / space development as gturnquist@pivotal.io...
Setting env variable 'spring.data.mongodb.uri' to
'${vcap.services.learning-spring-boot-mongodb.credentials.uri}' for app
learning-spring-boot in org cosmos-refarch / space development as
gturnquist@pivotal.io...
Binding service learning-spring-boot-rabbitmq to app learning-spring-boot
in org cosmos-refarch / space development as gturnquist@pivotal.io...

(the rest omitted for brevity)
```

Having applied these settings, we need to restart everything. To do so, we need the following script:

```
#!/usr/bin/env bash

cf restart learning-spring-boot-config-server

sleep 10

cf restart learning-spring-boot-eureka-server &
cf restart learning-spring-boot &
cf restart learning-spring-boot-comments &
cf restart learning-spring-boot-images &
```

Why the delay after restarting the Config Server? It's important that it's given a chance to be up and operational before the other applications. So, let's run it as follows:

```
$ ./restart.sh

Stopping app learning-spring-boot-config-server in org cosmos-refarch /
space development as gturnquist@pivotal.io...
Starting app learning-spring-boot-config-server in org cosmos-refarch /
space development as gturnquist@pivotal.io...

    state      since               cpu      memory       disk
details
```

```
#0    running    2017-01-11 10:11:07 PM    207.4%    426.7M of 1G    146M of 1G
```

```
Stopping app learning-spring-boot-images in org cosmos-refarch / space
development as gturnquist@pivotal.io...
Stopping app learning-spring-boot-eureka-server in org cosmos-refarch /
space development as gturnquist@pivotal.io...
Stopping app learning-spring-boot in org cosmos-refarch / space development
as gturnquist@pivotal.io...
Stopping app learning-spring-boot-comments in org cosmos-refarch / space
development as gturnquist@pivotal.io...

Starting app learning-spring-boot-eureka-server in org cosmos-refarch /
space development as gturnquist@pivotal.io...
Starting app learning-spring-boot-images in org cosmos-refarch / space
development as gturnquist@pivotal.io...
Starting app learning-spring-boot-comments in org cosmos-refarch / space
development as gturnquist@pivotal.io...
Starting app learning-spring-boot in org cosmos-refarch / space development
as gturnquist@pivotal.io...

App started

(the rest ommitted for brevity)
```

We can easily check their status like this:

```
$ cf apps

Getting apps in org cosmos-refarch / space development as
gturnquist@pivotal.io...
OK

name                                     requested state    instances
memory    disk    urls
learning-spring-boot                     started            1/1           1G
1G      learning-spring-boot.cfapps.io
learning-spring-boot-comments            started            1/1           1G
1G      learning-spring-boot-comments.cfapps.io
learning-spring-boot-config-server       started            1/1           1G
1G      learning-spring-boot-config-server.cfapps.io
learning-spring-boot-eureka-server       started            1/1           1G
1G      learning-spring-boot-eureka-server.cfapps.io
learning-spring-boot-hystrix-dashboard   started            1/1           1G
1G      learning-spring-boot-hystrix-dashboard.cfapps.io
learning-spring-boot-images              started            1/1           1G
1G      learning-spring-boot-images.cfapps.io
```

Let's take a peek. We can do so by visiting `http://learning-spring-boot.cfapps.io` (in an incognito tab to ensure a fresh session):

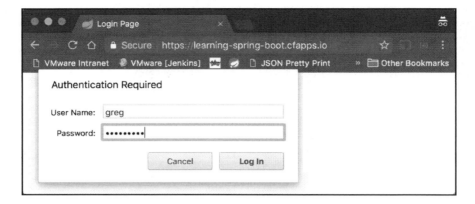

We will see the all too familiar login page.

If we log in as `greg/turnquist`, delete the default images and load up our favorites from earlier, we can expect to see this:

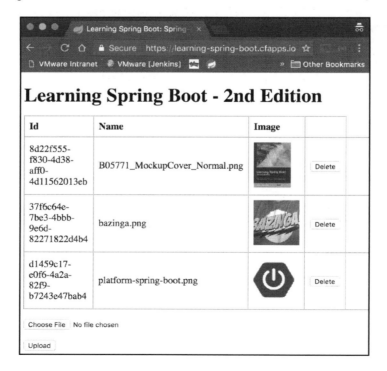

Our favorite chat channel is at the bottom of the page, as shown in the following screenshot:

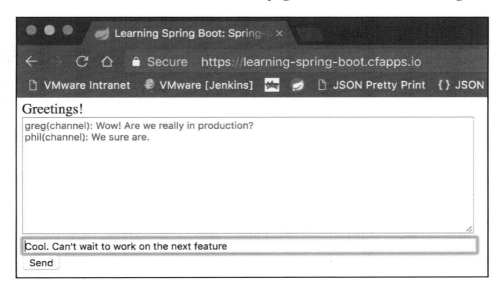

For extra maintenance, the following script can be used to delete all the apps (but not the related AMQP and MongoDB services):

```bash
#!/usr/bin/env bash

cf delete -f learning-spring-boot-config-server &
cf delete -f learning-spring-boot-eureka-server &
cf delete -f learning-spring-boot &
cf delete -f learning-spring-boot-comments &
cf delete -f learning-spring-boot-images &
cf delete -f learning-spring-boot-hystrix-dashboard &
```

Using the CF CLI, all the services are deleted in a background job.

 Doesn't Cloud Foundry support manifest YAML files? While it's true, manifest files have limitations that I prefer to avoid. Hence, I'd rather directly script the CF CLI operations directly, or use something ever more powerful.

Summary

In this chapter, we created profile-specific configuration settings to handle the WebSocket broker in either a local or cloud-based environment. We plugged in a custom configuration property bean and used it to grab necessary details from our cloud provider so our chat channel would work properly. We then built some BASH scripts to deploy things to the cloud, configure necessary properties, and restart/cleanup if needed.

This is just the beginning. We touched upon a lot of things in this book, including web apps, data access, testing, tools, messaging, microservices, security, and production. And we did it all *reactively*, ensuring we use resources more efficiently and effectively.

Think our social media platform is worth a billion dollars? Maybe, maybe not. However, by using the length and breadth of Spring Boot 2.0, Spring Framework 5, and its reactor-based paradigm end to end, we've learned a lot in how to build a scalable system.

Hopefully, I've whetted your appetite to go out and discover what else Spring Boot has to offer as you work on your next big project.

Please visit `https://github.com/learning-spring-boot/learning-spring-boot-2nd-edition-code` and "star" it. That way, you'll be alerted as Spring Boot 2.0 reaches GA release and this code base is upgraded to match. Also sign up for updates at `http://greglturnquist.com/books/learning-spring-boot` so you can be alerted to the latest news including code mods, contests, and more!

Index

C

callback hell 55
calls
    tracing 324
chat microservice
    about 256
    authentication, versus authorization 301
    securing 296, 297, 298, 299
chat service
    creating, to handle WebSocket traffic 246, 247, 248
    saved comments, broadcasting 249, 250, 251
    WebSocket handlers, configuring 253, 254
    WebSocket messages, brokering 249
circuit breaker solution
    URL 223
circuit breaker
    monitoring 226, 230, 232, 233, 235
classic Spring MVC
    versus reactive Spring WebFlux 45
client-side load balancing
    microservice, calling 210, 218, 222
cloud 333
Cloud Foundry
    about 333
    application, deploying to 27
    application, pushing to 342, 343, 345, 349
    reference link 342
    URL 28
cloud-native
    URL 27
code generation 70
Config Server
    microservice settings, offloading 235, 240
    securing 327, 328
    settings, offloading 242
configuration property bean
    about 335
    creating 335, 337
constructor injection 51, 157, 172
consumer groups
    URL 222
content delivery networks (CDN) 332
continuous integration (CI) 101
Cross-origin Resource Sharing (CORS) 254

custom finders
    creating 81, 85
custom health check
    writing 150, 153, 154
custom metrics
    creating 156, 159
custom Spring Boot autoconfiguration
    testing 125, 129, 133
customized metrics
    adding, for tracking message flow 183, 188

D

Debug mode 171
dependencies
    about 12
    testing 101, 102
Dependency Management Gradle plugin
    reference link 38
Dialect 315
direct exchange 177
distribution summary file 158
DRY (Don't Repeat Yourself) 111
DS (Discovery Service) 220

E

embedded Netty
    switching, to Apache Tomcat 44
    URL 44
embedded Spring Boot app tests 118, 125
Eureka Server
    securing 328, 329, 330
Eureka
    services, registering 203, 207
    services, searching 203, 207
    URL 210
exchanges 177
existing application
    messaging, adding as new component 167, 168, 169

F

fanout exchange 177
fat JAR 12
field injection
    URL 91

final product
    testing 281, 282, 283, 284
Flapdoodle 13
Flux
    used, for pulling data 76, 81
functional reactive programming (FRP) 268

G

Gateway API
    about 288
    creating 289, 291, 295

H

Homebrew
    reference link 164
hot code
    reloading, Spring Boot's DevTools used 136,
    140
hprof heap dump 160
HTTPie
    URL 48
Hystrix Dashboard 226

I

image ownership
    authorizing methods 308
    wiring 306, 308
    wiring in 305
images microservice
    method security 305
    securing 304, 305
immediately-invoked function expression (IIFE)
    255, 294

J

jOOQ 69
JPA (Java Persistence API) 69
JRebel
    reference link 137
JSON Viewer
    reference link 143
    URL 32
JsonPath
    URL 32

JsonSlurper
    URL 32
JSR 356
    versus Spring WebFlux messaging 284

K

kryo
    reference link 195

L

LiveReload plugin
    reference link 137
LiveReload
    URL 136

M

Matt Stine
    URL 202
message flow
    tracking, by adding customized metrics 183, 188
message producer/message consumer
    about 177
    AMQP fundamentals 177, 178, 179, 180, 181,
    182
    comments, displaying 171, 172, 174
    comments, producing 175
    creating 170, 171
messaging
    adding, as new component to existing application
    167, 168, 169, 170
method security 305
Micrometer module
    URL 159
Micrometer
    URL 34
microservice circuit breakers
    implementing 222, 224, 225
microservice
    about 201, 202
    calling, with client-side load balancing 210, 218,
    222
    session details, sharing with 301, 302, 303
    settings offloading, to configuration server 235,
    240, 242
MongoDB

S

SAM (Single Abstract Method) rules 52
saved comments
  broadcasting 249, 250, 251
  publishing, to chat service 244, 246
service discovery 203
service layer methods 310
service registry 204
session 249
session details
  sharing, with microservices 301, 302, 303
shaded JAR 12
Simple (or Streaming) Text Oriented Message
  Protocol (STOMP) 255
slice-based testing
  about 105
  embedded MongoDB, using 106, 110
  MongoDB database, using 110
social media platform
  building 8
Spring Boot Actuator 141, 156
Spring Boot application
  executing 14
  metrics 32
  pinging, for general health 31
  production-ready support, adding 30
  securing 286
Spring Boot DevTools
  about 171
  used, for reloading hot code 136, 140
Spring Cloud Config Server 235
Spring Cloud Config
  URL 242
Spring Cloud Gateway 289
Spring Cloud Stream
  logging with 198, 199
  reference link 188
Spring Cloud
  about 189, 191, 193, 195, 196, 197
  reference link 190
  URL 202
Spring Data repositories
  wiring up, with Spring Boot 72, 73
Spring Expression Language (SpEL) 308

Spring Initializr
  about 9
  reference link 36
  URL 9, 101
  used, for creating reactive web application 36,
  37, 38
Spring IO Platform
  URL 11
Spring Loaded
  reference link 137
Spring MVC
  advantages 46
Spring Security
  about 285
  prebuilt rules 309
  reference link 321
Spring Session
  benefits 287
  Gateway API, creating 289, 291, 295
  reference link 287
  using 286, 287, 288
Spring WebFlux 35
Spring WebFlux messaging
  versus JSR 356 284
Spring
  URL 141
starters 13

T

Thymeleaf template
  interacting with 60, 62
topic exchange 177
twelve-factor app
  URL 235, 332

U

uber JAR 12
unit testing 102, 105
user chatting 262, 264, 266, 268, 269, 270, 271,
  272
user interface (UI)
  about 286
  altering, with authorization checks 310
user-specific messages
  sending 273

89662700R00206

Made in the USA
San Bernardino, CA
28 September 2018